THE CULT OF MITHRAS IN LATE ANTIQUITY

LATE ANTIQUE
ARCHAEOLOGY

(SUPPLEMENTARY SERIES)

SERIES EDITOR

LUKE LAVAN

MANAGING EDITOR

MICHAEL MULRYAN

VOLUME 2

The titles published in this series are listed at *brill.com/laax*

THE CULT OF MITHRAS
IN LATE ANTIQUITY

DEVELOPMENT, DECLINE AND DEMISE *CA.* AD 270–430

BY

DAVID WALSH

BRILL

LEIDEN | BOSTON

Cover illustration: Modern Bull-Slaying Sculpture in the London Mithraeum. © Bloomberg.

Library of Congress Cataloging-in-Publication Data

Names: Walsh, David (Lecturer in Classical and Archaeological Studies),
    author.
Title: The cult of Mithras in late antiquity : development, decline, and
    demise ca. A.D. 270–430 / by David Walsh.
Description: Leiden ; Boston : Brill, 2019. | Series: Late Antique
    Archaeology (Supplementary Series), ISSN 2352-5177 ; VOLUME 2 | Includes
    bibliographical references and index.
Identifiers: LCCN 2018037207 (print) | LCCN 2018038584 (ebook) |
    ISBN 9789004383067 (ebook) | ISBN 9789004380806 (pbk. : alk. paper)
Subjects: LCSH: Mithras (Zoroastrian deity)—Cult. | Mithraism
Classification: LCC BL1585 (ebook) | LCC BL1585 .W335 2019 (print) |
    DDC 299/.15—dc23
LC record available at https://lccn.loc.gov/2018037207

Brill has made all reasonable efforts to trace all rights holders to any copyrighted material used in this work.
In cases where these efforts have not been successful the publisher welcomes communications from
copyright holders, so that the appropriate acknowledgements can be made in future editions, and to settle
other permission matters.

Typeface for the Latin, Greek, and Cyrillic scripts: "Brill". See and download: brill.com/brill-typeface.

ISSN 2352-5177
ISBN 978-90-04-38080-6 (paperback)
ISBN 978-90-04-38306-7 (e-book)

Copyright 2019 by Koninklijke Brill NV, Leiden, The Netherlands.
Koninklijke Brill NV incorporates the imprints Brill, Brill Hes & De Graaf, Brill Nijhoff, Brill Rodopi,
Brill Sense, Hotei Publishing, mentis Verlag, Verlag Ferdinand Schöningh and Wilhelm Fink Verlag.
All rights reserved. No part of this publication may be reproduced, translated, stored in a retrieval system,
or transmitted in any form or by any means, electronic, mechanical, photocopying, recording or otherwise,
without prior written permission from the publisher.
Authorization to photocopy items for internal or personal use is granted by Koninklijke Brill NV provided
that the appropriate fees are paid directly to The Copyright Clearance Center, 222 Rosewood Drive, Suite 910,
Danvers, MA 01923, USA. Fees are subject to change.

This book is printed on acid-free paper and produced in a sustainable manner.

Contents

Foreword   IX
List of Illustrations   X
List of Abbreviations   XII

Introduction   1
    Religious Change in Late Antiquity: Changing Scholarly Views   2
    The Cult of Mithras: A Brief Introduction   4
    The Cult of Mithras in Late Antiquity: Changing Scholarly Views   12
    The Structure of This Volume   13
    Selecting the Evidence   13
    A Note on Terminology   15

1 The Development of the Cult of Mithras in Late Antiquity   17
    The Location of Mithraea   17
    Mithraic Architecture   20
    Mithraic Iconography   22
    Patronage and Membership   25
    Mithraic Hierarchies   29
    Ritual Practice   30
        Initiation Rituals   30
        Sacrifices   31
        Feasts   31
        Votive Practices   32
        The Ritual Fragmentation of Objects   33
    Variations of the Name 'Mithras'   39
    Conclusion   39

2 The Decline of the Cult I: The Evidence   42
    Introduction   42
    The Decline in Construction/Restoration of Mithraea   44
    Mithraea and Wider Patterns of Construction and Repair in Late Antiquity   49
    Charting the Declining Use of Individual Mithraea   54
    Conclusion   55

3 The Decline of the Cult II: Explaining the Decline   56
    Introduction   56
    Declining Populations   56
    Changing Social Networks   58
    Changes in Mithraic Rituals   60
    Coercion by the Imperial Government   64
    Conclusion   65

4 The Fate of Mithraea   67

Introduction   67
Geographical and Chronological Variation in the Fate of Mithraea   68
Factors Contributing to the Fate of Mithraea   77
Christian Iconoclasm   78
'Barbarian' Incursions   85
Civil War   88
Imperial Legislation   89
Relocation of Mithraic Initiates   89
Natural Disasters and Accidental Destruction   90
Conclusion   92

Conclusion   94

Appendix A: Gazetteer of Mithraea Active in the 4th c. and Those That Exhibit Evidence of Christian Iconoclasm   101

A.   Britain   101
  A.1   *Borcovicium (Housesteads)*   101
  A.2   *Brocolitia (Carrawburgh)*   101
  A.3   *Londinium (London)*   103
B.   Germany   104
  B.1   *Biesheim*   104
  B.2   *Bornheim-Sechtem*   105
  B.3   *Gimmeldingen*   106
  B.4   *Reichweiler*   106
  B.5   *Rockenhausen*   106
C.   Noricum   106
  C.1   *Ad Enum (Pons Aeni)*   106
  C.2   *Lentia (Linz)*   107
  C.3   *Schachadorf*   108
  C.4   *St. Urban*   108
D.   Pannonia   108
  D.1   *Aquincum IV ('of Symphorus')*   108
  D.2   *Carnuntum I*   109
  D.3   *Carnuntum III*   109
  D.4   *Poetovio II (Ptuj)*   110
  D.5   *Poetovio III*   110
  D.6   *Poetovio V*   111
E.   Dalmatia   112
  E.1   *Arupium (Prozor) I and II*   112
  E.2   *Epidaurum (Cavtat)*   112
  E.3   *Jajce*   112
  E.4   *Konjic*   112
F.   Italy (Excluding Rome and Ostia)   113
  F.1   *Capua*   113
  F.2   *Ponza*   113
  F.3   *Spoletium*   114
  F.4   *Timavo*   114
  F.5   *Vulci*   115

CONTENTS

VII

G. Gaul 115
  G.1 *Augusta Treverorum (Trier)* 115
  G.2 *Burdigala (Bordeaux)* 116
  G.3 *Forum Claudii Vallensium Octodurensium (Martigny)* 116
  G.4 *Les Bolards* 117
  G.5 *Mackwiller* 117
  G.6 *Pons Saravi (Sarrebourg)* 118
  G.7 *Septeuil* 118
  G.8 *Tienen* 119
  G.9 *Venetonimagus (Vieu-en-Val-Romney)* 119
H. Spain 120
  H.1 *Lucus Augusti (Lugo)* 120
I. North Africa 120
  I.1 *Lambaesis* 120
J. The Eastern Mediterranean 121
  J.1 *Caesarea Maritima* 121
  J.2 *Doliche* 122
  J.3 *Hawarte* 122
  J.4 *Šaʿāra* 124

Appendix B: Mithraea Constructed and Repaired *ca.* AD 201–400 125

Bibliography 128
Index 138

Foreword

There are many people I need to thank who have helped and supported me during the course of writing both my thesis and this subsequent monograph. Firstly, there is the long list of those who have provided me with information, photographs/images, shown me around sites and museums, and read over various chapters of this work. These are: Roger Beck, József Beszédes, Jonas Bjørnebye, Neil Christie, Jitse Dijkstra, Richard Gordon, Alison Griffith, Marion Großmann, Michael Gawlikowski, Ines Klenner, Orsolya Láng, Ray Laurence, Marleen Martens, Roger Pearse, Peter Talloen, Sophie Jackson and Sadie Watson of MOLA, Eberhard Sauer, Ellen Swift, Cornleius Ulbert, Francois Wiblé, Greg Woolf, and Paula Zsidi. Thanks go to Lloyd Bosworth for drawing various images, and to Chris Newman for imagining a 4th c. mithraeum, especially for having to put up with my continuous requests for tweaks, as well as to Carole Raddato for allowing me to use her extensive catalogue of photographs.

I am tremendously grateful to John Beale and the School of European Culture and Languages at the University of Kent for providing me with a fee-wavier, without which I would not have been able to undertake this opportunity. Many thanks also go to the Society for the Promotion of Roman Studies for their generous bursary to help with research costs. Thanks also go to James Burchell and Andrew Martinovs for keeping me employed throughout, and to my flatmate Andrew Rawlinson, who probably now knows far more about cults in the Roman empire than he ever expected he would. Michael Mulryan has my immense gratitude for editing the manuscript, as does Mark Crittenden for his proof-reading prowess. Any errors that remain are my own.

Special acknowledgement must go to my supervisor Luke Lavan for his unwavering enthusiasm. Support for this Ph.D. topic was arranged through him, as a case study for a wider project on the end of paganism, to which the fate of the cult of Mithras has been seen as particularly significant.

Finally, the most important thanks go to my parents. I doubt they thought trips to the British Museum and the purchasing of many 'Horrible Histories' would result in this, but I hope this goes someway to repaying their endless faith and love. Any success I achieve is as much theirs as it is mine.

David Walsh
Centre for Late Antique Archaeology,
University of Kent,
March 2018

Illustrations

Figures

1 An artist's impression the exterior of the Londinium Mithraeum   5
2 Relief of the bull-slaying scene from Angera   6
3 Mithraic relief from Aquileia, Italy   6
4 Rock-birth statuette from Aquincum   7
5 Standard plan of a Mithraeum   7
6 An artist's impression the interior of the Londinium Mithraeum   8
7 Mithraeum of the Seven Spheres at Ostia (symbols substituted for images of the planets and signs of the zodiac)   9
8 Image from a series of frescos found in the Capua Mithraeum that depict Mithraic intiations. Pictured here appears to be the Pater (left), the intiate (centre), and the latter's sponsor (right)   10
9 The Altars at the Brocolitia Mithraeum. The altar on the left is hollow, which would have allowed the image of Sol on its face to be illuminated by a candle or lamp   10
10 Mosaic from the Felicisimus Mithraeum, Ostia, which depicts the seven Mithraic grades   11
11 Cross-section of the mithraeum found at Via S. Giovanni Lanza 128. Esquiline Hill, Rome   20
12 Comparative plan of various mithraea built and adapted from the late 3rd c. onwards   22
13 Comparative plan of various mithraea built and adapted from the late 3rd c. onwards   23
14 Mithraic relief found at Dardagana   24
15 Wall painting from the Hawarte Mithraeum: a man in Persian garb (Mithras?) holding the chains of a short, black two-headed demon, while standing in front of a large white horse   25
16 Wall painting from the Hawarte Mithraeum: city wall topped by various black heads, with rays of light descending on (or attacking) them   25
17 Mithraic votives ca. AD 271–300   34
18 Mithraic votives ca. AD 301–30   35
19 Mithraic votives ca. AD 331–70   36
20 Mithraic votives ca. AD 371–400   37
21 Distribution of coin finds at the Martigny Mithraeum ca. AD 268–94   38
22 Distribution of coin finds at the Martigny Mithraeum ca. AD 330–48   38
23 Distribution of coin finds at the Martigny Mithraeum ca. AD 378–402   38
24 Fragments of a Mithraic ceramic vessel from the Bornheim-Sechtem Mithraeum   39
25 The head of Mithras from the Londinium Mithraeum   40
26 The main relief (shaded areas indicate extant fragments) from Carnuntum III   40
27 Construction and repair of Mithraea ca. AD 201–400   45
28 Construction and repair of Mithraea ca. AD 271–300   46
29 Construction and repair of Mithraea ca. AD 301–30   47
30 Construction and repair of Mithraea ca. AD 331–70   48
31 Public Building v Mithraea in Italy ca. AD 131–400 (excluding Rome)   52
32 Public Building v Mithraea in Noricum and Pannonia ca. AD 131–400   53
33 Fate of Mithraea ca. AD 271–300   69
34 Fate of Mithraea ca. AD 301–30   70

ILLUSTRATIONS

35 Fate of Mithraea ca. AD 331–70 71
36 Fate of Mithraea ca. AD 371–400 72
37 Fate of Mithraea ca. AD 401–30 73
38 The Caesarea Maritima Mithraeum 74
39 Restored bull-slaying scene from the Pons Saraavi Mithraeum 75
40 Relief of the rock-birth from the Trier Mithraeum 76
41 Relief of the bull-slaying scene at the Doliche Mithraeum 79
42 Rock-birth statuette from Carnuntum 'III' 80
43 Headless Rock-Birth statue from Mithraeum 'I' at Carnuntum 80
44 Lion statuette from Mithraeum 'III' at Carnuntum 81
45 The altar decorated with the personifications of the winds and seasons from Carnuntum III 81
46 Headless Mithraic statuettes from the Dieburg Mithraea 86
47 The two-sided Mithraic relief from Konjic 91
48 Artist's impression of coins offered as votives in a mithraeum during the 4th c. 96

Abbreviations

Abbreviations are those used by the *American Journal of Archaeology* for periodicals, and the *Oxford Classical Dictionary* (3rd edn. 1999), A. H. M Jones, *Later Roman Empire* (Oxford 1964), G. W. H. Lampe, *A Patristic Greek Lexicon* (Oxford 1961) for ancient sources. Other abbreviations used are listed below:

CIMRM   M. J. Vermaseren, *Corpus inscriptionum et monumentorum religionis Mithriacae*, 2 vols. (The Hague 1956–60).

LTUR   E. M. Steinby ed. *Lexicon Topographicum Urbis Romae*, 6 vols. (Rome 1993–2000).

Introduction

In AD 308, the surviving emperors of the 'second tetrarchy' convened with their retired predecessors at Carnuntum, a major town and military fortification on the Roman empire's Danube frontier, in order to resolve the quarrels that had erupted between them regarding the issue of succession. During the course of their short stay, they paid for the repair of a 'mithraeum', a temple in which the followers of the god Mithras gathered to worship. This act is communicated to us via an altar that also refers to Mithras as the 'Protector of their *Imperium*'.

In the context of the early 4th c., such a dedication is notable for a number of reasons. Firstly, there are no extant references to any emperors acting as patrons of the cult from preceding periods, suggesting direct imperial support in such a manner was unprecedented. Secondly, by this time the construction and repair of temples had decreased significantly across the empire, with evidence for such activities particularly rare along the Danube from the early 3rd c. AD onwards. Subsequently, the repair of a temple would have been a rarity even without imperial involvement. Thirdly, the cult of Mithras was, it would seem, a highly secretive group who met in dark, windowless structures, as opposed to the ostentatious temples dedicated to other deities. One would expect an act such as this, orchestrated as it was by a group of emperors, to be as public as possible, yet mithraea were the antithesis of such a platform. In addition to the Tetrarchs' dedication, similar acts of restoration were undertaken on mithraea around the same time at nearby Virunum and Poetovio, by a *dux* and provincial governor respectively. At Lambaesis in North Africa, a governor had also made a dedication to Mithras a few years before. By the mid 4th c., the cult could even count a number of senatorial families among its ranks. The cult of Mithras in the early 4th c., it would seem, was very much a cult 'on the up'.

Yet, within a hundred years of the conference at Carnuntum, and Mithras being proclaimed as the protector of the emperors' *Imperium*, the cult had all but disappeared. Only two or three mithraea look to have still been in use in the early decades of the 5th c., and these were soon abandoned as well. Many mithraea that ceased to be used in the latter half of the 4th c. appear to have been left in a ruinous state, with their statues smashed and their reliefs mutilated. What went wrong for the cult?

If we are to follow the traditional narrative, the answer to this question was one of the major reasons the meeting at Carnuntum had been called: the rise of Constantine.

He was the son of the recently deceased Augustus in the West, Constantius Chlorus, who had, against the wishes of the established Tetrarchs, proclaimed himself Caesar in the West. Within a decade, Constantine would rule half the empire and within 20 years the whole Roman world. More so than for any of his other achievements, Constantine is remembered as the first Christian emperor, and the man who set in motion the transformation of the Roman empire from a polytheistic state to one dominated by monotheistic Christianity. Within decades of Constantine's reign, an increasing number of laws restricting polytheistic practice were being issued: bans on animal sacrifice (AD 341/56),[1] the closure of temples (AD 346/54/56),[2] a ban on private practice (AD 392),[3] and finally a complete destruction of temples (AD 435).[4] The monotheistic Christians, naturally intolerant of other faiths and fixated on the violent demise of false idols, were (apparently) greatly buoyed by the Christian emperors' desire to promote Christianity, and took it upon themselves, with the likes of Martin of Tours, Shenoute of Atripe and Theophilus of Alexandria leading them, to extinguish the fire of polytheism wherever they found it. The cult of Mithras, so we are told, regardless of its status in the early 4th c., soon found itself persecuted out of existence.[5]

But does this narrative really hold up to scrutiny? When one considers that the evidence for the Mithraic cult stretches from the Syrian Desert to Hadrian's Wall, can one really explain the demise of a cult that was so widespread with a single, overriding factor? What of areas of the empire where we lack any strong evidence for Christian presence at this time, such as along the Rhine and Danube frontiers, which actually tend to be the regions where the Mithraic cult was most prevalent? Did the rate and fashion of the decline of the Mithras cult vary in different regions?

Unfortunately, such a uniform approach to the demise of the cult is emblematic of the way in which many scholars have portrayed the cult of Mithras generally. That Mithraic communities had significantly uniform traits, at least until the turn of the 3rd c., is undeniable. The layout of many mithraea followed a set groundplan, we see the reoccurrence of the same Mithraic titles in different regions, the image of Mithras slaying the bull

---

1 *Cod. Theod.* 16.10.2, 6.
2 *Cod. Theod.* 16.10.14.
3 *Cod. Theod.* 16.10.12.
4 *Cod. Theod.* 16.10.24.
5 Sauer (1996), (2003); Clauss (2012) 157–67.

was the focus of the mithraeum, and sacrificial deposits of similar composition appear in mithraea across the breadth of the Roman world. Yet, was the cult truly a static entity regardless of place or time? Can we not detect regional forms of the cult emerging as we move into Late Antiquity? And if so, what ramifications might this have for how we understand the cult's demise?

It is the aim of this monograph to address these two themes. The first of these is to assess the extent to which the cult of Mithras evolved in Late Antiquity to become increasingly regionalised. In doing so, the following questions will be proposed: did Mithraic rituals, sacred architecture, structure or membership alter in Late Antiquity? If so, can we chart these evolutions following alternate paths across different regions? Would a member of the Mithraic cult who set out for Hadrian's Wall from Syria in the 4th c. meet identical Mithraic communities along the way, or would they have seemed strange and peculiar to him? As will be demonstrated, the picture that emerges of the Mithras cult in the 4th c. is one that is highly varied, rather than one that was a uniform homogenous body. In showing this, the stage is set to tackle the Mithras cult as it was at the time of its decline and demise, as opposed to addressing this via our image of the cult in the 2nd or early 3rd c.

This leads us to the second theme of this study, which is to establish how and why the cult diminished in the late 4th and early 5th c. In order to do so, we will explore not only the evidence for the cult itself, but also address the context in which it existed, in order to produce a more nuanced understanding of why it disappeared. How might changes in the urban fabric have affected the cult? What did the changing socio-political dynamics of the late Roman empire mean for the structure and membership of the cult? Did barbarian incursions affect its status? Can we find evidence of natural disasters playing a role in the abandonment of mithraea? Once again, the picture that emerges from this analysis is far more diverse than what scholars in previous generations had imagined.

Religious Change in Late Antiquity: Changing Scholarly Views

Before exploring the cult of Mithras in Late Antiquity, let us begin by reviewing how scholarly ideas regarding changes in the religious sphere of the 4th c. have altered over recent generations. For centuries, the transformation of the Roman empire from a world filled with a variety of temples, cults and rituals into one dominated by Christianity, had been seen as a largely violent process. Particular moments in the late 4th c. have often

been thought to have defined the struggle between the old 'pagan' world and the new Christian one, such as the destruction of the Alexandrian Serapeum, (AD 391), the Battle of the Frigidus (AD 394), and the death of the philosopher Hypatia (AD 415). As far back as the 1700s, these episodes were being given prominent places in the works of various Enlightenment scholars, such as Tolland, Voltaire, and Gibbon.[6] In the 20th c., studies by Deichmann and Fowden have had a strong influence in perpetuating this narrative of intolerance, with the former claiming temples were widely closed around the turn of the 5th c., and the latter arguing that many temples were converted into churches.[7]

Even some recent volumes have continued to present the end of temples as being the result of coercive Christianisation, with Ramsey MacMullen observing that post-Constantinian Christianity was "determined on [paganism's] extinction". Similarly, Robin Lane-Fox commented on the "robust history of Christian temple— and statue-breaking", and David Frankfurter refers to the destruction of non-Christian shrines in Late Antiquity as an "epidemic around the Mediterranean world".[8] For these scholars, the references we find in the literary texts to the destruction and desecration of temples by Christians are ample evidence that this was a period of intense struggle that swept across the Roman world. Of course, some examples of literary accounts of temples being destroyed or desecrated by Christians do reflect incidents that certainly happened; that the Serapeum of Alexandria was attacked by monks under the orders of the Bishop Theophilus is an accepted fact. However, this does not mean every account is accurate or even true, while even those that are, do not necessarily reflect the wider picture at the time. Authors have their biases, they receive news second, third or even fourth-hand, and of course occasionally employ 'artistic license' in order to hold the reader's attention. To rely on the historical texts alone is to see only one perspective.

With this in mind, it is perhaps unsurprising then that in recent decades there has been a notable shift in scholarly views on the end of non-Christian cults in Late Antiquity, as greater emphasis has been placed on the archaeological evidence. Richard Bayliss' study of the conversion of temples into churches has shown Deichmann's conclusions to be largely unfounded, as the former could only find 120 examples where temples had been converted into churches from across the entire Roman world. Only a third of these conversions occurred prior to the late 5th c., while Bayliss also found

---

6   Tolland (1722); Voltaire (1764); Gibbon (1781).

7   Deichmann (1939); Fowden (1978).

8   MacMullen (1997) 13; Lane-Fox (1986) 672; Frankfurter (1998) 278.

only four definite acts of desecration in the archaeological record.[9] Furthermore, many of the case studies included in the recent volume *The Archaeology of Late Antique 'Paganism'* have shown that evidence for the violent destruction of temples is relatively scarce in regions such as Gaul, Egypt, North Africa and Spain.[10] As a result, scholars are now approaching the *Lives* of saints with greater caution, realising that these texts served as panegyrics that exaggerate (or possibly even falsify) information.[11] As stated, none of this is to say temples were never destroyed by Christian iconoclasts, and that these events were all fabrications, indeed non-Christian authors, such as Libanius, also recorded instances of temple destruction by Christians.[12] Rather, it appears that such incidents were far less common than traditionally thought.

Instead, it is now becoming apparent that the transformation from polytheism to Christian monotheism in the Roman empire was a much more complex process, that went beyond the confines of the 4th c. and early 5th c. To begin with, there is a growing realisation that things had begun to change in the generations preceding Constantine, with the construction and restoration of temples already in decline.[13] For example in Noricum and Pannonia, temple construction entered into a period of rapid decline from the end of the 2nd c., while temple restorations there were uncommon after the Severan period.[14] Similar declines have been identified in Gaul, Egypt, Spain and North Africa. One may argue the instability of the '3rd c. Crisis' may have played a role in this, and this is undoubtedly true to an extent, but even when the empire regained a level of stability under the Tetrarchs, we still see little change in the fortunes of temples. Despite the Tetrarchs undertaking large restoration projects in various towns, while portraying themselves as Jovius and Herculius, they do not appear to have had any desire to display this via investment in temples. For example, at Gorsium in Pannonia, the Tetrarchs' restoration of the town following its devastation in the mid 3rd c. did not include the large imperial cult complex (possibly the centre of the cult in this region); instead they mined these structures for *spolia* to build secular buildings. Notably, despite his desire to

undermine Christianity, Julian appears to have followed a similar trend in his reign. He restored the occasional temple, but his building projects at Aphrodisias, Constantinople, and Tarsus failed to include any newly constructed temples.[15]

At the same time that funding for temples was dwindling, it appears that one of the key rites associated with them—animal sacrifice—was also declining in popularity, at least in connection to temples. Even prior to the 4th c., philosophers such as Porphyry were questioning whether blood sacrifices were beneficial or not, and perhaps even had dangerous consequences, such as attracting demons. Such distain for these activities looks to have spread in the 4th c., judging from the reaction to Julian's request for a large sacrifice at Antioch in AD 362 when the priest of the temple presented him with only a goose, much to the chagrin of the emperor who had dreamed of a lavish ceremony filled with mass slaughter. Even authors who were largely in support of Julian, such as the polytheistic Ammianus, considered Julian overzealous in his approach to such practices.[16]

Yet, while some elements of polytheistic worship had long been in decline, it is also now acknowledged that many pre-Christian traditions continued beyond the 4th c., such as festivals, ritual feasts at grave sites, and animal sacrifice in some rural communities.[17] Occasionally, these survivals have been described as either a form of 'pagan resistance' or a 'pagan revival',[18] but in reality the continuation of these activities appears to be more due to the fact that Christianity and 'paganism' were not mutually exclusive entities; many Christians were happy to embrace non-Christian elements of society and vice-versa. The Codex-Calendar of AD 354, with its lists of Christian holy days, martyrs and popes, alongside images of 'pagan' festivals, is a case in point. That the likes of Paulinus of Nola and Pope Gregory I recognised that animal sacrifice could not be stopped via coercion amongst rural communities, is also an indication that the Christian clergy were aware that a degree of flexibility was required. To quote Cameron, "[W]e should not confuse the end of paganism with Christianity, nor

---

9   Bayliss (2004). This work is not comprehensive and does not include many of the mithraea included in this study. On the rarity of temple to church conversion, see also Hanson (1978).

10   Lavan and Mulryan (2011).

11   For example, on the *Life of Porphyry*, see Hahn (2004) 202–209 and on the *Life of Shenoute*, see Dijkstra (2011) 398.

12   Lib. *Or.* 30.9.

13   On the decline of temple construction, see Lavan (2011). On a decline in animal sacrifice, see Bradbury (1995).

14   Walsh (2016).

---

15   Lavan (2011) xliv.

16   On the decline of sacrifice, see Bradbury (1995). On Julian and blood sacrifices, see Julian *Mis.* 25–26 and Amm. Marc. 22.12.6 and 22.4.3.

17   On the continuation of festivals, see Graf (2015); on graveside feasts, see MacMullen (1997) 110–20; on continued instances of animal sacrifice, see Trout (1995).

18   On 'pagan resistance', see MacMullen (1997); on revival, see Bloch (1963) and Watts (1998).

should we assume that it was active pagan opposition that kept certain practices alive".[19]

Finally, it is important to highlight that, while many strides have been made in our understanding of religious transformation in Late Antiquity, there are number of provinces that have yet to receive adequate attention in this regard. In the bibliographical essays provided in *The Archaeology of Late Antique 'Paganism'*, there is barely a single entry on the Danubian provinces or the Rhine frontier.[20] There are various reasons for this, such as little textual evidence to supplement the archaeological record in these areas, and the existence of the 'Iron Curtain' in the 20th c. inhibiting interaction between scholars until recent decades. However, these areas have provided an abundance of archaeological material that is just as important for the study of the religious landscape in Late Antiquity as Italy or North Africa. As will be shown, evidence from these regions is of great importance for the study of the cult of Mithras in this period.

The Cult of Mithras: A Brief Introduction

Having looked at broader issues in the study of religion in Late Antiquity, now let us turn to the scholarship of our focus: the cult of Mithras. Precisely when and where the cult of Mithras came into being is unclear, but it is evident that whomever founded the Roman cult took inspiration from the Persian deity Mithra, not only regarding the name of the god, but also his appearance (Phrygian cap and tunic), and his connection with the Sun. However, it must be stressed that the worship of these two deities was entirely separate, and that the Roman cult of Mithras never appears to have had any followers in Persia. The most likely explanation as to how the first seeds of the cult were planted in the Roman world is to be found in Plutarch, according to whom sailors under the command of Pompey encountered the secret rites of 'Mithras' being performed at Mount Olympus (Turkey).[21] It is more likely these men came into contact with the worship of Mithra, which Plutarch mistook for Mithras, and that they subsequently communicated some of its aspects back to the Roman world. The cult was certainly active in Rome by the late 1st c. AD, as is evident by a reference from the poet Statius (d. AD 96).[22] Whether or not the cult was actually formulated in Rome itself, as Clauss has argued, or

elsewhere, is almost impossible to discern at this time, and is not of major concern here.[23]

The cult first appears in the archaeological and epigraphic records in the late 1st c. AD on the Rhine frontier at Nida-Heddernheim. Here, a mithraeum was constructed at that time which was found to contain dedications by a centurion and cavalry soldier. A second mithraeum was built at Nida a short time later. Roughly contemporary to this activity are the first Mithraic dedications to appear on the Danube frontier, at Carnuntum and Novae, which were erected by a soldier and *portorium* slave respectively.[24] Over the next century, the cult achieved notable popularity along the Rhine and Danube frontiers, as well as on Hadrian's Wall in the Severan period, owing much of this success to a strong following among soldiers and customs-officials (*portoria*). The cult also had a measure of success in some civilian areas, such as eastern Gaul, Rome and Ostia. In the case of the latter two, the following the cult gained in these locations must have been relatively large, given the significant numbers of mithraea (*ca.*17 at Ostia and *ca.*19 in Rome) found at both to date.

However, there were areas where the cult appears to have had minimal appeal. Among the western provinces, Spain and North Africa have produced less than ten mithraea combined, while in Britain little evidence for the cult has been found outside the military zones, except for the Londinium Mithraeum (although this was seemingly funded by a veteran), which was set in an area populated by domestic buildings (fig. 1). Somewhat surprising is the lack of Mithraic material to be found across the entire eastern part of the empire. Several well-preserved mithraea have been uncovered around the Fertile Crescent, such as at Dura-Europos in Syria and Caesarea Maritima in Israel, but fewer mithraea have been found across the entire East than in Pannonia alone. Why there was such an imbalance between East and West is unclear, although (as will be discussed) the overt Persian elements of the cult may have proved a more difficult issue to reconcile among those on the doorstep of Persia, as opposed to those situated thousands of kilometres away on a different frontier. In any case, it is important to note that many of these eastern regions have been extensively excavated and tend to yield far more in the way of extant remains of structures than the Rhine or Danube regions, thus these regional discrepancies cannot be explained via an imbalance in the application of modern excavation.

---

19 Cameron (2011) 783. On the Codex Calendar of AD 354, see Salzman (1990).

20 Demarsin (2011); Mulryan (2011a).

21 Plut. *Vit. Pomp.* 24.5.

22 Stat. *Theb.* 1.719–20.

---

23 Clauss (2012) 26.

24 Clauss (2012) 26–27. Dedications at Nida-Heddernheim: *CIMRM* 2. 1092, 1098; Carnuntum: *CIMRM* 2. 1718; Novae: *CIMRM* 2. 2269.

INTRODUCTION 5

FIGURE 1   *An artist's impression the exterior of the Londinium Mithraeum.*
ARTIST: JUDITH DOBIE © MUSEUM OF LONDON ARCHAEOLOGY.

So much for a brief history of the cult, but what did the cult of Mithras actually entail? Nearly all of what we know regarding the cult comes from the archaeological and epigraphic evidence. There are almost no Mithraic literary sources, except for a couple of scraps of 4th c. Egyptian papyri that look to have come from a script for a Mithraic initiation ceremony.[25] As such, all surviving written accounts describing the cult emanated from outsiders. This means that, while we can piece together what appears to be a relatively accurate model based on the available evidence, it is important to remember there is much we do not know. Furthermore, given that many of the outsiders who wrote about the cult probably never witnessed a Mithraic ritual, some of their descriptions are certainly distortions of the reality.

In terms of a Mithraic narrative, the central image of the cult that would take pride of place in every mithraeum was that of Mithras slaying a bull (the 'tauroctony': figs. 2–3). This act is often depicted taking place inside a cave with stars decorating its ceiling. Usually, a dog and snake are shown in the image drinking the blood of the bull while a scorpion bites its testes, although occasionally a lion and a krater are also depicted. On either side of the image one would find the torchbearers: Cautes, with his torch raised, and Cautopates with his lowered. Often in the top-left of the tauroctony one finds Sol, while in the top-right Luna is depicted, and a raven appears between Sol and Mithras, acting as a messenger from the former to the latter. Although we have no written explanation as to what the image is attempting to convey, certain meanings are readily apparent. First, the death of the bull brings about the (re)birth of the universe, as indicated by the animals feeding on its life-force and (in some versions) corn and grape vines emerging from its tail or wound.[26] The cave in which the slaying of the bull takes place also appears to be a symbol of the universe: a dark sphere-like environment with an interior but no exterior. Another reading of the image is of the victory of light over dark and day against night. Given their positions within the image, Mithras is clearly related to Sol, while the bull is connected to Luna; indeed, the bull's body-shape is often that of a crescent moon.[27]

This image is the climax of a narrative that includes various other episodes, although these are less commonly depicted. The second most frequent Mithraic

---

25   Brashear (1992).

26   *CIMRM* 2. 1283, 1306, 1314, 1727.

27   Clauss (2012) 77–88.

FIGURE 2　*Relief of the bull-slaying scene from Angera.*
PHOTO BY CAROLE RADDATO.

FIGURE 3　*Relief of the bull-slaying scene from Aquileia, Italy.*
PHOTO BY THE AUTHOR.

FIGURE 4 *Rock-birth statuette from Aquincum.*
PHOTO BY THE AUTHOR.

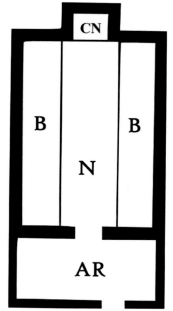

FIGURE 5 *Standard plan of a Mithraeum. A R - Anteroom; B- Bench C N - Cult Niche; N- Nave*
DRAWN BY THE AUTHOR.

image after the tauroctony is that of Mithras being born from a rock, often holding a torch and dagger (fig. 4). From the Rhine and Danube regions also come various representations of Mithras wrestling with and dragging the bull to the cave, as well as Mithras and Sol engaged in a feast after the sacrifice has been performed. Additionally, at some point during the Mithraic narrative (although precisely when is difficult to ascertain), Mithras shot an arrow into a rock and brought forth water. Unfortunately, whether Mithras' biography provided any moral lessons for, or restrictions on, the Mithraic initiates is unclear.[28]

Concerning where Mithraic communities met, we are fortunate that a large number of their temples (singular: mithraeum, plural: mithraea) have been found across the Roman world. These often follow a set-plan (fig. 5), although, as will be demonstrated in the course of this volume, exceptions would arise in the 4th c. The general plan though was of a small rectangular room containing a central nave, flanked by parallel benches, leading to a niche or altar. In addition to the main *cella*, additional rooms are sometimes found in mithraea that acted as storerooms, kitchens, or (possibly) for educating prospective members before they were initiated. Mithraea usually had no windows and were entirely artificially lit, although some mithraea have been found to contain shafts in their roofs that allowed light to shine on the altar or niche on certain days of the year when opened. The reason for this lack of natural light appears to have been to create a cave-like atmosphere (some mithraea were actually installed in caves) so as to replicate the setting of Mithras' most important act. Indeed, in Italy mithraea are often referred to in inscriptions as *spelaea*.[29] Furthermore, evidence has even been found indicating that the *cella* was decorated, so as to add to the cave-like effect (fig. 6), such as at Groß-Krotzenburg where rough basalt covered the ceiling.[30] In contrast, there is no evidence that mithraea had any form of external decoration, although occasionally the entrance way was covered by a portico.

Roger Beck has argued that the uniform topography of mithraea was imbued with significant meaning, which was specifically designed to facilitate certain ritual practices conducted within them. According to Beck, the standard plan of a Mithraic *cella* was intended to act as a map of the universe. In this idealised plan of a mithraeum, the cult relief served as the spring equinox, which faced the entrance that represented the autumn equinox. The side benches represented "… the ecliptic/ zodiac. But they also represent … the celestial equator", thus to stand in the centre of the nave would be to stand

---

28 Clauss (2012) 64–77.

29 Aquileia: CIMRM 1. 747; Milan: CIMRM 1. 706; Rome: CIMRM 1. 360, 412, 423. Outside of Italy, a mithraeum is usually referred to as a *templum*, e.g.: Lambaesis: CIMRM 1. 135; Vindobala: CIMRM 1. 842; Poetovio: CIMRM 2. 1614; Neusiedl am See: CIMRM 2. 1661, Aquincum: CIMRM 2. 1792–93.

30 Clauss (2012) 55. An inscription from Virunum refers to a mithraeum with a vaulted ceiling which was decorated, see AE (1994) 1334.

FIGURE 6 *An artist's impression the interior of the Londinium Mithraeum.*
ARTIST: JUDITH DOBIE © MUSEUM OF LONDON ARCHAEOLOGY.

at the centre of the universe. Of all extant mithraea, Beck has suggested that the closest a mithraeum came to recreating this layout was the *cella* of the 2nd c. Mithraeum of the Seven Spheres at Ostia (fig. 7). In this mithraeum, the seats of the benches were decorated with mosaics depicting the signs of the zodiac, while their sides were painted with representations of the planets (with the exception of the sun, which is represented by the tauroctony relief). At the end of the benches closest to the entrance, Cautes and Cautopates were depicted, with the former a symbol of the sun and the latter the moon, thus emphasising the roles of the respective benches: spring/autumn, heat/cold, exit/entry from earth, night/day.[31] Drawing on accounts from the philosopher Porphyry, Beck surmised that this layout was to facilitate Mithraic rituals which portrayed the passage of the soul across the celestial spheres.[32] Whether this was the case or not cannot be established for certain, yet the uniformity of mithraea across the Roman world indicates their layout and decoration must have had some form of ritual significance. This is important to bear in mind, for this would mean that a deviation from this plan—which is evident in some later mithraea—represents more than just aesthetic choice, but also one that infers alterations to ritual practices.

Furthermore, the fact that all mithraea were all designed to recreate a space, rather than actually *be* that space, meant no mithraeum held greater prestige than another. As Beck observed, "no mithraeum, as far as we know, was any more special or authentic than any other mithraeum". He also suggested the reason why there is such little evidence for any exterior decoration of mithraea was due to the symbolic nature of the mithraeum:

> A cave is an appropriate image of the universe because, like the universe, it is an inside without an outside. That is why, ideologically at least, the exterior of a mithraeum, in dramatic contrast to the

---

31 Gordon (1976) 129; Beck (2006) 102–15. The appearance of the planets in the order shown in the iconography of the Mithraeum of the Seven Spheres does not follow the standard order of the Roman planets, which Beck suggests was designed to reflect the arrangement of the planets on the spring equinox in AD 172.

32 Beck (2006) 151–52. Beck (2000) also believes that the image on one side of a Mithraic vessel from Mainz, which shows four Mithraic initiates in procession, is a depiction of such a ritual.

INTRODUCTION

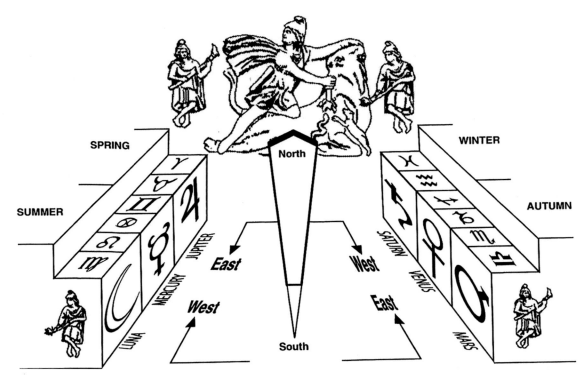

FIGURE 7   *Mithraeum of the Seven Spheres at Ostia (symbols substituted for images of the planets and signs of the zodiac).*
BECK (2006) 104 © OXFORD UNIVERSITY PRESS.

exteriors of standard Greek and Roman temples does not matter. Literally, it does not signify. Economic considerations no doubt played their part, but in an urban context an anonymous room or suite of rooms makes good symbolic sense.[33]

It has been estimated that the average mithraeum had seating for between 15 to 20 people, although there may have been those who stood, in which case the average number is probably closer to 40.[34] It is common for multiple mithraea to have coexisted at the same site, with the majority remaining small enough to limit congregation sizes to those mentioned. Examples of sites with multiple mithraea include: those already referred to at Rome and Ostia; at Aquincum and Poetovio, which have both produced five mithraea; at Nida-Heddernheim in Germany, where there were four mithraea; and at Carnuntum, which certainly contained at least two mithraea.[35] Undoubtedly, given that at Güglingen a timber mithraeum was found in close proximity to a masonry-built mithraeum, there are no doubt places where multiple mithraea coexisted, but only one or two of which have been found.[36] It is highly unlikely that the congregations using these mithraea formed and operated autonomously of each other, particularly as many of these settlements were not of considerable size. That the appearance of new mithraea was often the result of a pre-existing congregation dividing is indicated by the two Mithraic inscriptions discovered at Virunum, which date to the late 2nd/early 3rd c. These demonstrate that a Mithraic community, upon reaching *ca.*100 members, split into two smaller congregations.[37] A repetition of this elsewhere would explain the appearance of numerous mithraea in close proximity to each other, and also explain the lack of many pre-existing mithraea expanding or being abandoned in favour of new, larger mithraea.[38]

---

33   Beck (2006) 106.
34   Volken (2004) 2.
35   The two mithraea discussed in this work are referred to as Carnuntum I and III, following their labelling as such in CIMRM. I am aware that Carnuntum II (CIMRM 2. 1681) is far from certain in its identification, but for ease of relating this work to Vermaseren's corpus, I have maintained these pre-existing labels.

36   Rome: Griffith (1993); Ostia: White (2012); Aquincum: CIMRM 2. 1742–72; Póczy (2005) 215; Poetovio: CIMRM 2. 1487–1618, Vomer-Gojkovič (2001); Nida-Heddernheim: Huld-Zetsche (1986); Carnuntum: CIMRM 2. 1664, 1681, 1682; Güglingen: Kortüm and Neth (2005).
37   Piccottini (1994).
38   Some mithraea were expanded in size, but rarely by very much, see Dura-Europos: CIMRM 1. 34; Capua: Vermaseren (1971); Brocolitia (Carrawburgh): Richmond *et al.* (1951); Poetovio III: CIMRM 2. 1578.

FIGURE 8 *Image from a series of frescos found in the Capua Mithraeum that depict Mithraic intiations. Pictured here appears to be the Pater (left), the intiate (centre), and the latter's sponsor (right). After CIMRM 1.188.*
DRAWN BY LLOYD BOSWORTH.

FIGURE 9 *The Altars at the Brocolitia Mithraeum. The altar on the left is hollow, which would have allowed the image of Sol on its face to be illuminated by a candle or lamp.*
PHOTO BY THE AUTHOR.

Regarding recruitment, the cult of Mithras, at least until the 3rd c., was certainly male-only.[39] In order to join the cult, prospective members would have to undergo an intensive initiation ritual. Judging from the iconography, this involved the initiate being stripped, blindfolded, and having their hands tied (fig. 8). They would then have swords, torches, and bows and arrows pointed in their faces (or at least this was what they thought what was occurring with the blindfold on). Once the initiate had reached an intense emotional state, the blindfold was pulled away to reveal the central image of the cult, Mithras slaying a bull. This was bathed in light, or at least this was the impression given by the candle or lamp hidden behind the relief; there is also evidence for curtain railings or screens that could hide the relief.[40]

Archaeological evidence relating to these rituals has not been found in many mithraea, but some German mithraea have been found to contain swords, arrows, and crowns. The second mithraeum at Güglingen was destroyed in the early 3rd c. while still in use, and amongst the finds recovered from the temple were two swords (one of which had been placed across an altar), a crown, and arrow fragments. The Künzing mithraeum, which was destroyed around the same time, also yielded a complete sword, a fragment of another sword, an arrowhead, and a knife. At the mithraeum of Riegel, a sword was found that was bent in a semi-circle in the middle of the blade, suggesting it could have placed on someone to make it appear as though they had been run-through with it.[41] In regard to the illumination of the cult image or another relief: at Koenigshoffen columns that supported a curtain rail were found on either side of the relief; at Mithraeum II in Nida-Heddernheim, indentations in front of the cult-niche indicate some form of barrier that divided it from the nave; and at Ša'āra, door jambs were found in front of the apse where the cult image was held.[42] Hollowed out Mithraic altars, such as those found at Brocolitia and Koenigshoffen, also appear to have been used to produce similar effects (fig. 9), with the image emanating light in the dark sanctuary.[43]
Once a new initiate had passed this test they were admitted into the lowest of seven grades—that of the *corax* (raven)—and would subsequently progress up the Mithraic hierarchy, as depicted in the mosaic of the Mithraeum of Felicissimus at Ostia (fig. 10). The seven grades consisted of: *corax, nymphus* (bridegroom),

---

39 A number of studies have explored the possibility of women joining Mithraic communities, but overall few scholars have accepted this. See: Gordon (1980); David (2000); Chapula (2005); Griffith (2006).

40 Clauss (2012) 98–101. Much of the interpretation of what Mithraic initiations consisted of, is based on the frescoes found in the mithraeum under S. Maria Capua Vetere in Campania, which date to the early 3rd c., see Gordon (2009). The use of a bow and arrow in initiations was perhaps more often utilised among Mithraic communities on the Rhine, given that we know of it only from the 'Mainz Vessel', see Beck (2000).

41 Güglingen: Kortüm and Neth (2002); Künzing: Schmotz (2000); Riegel: Cammerer (1976).

42 Koenigshoffen: CIMRM 2. 1335; Nida-Heddernheim II: CIMRM 2. 1108; Ša'āra: Kalos (2001) 239. At Caesarea Maritima, small holes run in a line across the vault-roof perpendicular to the nave, and 4.5 m from the eastern end, where the cult image would have stood. It is possible this denotes some form of divider that existed to separate this area from the rest of the mithraeum, see Bull (1978) 78.

43 Brocolitia: CIMRM 1. 847; Koenigshoffen: CIMRM 2. 1366. It is likely that incense was burned during the initiations, as well as during other Mithraic rituals perhaps: see Bird (2007).

FIGURE 10 *Mosaic from the Felicisimus Mithraeum, Ostia, which depicts the seven Mithraic grades.*
PHOTO BY THE AUTHOR.

miles (soldier), *leo* (lion), *perses* (Persian), *heliodromus* (Runner of the Sun), and the *pater* (father). As the holder of the highest grade, the *pater* seems to have been the leader of the community and the one who conducted the initiation ceremonies, and it is the holders of this title who appear most frequently in Mithraic inscriptions. The prevalence of the *pater* grades in Mithraic inscriptions is probably due to the leaders of the community taking precedence over other members when it came to commemorations. That the second most common is *leo* suggests that many members did not progress beyond the halfway point of the Mithraic ladder.[44] Concerning the Mithraic hierarchy and that of secular status, there appears to have been little difference, with those holding the highest secular offices also acting as *patrēs*; it would not do to have a slave thinking himself better than a centurion. Furthermore, despite no evidence to suggest direct imperial involvement in the cult prior to the early 4th c., one of the most common recipients of Mithraic dedications was the emperor.[45] Thus, although the cult of Mithras was relatively unique when compared with other cults in the Roman empire, it displays no indication of encouraging deviance from what were considered the acceptable norms of behaviour in Roman society.

Other than initiation ceremonies, the cult also engaged in ritual feasts that mimicked the meal enjoyed by Sol and Mithras after the latter had slayed the bull. Judging from the faunal remains found in mithraea, these feasts consisted largely of chicken and piglet.[46] From the iconographic evidence, we can discern that the initiates involved in these rituals would play certain roles in the Mithraic narrative, with the *heliodromos* as Sol, the *pater* as Mithras, and other grades acting as attendants at the meal. Whether these events were regular occurrences is unclear but, judging from the remains of a large feast that took place in the mithraeum at Tienen, the summer solstice may have been such an occasion for one, which comes as little surprise given the close relationship between Sol and Mithras.[47]

Finally, the importance of sacrifices in the cult of Mithras remains unclear, with evidence for such activities existing in some mithraea, but the evidence for them overall being rather patchy. Among the wall paintings of the *Santa Prisca* Mithraeum in Rome, members of the Mithraic congregation are depicted presenting cocks, a bull, and a boar to the *pater*, perhaps as sacrificial animals.[48] Given that many mithraea were too small for a bull to enter, the inclusion of the animal in this scene is likely to have been an idealised image, but there is evidence to infer that the presentation of cocks and boars as sacrifices may have occurred.[49] The remains of birds deposited in a ritual fashion have been found in various mithraea: in one of the mithraea at Nida-Heddernheim a cistern was found to contain the bones of a cock, while at Pons Saravi a pot was found in the corner of the *cella* containing ash and bird bones. Furthermore, the burnt bones of a fowl were found in a pot deposited in late 3rd c. strata next to the altar of the Londinium Mithraeum, while at Brocolitia (Carrawburgh) a bird skull was

---

44 St Jerome also provides us with this information in Jer. *Ep* 107.2. For the mosaic from the Mithraeum of Felicissimus, see Clauss (2012) 124–31. Clauss argues that not all initiates held a grade, but rather that these were actually priesthoods held by a select few in Mithraic communities as, although such a view is not widely accepted.

45 Gordon (1972). Mithraic initiates honouring emperors: *CIMRM* 1. 53, 142, 161 347, 510, 626, 876, 2. 2350.

46 Gaidon-Bunuel and Caillat (2008) 265.

47 Lentacker, Ervynck and van Neer (2004). The belief that this feast took place on the summer solstice is based on the breeding patterns of pigs and sheep. These animals, remains of which were found in the mithraeum at Tienen, would have been born around April, and their age at time of death indicates that the deposition occurred during June or July.

48 *CIMRM* 1. 481.

49 Alvar (2008) 346.

buried under one of the altars when the temple was reconstructed at the turn of the 4th c. As for the remains of boars: at the *Foro Boario* mithraeum, two tusks of a boar were found in an amphora placed in a pit dug at the entrance,[50] while, as noted above, the presence of young pig remains—albeit not strictly the same animal—have also often been found in the excavations of various mithraea. Additionally, what appear to be sacrificial knives have been found within several mithraea.[51]

The Cult of Mithras in Late Antiquity: Changing Scholarly Views

Of the various non-Christian cults that were still active in Late Antiquity, the cult of Mithras has arguably received more attention than most. The majority of scholars have been content to see the disappearance of the cult as the result of the traditional narrative of violent Christian persecution. In the earliest days of Mithraic studies, Cumont commented that the "ruins of Mithraeums (*sic*) bear witness to [the Christians] devastating fury", and this view has been echoed by many up to the present day.[52] Among the most prominent works of recent times to adhere to this narrative are those of Eberhard Sauer, who suggested that the cult of Mithras was "the most hated cult and first victim of the Christian persecution of paganism". Manfred Clauss was content to accept without scrutiny when updating his original volume on the Mithras cult in 2012, a revision that Roger Beck referred to as "the most successful of Clauss' additions [to the original publication]".[53] In his study, Bayliss also noted that mithraea were the most common type of temple to have met a violent end, although does not provide much evidence to substantiate this claim.[54]

At first glance, the evidence for this narrative does appear convincing, with many mithraea providing a *terminus post quem* for their abandonment of the late 4th c. (i.e. contemporary to the 'anti-pagan laws'

of Theodosius), having had their reliefs and statues smashed or mutilated. The historical texts also appear to concur, recounting how mithraea were desecrated at Rome and Alexandria, while various Christian authors made their disdain for the cult abundantly clear.[55]

However, there are some dissenting voices that have begun to question whether there might be other explanations for the demise of the cult. Richard Gordon produced a strong critique of Sauer's initial volume, pointing out that many of the mithraea Sauer had looked at had failed to produce any convincing diagnostic evidence for Christian iconoclasm (i.e. no crosses carved into any walls). Furthermore, Gordon also questioned Sauer's selection of provinces—Britain, Gaul and parts of Germany—arguing they did not provide enough evidence to be considered representative of the Mithras cult in the 4th c. Subsequently, he questioned why Sauer failed to look at Italy, Dalmatia or Pannonia, which have produced significant Mithraic evidence dating to this period.[56] Indeed, given that no study has ever discussed how the cult of Mithras came to an end in areas where it was particularly prevalent, such as Pannonia, Noricum, and Dalmatia, a large amount of material has been overlooked in attempting to ascertain how and why the cult ceased to exist.

As mentioned, another issue is the lack of attention paid to any apparent changes that occurred within the cult itself during this period. Often when the status of the Mithras cult in the 4th c. is discussed it is dismissed within a page or so, with one left believing that the cult was much the same as it was in the early 2nd c. Any study presenting the cult in such a fashion immediately raises concerns regarding any conclusions that it may reach on the fate of the cult, for it is failing to take into account the nuances of different Mithraic communities, and how this might have affected the decline of the cult on a regional basis.

Furthermore, little attention has been paid to the context of mithraea in the 4th c.: what happened to the structures they neighboured? What changes occurred in the social networks of cult members? Indeed, nearly all the works which claim that Christian iconoclasts were the driving force behind the damage and destruction of mithraea rarely attempt to ascertain whether there is *any* evidence of a Christian presence in the area

---

50 Nida-Heddernheim: Huld-Zetsche (1986) 21; Pons Saravi: Walters (1974) 19; Londinium: Macready and Sidell (1998) 209; Brocolitia: Richmond *et al.* (1951) 35–36; *Foro Boario: CIMRM* 1. 434.

51 Taunum: *CIMRM* 2. 1069; Ober-Florstadt: *CIMRM* 2. 1080; Nida-Heddernheim II: *CIMRM* 2. 1115.

52 McCormack (1956) 203 (orig. Cumont (1913) 215). See also, Turcan (1984), (1996) 246; Winter (2000).

53 Sauer (1996) 79, (2003); Clauss (2012) 161–66. Clauss includes the mithraeum at Fertörakos among the mithraea abandoned in the late 4th c., yet it had clearly been turned into a mausoleum by this time, see *CIMRM* 2. 1646.

54 Bayliss (2004) 17.

55 Alexandria: Ruf. *HE.* 11.2; Sozom. *Hist. eccl.* 5.7; Socrates, *Hist. eccl.* 3.2.3. Rome: Jer. *Ep.* 107. 2. Christian authors hostile to the cult of Mithras: Justin *apol.* 1.66; Tert. *De Prae. Hae.* 40.3–4; Firm. Mat. *De Err. prof. rel.* 4.

56 Gordon (1999). For other works questioning the narrative of Christian iconoclasm directed at mithraea, see Martin (1989); Nicholson (1995).

INTRODUCTION

at the time. This has been another flaw in many studies that have looked at the end of the Mithras cult, for how can one establish why the cult came to an end with any reasonable plausibility if one does not know the context in which it existed at the time? It is by addressing these issues that this study will achieve a greater understanding of the cult of Mithras in Late Antiquity.

The Structure of This Volume

This monograph contains four chapters. The first of these looks at how—contrary to the way it has often been presented—the cult of Mithras had become increasingly regional by the early 4th c. By looking at various aspects of Mithraic communities—such as the location of mithraea, the architecture and decoration of these buildings, who was initiated into these cult communities, and what rituals they practised—it is apparent that if a Mithraic initiate travelled across the Roman world in the mid 4th c., the Mithraic communities they encountered would have been familiar in some ways, but also very discrepant in others. For example, the cult of Mithras in Gaul became increasingly equated with healing sanctuaries, on the Danube Mithras was the unconquerable patron of the army, while the Mithraic community on the eastern fringe of the Roman world was heavily influenced by neighbouring Persia. Furthermore, it will also be illustrated that there were some significant developments within certain Mithraic communities, particularly in regard to ritual practice, that suggest major changes occurred in how these groups operated.

Having set the stage by establishing what the cult (or cults) of Mithras entailed at the dawn of Late Antiquity, chapter two moves onto exploring when the cult began to enter into a decline, by utilising quantitative evidence regarding the construction and repair of mithraea. Rather than any indication of sudden persecution bringing such activities to an abrupt end, it is clear that support for the cult declined at a gradual rate, beginning in the early 4th c. and culminating in the early 5th c. However, what will also be demonstrated is that this decline was not uniform across the Roman world, with some areas already exhibiting diminishing support for mithraea in the late 3rd c. Of course, one cannot present such data in isolation, and in this chapter the building patterns of other temples and secular buildings are also illustrated. It has been shown here that, rather than the decline in the construction and maintenance of mithraea being the product of a general decline in building activity, the former follows its own different pattern. This indicates that it was largely an increasing lack of

desire amongst Mithraic worshippers to build and repair their mithraea, as opposed to external factors preventing them from doing so, that caused this.

In chapter three, this decline in support for mithraea will be explained by utilising the evidence outlined in chapter one. By applying sociological theory to certain aspects of the evidence, such as the changes in social networks of Mithraic worshippers and the development of Mithraic rituals, it is apparent that the cult no longer had the ability to foster commitment amongst its adherents to the extent it once did. Furthermore, the general decline in the populations of areas in which the cult was particularly prevalent, also limited the numbers that could be attracted to the cult. As such, the support for mithraea began to diminish.

The final chapter addresses the fate of mithraea, illustrating how and when these temples went out of use across the Roman world, from the late 3rd c. to early 5th c. While in many cases mithraea appear to have simply been abandoned without any items left within them, in the case of those that exhibit a more violent end, we will explore what factors may have played a role in this. From this, it will become clear that Christian iconoclasts were unlikely to have been responsible in the majority of cases, although there are a few examples where this is plausible. Rather, in many cases, barbarian incursions, civil wars, the relocation of Mithraic initiates, and natural disasters also played a role.

Selecting the Evidence

Given that this study reviews Mithraic evidence from across the entire Roman empire in the late antique period, inevitably limits have to be set on which data to include. As a result, the mithraea discussed in this study have been selected because they have produced reliable evidence indicating that they were being used as mithraea past the year AD 270. I have begun this study with the year 270 for largely practical reasons, given that it is often difficult to precisely date archaeological contexts, and by using this date I am able to incorporate all information that is roughly dated to the late 3rd c. By 'reliable' evidence, I mean epigraphic or iconographic material which explicitly refers to Mithras, the torchbearers, or the Mithraic grades that can be dated to 270+. If a building has produced no such evidence it will have been excluded, even if it has the ground-plan of a mithraeum.[57] As will be demonstrated, mithraea were reused for other purposes during this period, and thus it

---

57 A standard ground-plan for a mithraeum would include a room with a central aisle flanked by two parallel benches. At

cannot be said with any certainty that, even if a building did serve as a mithraeum initially, it was still being used as such in the 4th c. if there is no diagnostic evidence for this. Furthermore, structures are not included even if they have produced faunal evidence that is suggestive of a mithraeum, (e.g. a significant number of chicken bones), as this evidence has rarely been published with any chronological distributions illustrated; thus, it is possible that they originate from earlier phases of occupation. Sites that have been omitted, but which may have served as mithraea in this period include:

Aquae Mattiacae (Wiesbaden), Germany
This mithraeum was dug into a hillside on the edge of the Roman town. It measured 13.10 m × 7.30 m and consisted of the main cult room and an anteroom cut into the natural rock. The mithraeum was constructed in AD 218, as indicated by a votive altar. *Spolia* was taken from the mithraeum and used in the construction of the city wall sometime in the 4th c. As no other dating evidence was retrieved from the site, it is plausible that the mithraeum was still in operation past AD 270, but it also may have been long since out of use.[58]

Königsbrunn, Raetia
During excavations carried out in 1976–77, the tufa foundations of seven small buildings were found on a hillside overlooking the Lech Valley, *ca.* 500 m away from the *Via Claudia.* It appears these structures were part of *villa rustica* complex, with the main villa (which was not uncovered) likely to have been located on a higher terrace. One of these buildings, measuring 9.80 m × 9.10 m, bears the ground-plan of a mithraeum, although no specific Mithraic artefacts or inscriptions were recovered, although fragments of wall-plaster bearing red and white-green stripes, a decorative pattern evident in other Mithraic temples, were present. In the structure 98 coins were found, the latest minted in AD 367. Most of the coins were deposited in front of the niche, though there were some other small concentrations: one next to the north bench and the other at the end of the nave near the entrance.[59]

Orbe, Gaul
The structure was built near a large rural villa. The main room was of the standard mithraeum ground-plan, with the central nave terminating at a rounded apse. The main room was accessed via an anteroom, which appears to have been separated from the *cella* by a wooden door or a curtain, given the remains of a wooden threshold along the floor. Under this threshold, a small pit had been dug, which had been filled with charred ceramics and animal bones. Other rooms in the structure have been identified by the remains of wooden floors, some of which are likely to have been storage areas given their limited space. From AD 330 onwards a large number of coins were deposited in front of the apse. The only other finds were ceramics, which place the construction of the building in the Antonine period. The numismatic data indicate that it was abandoned in the early 4th c.[60] No specific Mithraic materials were found though.

Segontium (Caernarvon), Britain
This building, which had the ground plan of a mithraeum, was located on the slope of a hill close to a fort. A date for the construction of the building cannot be established precisely, but it is most likely to have been in the early 3rd c. when extensive construction work was undertaken at Segontium. A coin of Faustina I (AD 138–61) was uncovered below the surface-layer of one of the benches, but it had been disturbed post-deposition, and thus is of limited dating value. The building was altered several times during its occupation, but it is only the third phase of this can be dated securely as pottery sealed in this layer dates to the turn of the 4th c. There is no evidence to inform us when the structure was abandoned, but the decision to vacate it does not appear to have been due to an imminent threat as the last layer of occupation was covered by a thin stratum with no finds. Above this, however, there was evidence for the burning of oak beams, which had probably served as part of the roof frame. In this layer, a coin of Constans (AD 337–50) was found, thus the destruction of the building appears to have coincided with the arrival of a new garrison in AD 350.[61]

Serdica (Sofia), Thrace
A cellar of a house was adapted so that it had the ground-plan of a mithraeum, but when this adaption occurred is unknown, and no Mithraic material was found therein. It was subsequently turned into a storage space, the use of which could apparently be dated by two coins of Arcadius (AD 383–408), although I have not been able to establish the context of these.[62]

---

the end of the aisle would be a niche or plinth where the cult image was situated.

58   *CIMRM* 2. 1230–38; Schwertheim (1974) 86; Clauss (1992) 105–106.
59   Bakker (1994); Overbeck (1985).

60   Luginbühl, Monnier and Mühlemann (2004).
61   *CIMRM* 2. 2374; Boon (1960); Clauss (1992) 81.
62   *CIMRM* 2.2322–24.

INTRODUCTION

Sidon, Syria

The story surrounding a set of statuettes said to be from this site, which are now in the Louvre, is highly peculiar. In the late 1800s a man by the name of Durighello claimed to have discovered a mithraeum at Sidon, although due to his troubles with the authorities he refused to ever disclose its location. He did provide a description of the mithraeum, which if true would make it unlike any mithraeum ever found: it apparently contained at least eight rooms! Durighello did, however, produce the aforementioned statuettes, which consisted of: a relief of the tauroctony; a statue of the tauroctony; a statue of Mithras carrying the bull; three statues of Cautes and one of Cautophates; a statue of Aion; a statue of Hecate; and two statues of Venus, one in bronze. Some of the statuettes bear inscriptions stating they were paid for by Fl. Gerontios in the year '500', although there has been some deliberation as to what year this is in the modern calendar. If it is taken from the Seleucid calendar then it would be the equivalent of AD 188, while Ernest Will observed that, based on the local calendar of Sidon, which is established from stelae found in the town, the date is more likely to have been AD 398. Will also argued that the name Gerontios is far more common at the turn of the 4th c. than during the 2nd. Unfortunately, given the circumstances surrounding their discovery it is difficult to say with any certainty where these statuettes came from, and if there was indeed a mithraeum active in Sidon at the turn of the 5th c.[63]

Vindobala (Rudchester), Britain

This mithraeum, which was situated on a hillside outside of the fort, was constructed sometime in the early 3rd c. It measured *ca.*6.02 m × 12.00 m. When it was abandoned is unclear, due to heavy disturbance of the site. Unstratified ceramics indicate some presence here in the 4th c., but how this relates to the mithraeum is unknown.[64]

Additionally, while I utilise evidence from Ostia, particularly mithraea built in the late 3rd c., it is a fact that nearly all of these structures were excavated long before the application of modern methods, which means that it is unclear how long they were used for. Undoubtedly, some may have been used long into the 4th c., but equally some may have been abandoned not long after they were first consecrated. Thus, this work is not utilising any evidence from Ostian mithraea when discussing the cult in the 4th c.[65]

A Note on Terminology

It is also worth making some brief remarks regarding the use of certain terms in this study. First, I must state that I have endeavoured throughout this study not to use 'Mithraism' and 'Mithraist'. This is primarily because these are modern labels (to its contemporaries it would have been the Mysteries of Mithras and its followers known as 'Persians') that instil preconceived notions. As we do not know of any central Mithraic doctrine, or particular parameters for how Mithraic initiates had to live their lives, the use of the term Mithraism risks drawing parallels with modern religious '-isms', such as Judaism, Hinduism or Buddhism, that are a "differentiated social [entities that offer] a distinctive view of the world, including history and fate, one that demands exclusive adherence from its members and claims sole authority in matters cosmological and ethical".[66]

Secondly, I have attempted to avoid using the term 'mystery-cult' as much as possible. This is a label that has been applied to a number of religious organisations between the 7th c. BC and 4th c. AD, among which, in the Roman period, includes the cult of Mithras, as well as that of Isis/Sarapis, Magna Mater and Dionysus. However, much like terms such as 'Mithraism' and 'Mithraists', the application of the phrase 'mystery-cult' is an entirely modern invention. Indeed, we do not know whether people in the Roman world grouped together cults such as those of Isis, Mithras and Magna Mater. Certainly, these cults had mysterious elements to them, all involving initiation rites that were kept hidden from the outside world, but there was also a significant degree of variation between them. To begin with, the likes of Mithras, Isis and Magna Mater appeared in the Roman world at different times and by various means. Magna Mater was officially inducted into the Roman religious sphere by the Senate at the end of the 3rd c. BC, some three hundred years before we see the first appearance of the Mithraic cult, the origin of which remains largely unclear. In the case of Isis, her cult has a history stretching back to Hellenistic and ancient Egyptian worlds, probably entering into the Roman sphere via merchants and sailors from the East.

Such cults were also distinct from each other when it came to their architecture; one would not have found large ostentatious temples dedicated to Mithras as one would Isis or Magna Mater. Furthermore, the cult of Mithras did not hold public celebrations as the other two did, such as the *Megalesia* or *Isidis Navigium*. Finally, in

---

63   *CIMRM* 1.74–87; Will (1950); Clauss (1992) 242–43.

64   *CIMRM* 1. 838–43; Gillam and MacIvor (1954); Clauss (1992) 83.

65   I am aware of the recent discovery of a supposed mithraeum at Ostia that dates to the 4th c. (see David (2016)), but at the

---

time of writing I have seen no major publication that discusses it.

66   Woolf (2014) 66.

the case of Magna Mater, certain priests of the cult called *galli* would castrate themselves, but there is no evidence that there was a desire to do so amongst the followers of Mithras or Isis to go to such lengths to display their dedication; in the case of priests of Isis, a shaven head was the limit. Thus, in using the term 'mystery-cults', we once again risk creating a template for these cults that they did not adhere to.[67]

In broader terms, it worth noting that there are similar issues with the application 'pagans' and 'paganism' to describe polytheistic cults in Late Antiquity.[68] In literal terms, 'pagan' meant 'rustic' and was applied by Christians to the whole spectrum of non-Christian cults in the Roman world. Although undoubtedly there was a great deal of interaction and exchange between cults, particularly as people could be a member of several at one time, such a term obviously does not do justice to the wide range of beliefs and practices that existed in the Roman empire. As Greg Woolf put it, "[P]aganism is the most obvious version of a catch-all category defined only in negative terms".[69] Consequently, if one seeks to ascertain how 'paganism' declined and fell, the resulting possible answers are innumerable:

> [S]o when did paganism really, finally, end? If we define paganism as the civic cults of the pre-Christian Graeco-Roman World, official Roman paganism really did effectively end with the disappearance of the priestly colleges in the early 5th c. To use the term in the wider but well-established sense of any and all religious beliefs and practices that preceded conversion in what became Christian societies, Gothic paganism ended in the mid-4th c., Viking paganism not until the mid-twelfth.[70]

Indeed, how, why and when different 'pagan' cults and practices came to an end was highly variable, both in relation to each other and within themselves. Once again, archaeological investigation has been highly beneficial in highlighting this. For instance, the cult of Jupiter Dolichenus appears to have largely disappeared from the Danube and Rhine regions by the 3rd c., but at Vindolanda on Hadrian's Wall a dolichenum remained in use until the late 4th c., while recent work on the Aventine in Rome has yielded a dolichenum that was abandoned in the AD 330s.[71] How is it that temples to the same deity came to meet different fates at different times? Arguably, the best way to ascertain why this was is to place the respective cult communities in their socio-cultural setting, assess how this altered over time, and what effect this may have had on the cult community. Cults do not remain static, geographically or chronologically, but are continuously forced to react to the changing world around them. Indeed, Greg Woolf has suggested that deities should be viewed in the same way as objects, in that they have a 'cultural biography', with them "... undergoing processes of utopianization and processes of localization, their transformations entangled on each occasion with shifts in the social and political geography and identity characteristic of world empires and diaspora".[72] Sometimes, dramatic shifts in the context in which cults exist might force a cult to adapt in ways that are to its detriment, and lead to its decline. As will be highlighted in this study, significant variations began to emerge in the cult of Mithras across the 3rd and 4th c., with Mithras meaning different things to different people in different places, in ways that may not have always been beneficial to the cult's long-term prospects.

---

67 For critiques of applying the term 'mystery-cult' to Graeco-Roman religions, see Sfameni Gasparro (2011).

68 Lee (2000) 8–9; Cameron (2011) 1–32; Jones (2012).

69 Woolf (2009) 22.

70 Cameron (2011) 783.

---

71 On the end of the cult of Jupiter Dolichenus along the Danube and Rhine frontiers, see Tóth (1973). Vindolanda: Birley and Birley (2012); on the Aventine: Chioffi (1996) 132.

72 Woolf (2014) 85.

CHAPTER 1

The Development of the Cult of Mithras in Late Antiquity

By the turn of the 4th c., the cult of Mithras stretched from the Syrian Desert to Hadrian's Wall. Given that the cult was so widespread, it would be unsurprising for a degree of regionalisation to occur amongst different Mithraic communities, even if initially they had all started out as relatively homogenous. Such developments might be forced upon these communities, with changes in their architecture, ritual practice, or membership occurring as a reaction to the alterations in the world around them. Conversely, there may have been a desire among the patrons or members of the cult to highlight certain qualities of Mithras and/or his cult for particular reasons relating to the context in which they operated. In either case, this may have led to one Mithraic community developing certain characteristics that would seem peculiar to their contemporaries, both elsewhere and to those who had come before them in the same location. If a Mithraic initiate in the 4th c. had set out from Syria and travelled to Rome via Dalmatia, then headed north to the frontiers, and from there onto Gaul, would he have encountered the same approach to the cult of Mithras in every area, or would he have encountered alternative versions of the cult? Could a Mithraic initiate from a Mithraic community on one side of the Roman world slip seamlessly into another on the other side? And would a Mithraic initiate of the early 2nd c. find Mithraic worship in the 4th c. largely unchanged or significantly different?

In this chapter, I will demonstrate how the archaeological and epigraphic evidence indicates that our hypothetical Mithraic initiate may well have been perplexed by what he encountered on his travels. Given that regionalisation can occur on various levels—with similar developments taking place across large regions, while others occur only within individual provinces, and some simply within a single settlement—approaching this topic on a region-by-region basis would be problematic. Thus, this chapter is arranged via a thematic structure, which begins with the broader context of mithraea, before moving onto the architecture and decoration of these buildings, then to those who occupied them, and finally what ritual acts these people were performing therein. A brief discussion regarding the different forms of Mithras' name that appear in Late Antiquity is also included at the end. Vitally, what this information demonstrates is that this regionalisation involved considerable changes in how many Mithraic communities operated which, as we shall go on to see in later chapters, contributed to the decline of the cult in the 4th c.

The Location of Mithraea

The most obvious place to begin when discussing the cult of Mithras is by asking where does one find mithraea and how does their context vary? As highlighted in the introduction, despite drawing upon the Persian deity Mithra, there is little evidence relating to the Mithras cult from the eastern half of the Roman empire and the majority of this pre-dates the 4th c. period. Mithraea in this half of the empire have been discovered at Doliche (Turkey), Ša'āra (Syria) and (most famously) Dura-Europos (Syria), but all three had been abandoned by the mid 3rd c. In addition, a mithraeum at Caesarea Maritima (Israel) only remained in use until the late 3rd c.,[1] thus by the early 4th c. only one mithraeum is known to have been active in this entire area of the empire: the Hawarte Mithraeum. Given that there is no contemporary Mithraic activity evident within thousands of kilometres of this temple from the early 4th c. onwards, one would think that this community operated in a largely autonomous fashion from its contemporaries.[2] Indeed, as will become apparent through outlining the various unique aspects of this mithraeum in the course of this chapter, this Mithraic community did indeed become notably distinct from Mithraic activity elsewhere.

For now, let us turn our attention to the western provinces where the situation was rather different. Here, many mithraea are evident across the region, although their distribution is by no means even. In Gaul for instance, evidence for the cult of Mithras is largely concentrated in the eastern half of the province, with only occasional examples appearing in the West. Most of the Gallic mithraea were constructed around the beginning of the 3rd c., with many of these remaining in use until the final decades of the 4th c. Among these temples the level of excavation undertaken varies considerably from site to site, but an evident trend that has emerged is their close proximity to water features, most often

---

1 Doliche: Winter (2000); Schütte and Winter (2004) Gordon (2007); Dura-Europos: *CIMRM* 1. 34–69; Clauss (1992) 238–42. Ša'āra: Kalos (2001).

2 Gawlikowski (2007) 337.

natural springs, and other sanctuaries. At Les Bolards, a hypocaust was found near the mithraeum, as were a number of bronze *ex votos* relating to eye diseases, which may indicate a temple area connected to healing waters drawn from the natural spring of La Courtavaux, situated 2 km away. At Venetonimagus, to the south of the mithraeum lay the remains of what may have been a bath-house that perhaps drew upon a natural spring that was to be found close by. The fragments of a colossal statue were also recovered close to the mithraeum, leading Walters to suggest that this area may have served as a sanctuary complex dedicated to healing waters that was similar to that of Apollo-Moritagus at Alise-Sainte-Reine.

At Septeuil, just north-west of Paris, in the mid 4th c. a mithraeum was installed within a former nymphaeum that enclosed a natural spring. Once again, this mithraeum was neighboured by a large building that may have served as either a temple or a bath-house. Another mithraeum was built at Mackwiller, possibly located on private land that formed part of an estate, which overlay a natural spring and was neighboured by a small wooden temple that was also perhaps related to the spring. The Pons Saravi Mithraeum also lay next to a natural spring, while the worship of the local deities Nantosvelta and Sucellus appears to have occurred close by, given that altars dedicated to these deities were found just 20 m from the temple. At Forum Claudii Vallensium Octodurensium (hereafter referred to by its modern name Martigny, for brevity), excavations have shown that the mithraeum lay on the north-west edge of a collection of structures that included a bath-house and a Gallo-Roman temple, while to the west of the mithraeum lay a nymphaeum. Finally, a mithraeum was installed in the *Altbachtal* temple precinct at Augusta Treverorum (hereafter referred to as Trier), the capital of the Gallic provinces, around the turn of the 4th c. The identity of the gods to which neighbouring temples in this instance were dedicated is unknown, but a short distance from the mithraeum we once again find a bath-house.[3]

Evidently, there was a clear preference for locating Gallic mithraea close to natural water features, which in turn led to them neighbouring bath-houses and

temples. Subsequently, it appears that these mithraea found themselves associated with buildings that represented divine healing. However, this is not to claim that the site of these mithraea was initially chosen with the intention of connecting Mithras with such powers. The desire to locate mithraea close to such features is most likely due in part to the Mithraic narrative, in which Mithras shot an arrow into a rock and water poured forth, while the use of water in Mithraic rituals, probably for purification, may also have driven Mithraic initiates to erect their temples near to springs.[4] What would be more fitting than to use such water, flowing forth from the rock as if drawn from it by Mithras himself? Indeed, various mithraea across the Roman world were situated near springs or other water features, such as at Poetovio and at sites along Hadrian's Wall (see Appendix A), but rarely does one find other cases where this led to so many mithraea located within a particular area being situated so close to other temples and bath-houses.[5] Over time, it is plausible that an association would have formed between the cult of Mithras and the surrounding buildings, with Mithras subsequently recognised as a god who could save the sick. Indeed, this does appear to have been the case judging from the cult membership and finds from mithraea in this region (see below).

What then of the Danubian provinces? In the provinces of Noricum and Pannonia, mithraea were mainly concentrated in the northern, militarised areas. Major towns to the south, such as Aguntum, Mursa, and the imperial capital of Sirmium, have produced almost no Mithraic evidence. In contrast, towns in the north, including Aquincum, Carnuntum, and Poetovio, were hubs of Mithraic activity, with numerous mithraea found in and around these settlements, as was a range of individual Mithraic finds.[6] Mithraea also existed at Virunum, the original administrative centre of Noricum, and at Schachadorf near Ovilava, which replaced Virunum as the administrative centre. Additionally, mithraea were present at the town of Lentia and at Ad Enum, the latter a site lying across the River Inn from a pottery manufacturing centre and the customs station

---

3   For <u>Les Bolards</u> and <u>Venetonimagus</u>, see Walters (1974) 5–17. <u>Mackwiller</u>: Hatt (1955); <u>Martigny</u>: Wiblé (2008) 82, 117, 123, 175; <u>Pons Saravi</u>: Walters (1974) 18, 22–23; <u>Septeuil</u>: Gaidon-Bunuel (1991) 51; <u>Trier</u>: Ghetta (2008) 83–85. Gallic mithraea were not always found in such locations. The mithraeum at Tienen was located on the fringe of a *vicus* amongst pottery workshops, while at Burdigala a particularly large mithraeum was built within a residential area: <u>Burdigala</u>: Gaidon-Bunuel (1991) 51; <u>Tienen</u>: Martens (2004) 26–28.

4   On the water-miracle and the presence of basins in mithraea for purification rituals, see Clauss (2012) 72–74.

5   The Londinium Mithraeum had a well located within it, see Shepherd (1998) 70. At Brocolitia, the mithraeum was built near Coventina's Well and an open-air nymphaeum. At Borcovicium, the mithraeum was built over a natural spring, as was another building situated next to it. For the environment of both Brocolitia and Borcovicium, see Allason-Jones (2004) 185.

6   <u>Aquincum</u>: *CIMRM* 2. 1742–96; <u>Carnuntum</u>: *CIMRM* 2. 1664–1722; Gugl and Kremer (2011); <u>Poetovio</u>: *CIMRM* 2. 1487–1618, Vomer-Gojković (2001).

of Pons Aeni, which was replaced by a fort in the mid to late 3rd c.[7]

Some of these mithraea, such as Mithraea I and II at Poetovio, were built over or close to natural springs as their contemporaries in Gaul were, but overall it is much rarer to find mithraea located near to springs in Noricum or Pannonia.[8] In fact, many of the mithraea appear to have been constructed irrespective of such features in the landscape, with none of the extant mithraea at Aquincum or Carnuntum located over or adjacent to springs; rather the mithraea situated here were constructed in and around the towns and forts. Of all the mithraea in this region, the setting of the Lentia Mithraeum is perhaps the most unique, for it was constructed shortly after AD 275 next to a temple to *Dea Roma* and the *Genius Augusti*, in what appears to be the central temple area of the town.[9] For a mithraeum to hold a relatively prominent position was unusual and, whether it was intended or not, suggests a close relationship between the cult and deities that were emblematic of Roman power. We do not see this in the aforementioned evidence found in Gaul and Hawarte.

In contrast to the strong correlation between the presence of the military and the distribution of the Mithraic evidence on the Danube in the Late Roman period, along the German *limes* such a relationship is less apparent than in previous times. That the cult of Mithras initially spread to Germany via the army is relatively certain, for, as noted previously, the earliest datable Mithraic evidence was found at forts in this region. However, the relinquishing of territory across the Rhine to Germanic tribes in the mid 3rd c. saw a number of mithraea, including those at Dieburg, Nida-Heddernheim and Stockstadt, abandoned.[10] Subsequently, the mithraea still active in the Rhine area in Late Antiquity show little connection to the military, situated as they were either in rural locations (Gimmeldingen and Reichweiler) or on private estates (Bornheim-Sechtem and Rockenhausen).[11]

Among the mithraea mentioned thus far, some, such as at Reichweiler, were connected to natural rock faces onto which the central relief had been carved, but the majority were stand-alone buildings or installed within large pre-existing structures. In Dalmatia, however, nearly all mithraea were to be found in rural areas either abutting cliff-faces or installed within caves, with the main relief either carved into the natural rock or attached to it. The Jajce Mithraeum was erected against a rock-face on the bank of the Pliva River; two mithraea found at Arupium were also set against rock-faces; the Epidaurum Mithraeum was located within a cave. The exception is the mithraeum at Konjic, which was a standalone structure, and its main relief was not attached to or carved into the natural rock, but it was still constructed on a hillside away from a populated area. That many of these mithraea were located in mountainous regions suggests that they were not readily accessible to those who did not know of their whereabouts. To these can be added the mithraeum at Timavo, for although this mithraeum was located in northern Italy it was also situated in a cave overlooking the coast that, like the mithraeum at Epidaurum, contained a well. Furthermore, given that this mithraeum lay in closer proximity to the Dalmatian mithraea than those of Rome and its hinterlands (which is where the majority of Mithraic evidence in late antique Italy was situated), the Mithraic congregation that used this site were perhaps more closely linked with the former. However, the foci of worship in the Timavo Mithraeum were two statuettes of the bull-slaying scene, rather than a relief attached to the natural rock face.[12]

It is unclear as to why these Dalmatian Mithraic communities preferred to erect their mithraea in such contexts. It may have been for ritual reasons, as was the case with the close relationship between Gallic mithraea and natural springs. Indeed, given that mithraea were designed to replicate the cave in which Mithras slayed the bull, installing a mithraeum within an actual cave would be an entirely reasonable thing to do. Furthermore, Mithras' birth from the rock may have stimulated a desire among some Mithraic groups to place themselves as close to the 'natural' environment as possible, as opposed to the built-up confines of a town or small settlement. In any case, once again we find mithraea in a certain region that have defining characteristics that distinguish them from those we have seen elsewhere.

---

7   Kellner (1995) 498. The mithraeum at Ad Enum is often incorrectly referred to as the Pons Aeni Mithraeum.

8   Clauss (2012) 73.

9   The identification of the neighbouring temple as one dedicated to *Dea Roma* and the *Genius Augusti* was established by the discovery of two statue bases, see Karnitsch (1956) 205. Based on its ground-plan, another building situated next to the mithraeum may have been dedicated to the Capitoline Triad (with the terminus of the supposed *cella* divided into three), although this is unconfirmed, see Karnitsch (1956) 16–17.

10   Dieburg: *CIMRM* 2. 1246; Nida-Heddernheim: *CIMRM* 2. 1082, 1108, 1117; Stockstadt: *CIMRM* 2. 1158, 1209.

11   Bornheim-Sechtem: Ulbert (2004) 81–82; Gimmeldingen: *CIMRM* 1. 1313; Reichweiler: Bernhard (1990); Rockenhausen: Schwertheim (1974) 135.

12   Arupium: *CIMRM* 2.1851–52; Epidaurum: *CIMRM* 2. 1882; Jajce: *CIMRM* 2. 1901; Konjic: *CIMRM* 2. 1895; Timavo: Pross Gabrielli (1975) 7.

Finally, we turn our attention to Rome, where at least 16 mithraea were in use across the 3rd and 4th c. Examples of those in use in Rome at the turn of the 4th c. include mithraea in the *Crypta Balbi, Foro Boario*, the *Castra Peregrinorum* (under *S. Stefano Rotondo*) and *Ospedale San Giovanni*. Each of these mithraea were located in different contexts, but all share the fact that these were relatively busy, public areas: the *Crypta Balbi* Mithraeum was situated inside a large *insula*; the *Foro Boario* was a commercial hub; the mithraeum at the *Castra Peregrinorum* was attached to a barracks; and at *Ospedale S. Giovanni* the mithraeum was located near a number of granaries.[13] In nearby Ostia, nearly a third of the mithraea uncovered in the town ('of Fructosus', 'Porta Romana', in the House of Diana, 'of Felicissimus', and 'of the Serpents') were also installed in the late 3rd c., making it likely that at least some remained in use until the early decades of the 4th c., although as discussed there is no extant evidence to confirm this.[14]

During the course of the 4th c., three more mithraea were erected in Rome by senatorial groups on their own property (in the house of the Senator Fl. Septimius Zosimus at *Via Giovanni Lanza* 128 on the Esquiline Hill, and two in/around the house of the Olympii on the Campus Martius) along with the mithraeum installed within the sanctuary area of Magna Mater and Attis on the Vatican Hill.[15] The context of these are considerably different from their contemporaries both in Rome and elsewhere, being located as they were on expensive properties. However, as no extant remains of the mithraea located on the Campus Martius and the Vatican Hill have yet been found (we only have

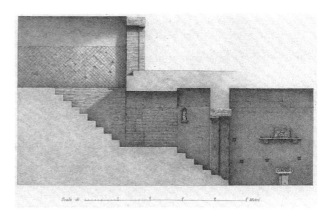

FIGURE 11 Cross-section of the mithraeum found at Via S. Giovanni Lanza 128. Esquiline Hill, Rome. Visconti (*1885*) plate 5.

inscriptions currently) it is difficult to assess their relationship with their environment. That being said, the Vatican Hill Mithraeum may have been visible to non-members, given that the inscriptions found in that location are essentially long lists of the achievements of the congregation's members, and as such appear to have been composed so as to be viewed by a large audience (see below).[16] In the case of the mithraeum at *Via Giovanni Lanza* 128, however, it does look to have been a highly private sanctuary, not only because it was located within a house, but also due to the fact it was situated at a subterranean level, having to be accessed via a staircase (fig. 11). In order to do so, one would have had to pass a small *lararium* dedicated to a whole host of other deities; that the worship of Mithras was conducted away from this suggests an intention on the part of the owner(s) to limit accessibility to the mithraeum.[17]

Thus, in Rome itself we find notable variations in the spatial contexts of mithraea: examples next to barracks, in private houses, connected to sanctuaries of other gods, in a densely populated *insula*, and commercial hubs. One might go so far as to say the variation among the mithraea found in Rome is reflective of mithraea across the Roman empire in Late Antiquity. Indeed, it is difficult to imagine a Mithraic initiate from Hawarte comprehending the prominence of the mithraeum at Lentia, while an initiate who attended the mithraeum at the *Foro Boario* would probably have felt out of place in the mithraeum situated on the property of the Olympii.

Mithraic Architecture

Many of the mithraea in use during the 4th c. appear to follow the standard mithraeum plan, in which the

---

13 For a good overview of mithraea active in late antique Rome, see Bjørnebye (2007) 25–53. I am hesitant, however, to agree with Bjørnebye's suggestion that the mithraeum located in the Baths of Caracalla was still active until the late 4th c., which he appears to base on the fact that the baths themselves were still in use. Even if Bjørnebye is correct in this regard, I find it dubious to assert that it would still be attracting a 'full-house' of at least 100 Mithraic initiates 150 years after its initial construction. See also: <u>Castra Peregrinorum</u>: Lissi-Caronna (1986); <u>Crypta Balbi</u>: Ricci (2004); <u>Foro Boario</u>: *CIMRM* 1.434–56, Griffith (2003) 77–82; <u>Ospedale San Giovanni</u>: Santa Maria Scrinari (1979).

14 White (2012) 442–43.

15 <u>Via S. Giovanni Lanza 128</u>: *CIMRM* 1.356–60; Gallo (1979). The inscription referring to the mithraeum built by Zosimus was found reused in a church near to *Via S. Giovanni Lanza* 128. Given the growing interest in the cult of Mithras among the elites of Rome in the 4th c., it is entirely possible that the Zosimus inscription refers to a different sanctuary, but, given the close proximity between the temple and the inscription find-spot, it is highly likely they are related.

16 Cameron (2011) 142–48.

17 *CIMRM* 1. 356.

cella contained a central nave flanked by two parallel benches (figs. 12–13). As outlined previously, according to Beck's analysis this standard mithraeum plan had, at least initially, an important ritual significance. Yet there are some mithraea which appeared in the late 3rd and early 4th c. that abandoned this traditional format, suggesting not only a growing variation in architectural style, but also alterations to ritual practice connected to the topography of the mithraeum.

To begin with, let us return to the Hawarte Mithraeum (fig. 12.10). Here, there was only a single stone bench, running in an 'L' shape along the eastern and southern walls of the *cella*, with the entrance to the room lying in its western wall. Furthermore, unlike most other mithraea, the fact that the Hawarte Mithraeum was installed in a cave system means that the ceiling of the *cella* survives, in which was found an aperture that would allow light to shine onto the main relief. Another example where the ceiling of a mithraeum was still extant at the time of excavation is the Caesarea Maritima Mithraeum. Here, light would have shone on to the altar in front of the cult relief at mid-summer. Unfortunately, as the preservation of the ceilings of mithraea located in the West is uncommon, it is unclear whether such use of light was a feature confined to these eastern Mithraic communities or was employed throughout the Roman empire. However, that western mithraea situated in caves, such as at Epidaurum, St Urban and Timavo, have not produced any evidence for the presence of such shafts does infer that such a design feature was perhaps limited to the East.[18] Additionally, as fig. 9 makes apparent, mithraea varied notably in alignments, suggesting the path of the sun was not foremost on the minds of those constructing them.

In Rome, the mithraeum at *Via Giovanni Lanza* 128 also had an unusual architectural form. The room in which the mithraeum was situated was very small (*ca.* 6 m²), but what is particularly strange about this mithraeum is that it does not appear to have had any benches *at all*. In this regard, like Hawarte, it does not adhere to Beck's template for the ideal mithraeum, implying a departure from traditional ritual practice. Of course, the benches may have been made of wood and decayed over time, but there was no indication of any fittings having existed where the benches should have been.[19] It is unfortunate that the mithraea erected in

the house of the Olympii and on the Vatican Hill in the 4th c. are not extant, leaving us to wonder whether they too differed from the traditional mithraeum plan.

Some of the Dalmatian mithraea also have odd traits. The Konjic Mithraeum (fig. 12.1) was peculiar in that it appears to have contained just one bench running along its northern wall, to the left-hand side of the nave, with no evidence of a counterpart along the opposite wall. At Jajce (fig. 12.7) the mithraeum also had one bench that ran along the left-hand side of nave, although as this mithraeum was on a different alignment to that at Konjic, here the bench was attached to the southern wall.[20] The general shape of the Jajce Mithraeum is also atypical, for, if we include the rock-face it abutted, it had five sides, as opposed to the usual rectangular/square shape of other mithraea. It is also worth acknowledging that the mithraeum constructed at Lentia in the late 3rd c., was not found to contain any benches in its *cella* (fig. 12.6). However, given the evidence for burning in this room, it might be that the benches were made of wood and were thus destroyed.[21]

If the plan of a mithraeum was indeed intrinsic to the ritual activities held therein, then the departure of these mithraea from the standard *cella* plan is of considerable importance, as it may infer considerable ritual differences among these Mithraic communities, which are not apparent to us via the extant materials. In any case, mithraea that failed to include the standard *cella* plan would not be able to host Beck's hypothesised ritual procession of the soul through the celestial spheres, for by removing one or both benches this would also remove parts of the celestial map through which the soul moved. Notably there are no earlier examples where such variation is evident, thus indicating that this only began to occur in the late 3rd c. One wonders whether if the cult of Mithras had continued to flourish for a few more centuries, rather than having died within a century, if such variation would have become more commonplace among newly erected mithraea.

Additionally, at Gimmeldingen the term *fanum* was used to denote a mithraeum erected in AD 325, a structure that was constructed from wood and so sadly no longer extant. Such terminology is highly unusual, given that mithraea were typically referred to as being either a *templum* or a *spelaeum*.[22] Does the use of the

---

18   Hawarte: Gawlikowski (2007) 349–50; Caesarea Maritima: Bull (1978) 79.

19   *CIMRM* 1. 356. The remains of torches made of fair-wood were found in the room, thus one would expect some remnants of the benches to be extant had they been made of wood.

20   At Konjic, Vermaseren states only one bench 'survives', but this appears to be based on the assumption that there must be two benches to follow the standard plan, rather than from any extant evidence, see *CIMRM* 2. 1895.

21   Karnitsch (1956) 206.

22   Clauss (1992) 42.

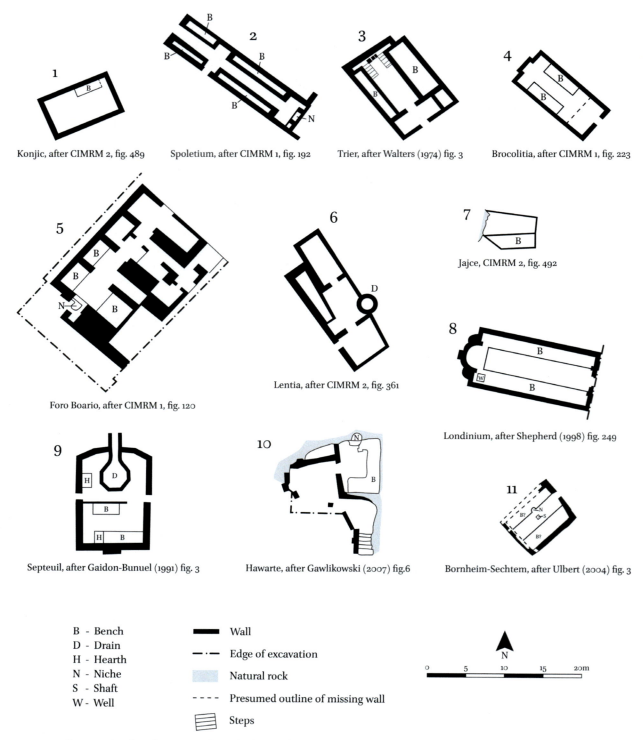

FIGURE 12 *Comparative plan of various mithraea built and adapted from the late 3rd c. onwards.*
DRAWN BY LLOYD BOSWORTH.

term *fanum* indicate this was a mithraeum constructed in the style of a Gallo-Roman temple? If so, this would represent a considerable break with the traditional arrangement of a mithraeum. Alternatively, was this simply a unique term applied to what was a typical mithraeum? Unfortunately, we will never know.

Mithraic Iconography

In the majority of cases, the mithraea in use during the 4th c. have not produced images that depart from the standard Mithraic iconography. The bull-slaying scene is still prevalent, while other common images,

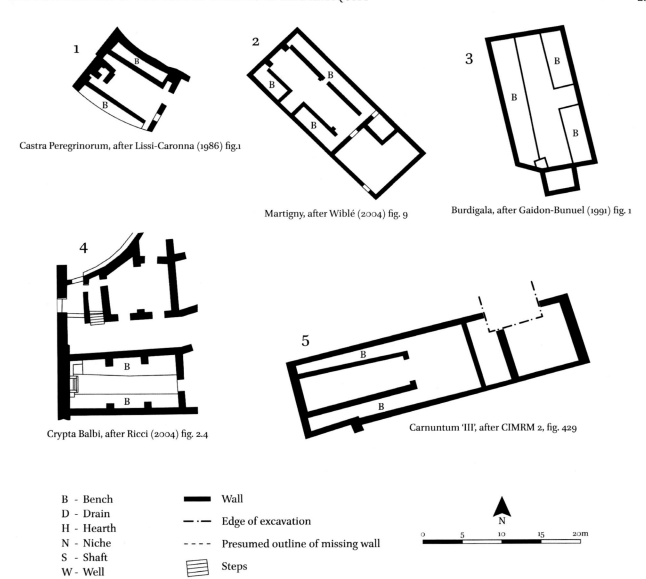

FIGURE 13   *Comparative plan of various mithraea built and adapted from the late 3rd c. onwards.*
DRAWN BY LLOYD BOSWORTH.

such as Mithras emerging from the rock and individual depictions of Cautes and Cautopates, still regularly occur. This was even the case in the mithraeum at *Via Giovanni Lanza* 128, which, despite its unusual layout, produced a relatively standard bull-slaying image alongside two statuettes of the torchbearers.[23] One may find a degree of variation among these images, but this is not something that is specific to later periods, for in the 2nd c. certain Mithraic iconographical traits emerged in different areas. The most notable of these was the so-called Danubian style, where the central bull-slaying image was bordered by other, smaller images depicting episodes from Mithras' life.[24]

There are, however, some particularly unique Mithraic images belonging to the period of Late Antiquity. As has been discussed, a notable quirk of the Dalmatian mithraea was the desire of initiates to inscribe or attach the main bully-slaying image onto the face of natural rock, although the actual images themselves are relatively standard. However, a rather unusual individual relief, relatively small in size (surface area 0.35 m²), was found at Dardagana along with some coins from the reign of Valentinian I, thus making it likely to have been manufactured in the 4th c. (fig. 14). The image shows Mithras slaying the bull (the latter is now mostly missing) flanked by the torchbearers, who are both holding croziers, rather than their usual torches; these are both pointed downward, as opposed to one pointing up and the other down, as was standard. Sol and Luna are also

---

23   *CIMRM* 1. 257–59.
24   Clauss (2012) 74–77.

FIGURE 14 *Mithraic Relief found at Dardagana. After Kosorić (1965) fig. 1.*
DRAWN BY LLOYD BOSWORTH.

pushed together in the top-left of the relief, rather than situated in the right and left corners respectively, and the snake in this depiction has a halo around its head.[25] As to why this depiction contains such unusual aspects is unclear, but the relief is by far one of the most unique Mithraic images ever found.

By far the most strikingly unusual 4th c. Mithraic iconography comes from the Hawarte Mithraeum. Both the ceiling and walls of the *cella* were plastered then painted, as were the walls of the anterooms. Five stages of painting can be detected, but only the last two can be distinctively analysed. There does not appear to have been any considerable differences between these two final phases, with the images of Period V the same as those of Period IV, just redrawn slightly. Depicted are various scenes from the life of Mithras, as well as a battle between good and evil. The images relating to the latter were found in the anterooms, and include: lions devouring demons; a man in Persian garb (Mithras?) holding the chains of a short, black two-headed demon, while standing in front of a large white horse; and a city wall topped by various black heads, with rays of light descending on (or attacking) them (figs. 15–16). Such images are unparalleled in any other mithraea and, as Richard Gordon has argued, are likely to be the product of a distinctly local tradition, which has been influenced by Zoroastrian beliefs from nearby Persia.[26]

In contrast, in the *cella* the walls were painted with the standard depictions of scenes from Mithras' life. These include images of: the rock birth; the tauroctony; Mithras in a tree; and Mithras holding an arrow. However, there are still some images in this room that are not common in other Mithraic contexts, including: wall paintings depicting items which may represent the seven Mithraic grades (located underneath the tauroctony painting);[27] hunters on horseback dressed in Phrygian hats chasing animals; Helios; Transitus; and Zeus. Little of the ceiling painting in the *cella* survives, but from the Period IV phase an inscription could be discerned, which read 'The fortune of the [invincible] Mithras [wins!]', which may be an adaption of a hippodrome chant. The division of these various images between the anterooms

---

25 Zotović (1973) n. 22.

26 Gordon (2001) 106–16.

27 The surviving images included: a krater between a leaping lion and a serpent, an oil lamp, a fire-shovel, "an egg-shaped black object", a round jar, a crown and an arrow: see Gawlikowski (2007) 357–58.

FIGURE 15 *Wall painting from the Hawarte Mithraeum: a man in Persian garb (Mithras?) holding the chains of a short, black two-headed demon, while standing in front of a large white horse. Gawlikowski (2004) fig. 9.*

FIGURE 16 *Wall painting from the Hawarte Mithraeum: city wall topped by various black heads, with rays of light descending on (or attacking) them. Gawlikowski (2004) fig. 12.*

and *cella* suggest a particular spatial arrangement was involved in their composition, perhaps providing some form of narrative. It is a shame that in this case much of the central bull-slaying image was lost, for one wonders if this displayed any radical differences to the traditional depiction, although from what could be discerned it followed the standard format.[28]

Patronage and Membership

We have seen how local variants of the Mithras cult are inferred via the location, structure and decoration of mithraea, but what of the people therein? What can this information tell us about the status of Mithraic communities in Late Antiquity? Before undertaking this analysis, it is important to highlight that the number of inscriptions relating to the cult of Mithras follows the general pattern of decline in the epigraphic habit in the 4th c. In many cases, this means we only have the odd inscription that attests to a Mithraic initiate or initiates at this time. In some instances, such as from the mithraea of Hawarte and Dalmatia, we have nothing, which is particularly unfortunate given that, as we have seen, these are among the most distinct in terms of location, architecture and decoration.

Let us begin by returning to Gaul: given that mithraea here were often located at and around sites connected to springs and what appear to be sanctuaries related to healing, is this reflected among the membership of these Mithraic communities? At Venetonimagus, this is indeed the case. Here, the *pater* C. Rufius Virilis erected an altar around the turn of the 4th c. which mentions his father, the *pater patrum* C. Rufius Eutactus. The latter's occupation is listed on another inscription as being a doctor, which provides the only known instance of a Mithraic initiate to hold such a position.[29] What this would mean for Eutactus' status in the secular world is unclear. Occasionally, doctors could obtain a significant level of social status, such as Claudius' personal physician Xenophon, who provided new buildings and restored others at his home on the island of Cos.[30] However, they rarely reach such heights, and there is nothing to indicate whether Eutactus' status in the Mithraic community was achieved due to financial power. Indeed, it is unlikely to be a coincidence that the single example we have of a doctor serving as the leader of a Mithraic community originates from a region where mithraea were often situated next to springs and healing sanctuaries; rather, the most plausible explanation is that it was this link between mithraea and neighbouring features that resulted in Eutactus becoming the leader of its community. Unfortunately, we have little in the way of inscriptions elaborating on the secular status of Mithraic initiates elsewhere in Gaul during the 3rd to 4th c., including at the many sites listed that were connected to natural springs. Two individuals from the Trier mithraeum, Martius Martialis and Nicasius, are known to us: the former was the *pater* of the community, while Nicasius probably served as slave. Neither infers any connection to healing, but the location of the Trier Mithraeum is not suggestive of this in any case. However, it is worth noting that an inscription from Angera, although providing neither a date nor a dedicatee, does describe Mithras as the 'helper' (*adiutor*), a word not found elsewhere in Mithraic inscriptions.[31]

In Germany, as discussed above, the distribution of late Mithraic sites suggests that the connection between

---

28 Gawlikowski (2007) 352–60.

29 *CIMRM* 1. 911. For Eutactus' profession, see *CIL* 13. 2509.

30 Jackson (1988) 56–57.

31 Angera: *CIMRM* 1. 717; Trier: *CIMRM* 1. 985, 987, 987bis.

the cult and the military in this region was not what it once was. Unfortunately, there is little epigraphic evidence to supplement this observation; only two Mithraic initiates are known to us in the epigraphic record (both from Gimmeldingen), and neither of them reveal their secular status.

However, along the Danube frontier, inscriptions do attest to the continuing importance of the cult amongst the army into the 4th c. In the mid 3rd c., the mithraea in Poetovio record various military personnel frequenting Mithraea II and III, including Flavius Aper who acted as the commander of the *V Macedonica* and *XIII Gemina*.[32] By the turn of the 4th c., little appears to have changed in this regard. At Poetovio, four altars bearing *ex voto* inscriptions were found alongside the aforementioned inscription attesting to the restoration of a mithraeum (IV) by a *dux*. They provide no details about the men who dedicated them other than their names and that two of them were brothers, but given the prevalence of the military in the mithraea of Poetovio and the presence of the *dux* among them, it is likely they were soldiers. Furthermore, there is an inscription from Virunum, dating to the Tetrarchic period, that refers to a *speculator legionis*, who donated an altar as an *ex voto* with the permission of an unnamed *pater*. In AD 297 another veteran erected an altar at Ulcisia Castra in Pannonia, while a small stone altar recovered from the Lentia Mithraeum, thus post-dating AD 275, was dedicated by a veteran. Finally, a fragment of an inscription carved on a Mithraic relief, found at Axiopolis in Moesia, informs us it was commissioned by a *dux*. It probably dates to the Tetrarchic period, but unfortunately nothing more about the man is known (not even his name), nor do we know if this was a votive inscription or a gift to a Mithraic community by a non-initiate.[33]

In addition to these finds, a marble relief from the Tetrarchic period found at Stifis, North Africa, which was commissioned by the entire *II Herculia*, can be added to the Danubian corpus. The legion in question was originally from the Danube and came to North Africa in AD 298/99, when they accompanied the emperor Maximian to Mauretania, but subsequently returned to the northern frontier thereafter.[34] Interestingly, given that an entire legion paid for this, rather than an individual soldier, it is possible that Mithras was seen as something akin to a patron deity of the entire group.

Non-military dedications also attest to the importance of the cult in the Danube region, such as the

inscription found at Virunum referring to the restoration of a mithraeum in AD 311 by the governor.[35] However, the most outstanding Mithraic inscription from the region is the Tetrarchic dedication from Carnuntum, describing Mithras as the 'Protector of their *Imperium*' and referring to their restoration of a mithraeum. There is no evidence to suggest that the Tetrarchs lavished extravagant sums on the Mithraic community; the altar bearing this inscription had been taken from a different context and re-carved, while there is no evidence for any substantial repairs to Mithraeum 'III', which is generally assumed to be the mithraeum referred to in the inscription.[36] Yet, regardless of how much their benefaction cost, the very fact that the Tetrarchs (who were not, as far as we know, members of the cult) were willing to fund a Mithraic community in any way was largely unprecedented, while their decision to call Mithras the 'Protector of their *Imperium*' was unlikely to have been undertaken on a whim. Indeed, when placed in the wider context of both mithraea and temples in general in the Danube region, the motivation behind this was clearly to send a message, not only to the Mithraic communities at Carnuntum but across this frontier.

Firstly, that this mithraeum is also one of the biggest examples ever found (*ca.* 298 m^2) and contained one of the largest images of the tauroctony in the Roman world (surface area of 2.75 m × 3.88 m), also infers that this dedication was designed to make an impact on the Mithras cult beyond the town.[37] Secondly, that the only two other instances of the Tetrarchs restoring temples in this region were those dedicated to Jupiter and Victory at Aquincum and Bedaium respectively suggests that the Tetrarchs were intending to show that they considered Mithras pre-eminent among other gods in this region.[38] What was the message they were trying to convey? As discussed, it is apparent that Mithras was viewed in high esteem by much of the soldiery in this region, a soldiery that had regularly proven problematic in securing stability in the empire, for they had earned a record of

---

32 Clauss (1992) 165–69.

33 <u>Axiopolis</u>: *CIMRM* 2. 2280; <u>Lentia</u>: *CIMRM* 2. 1419; <u>Poetovio</u>: *CIMRM* 2. 1615–17; <u>Ulcisia Castra</u>: Clauss (1992) 188; <u>Virunum</u>: *CIMRM* 2. 1434.

34 *CIMRM* 1. 149.

35 *CIMRM* 2. 1431.

36 I believe that the large altar decorated with various deities found in this mithraeum (*CIMRM* 1. 1685) was brought to the temple as part of this restoration process. The size and decoration are highly unusual in a Mithraic context, even though mithraea have been found to contain representations of other gods. Certainly, as with the Mithraic altar bearing the Tetrarchs' inscription, the reuse of an altar from a different context would not have been unusual.

37 *CIMRM* 2. 1683. The total surface area the mithraeum covered is calculated from the sum of the size of the various rooms that appear to have made up the mithraeum. The *cella* of the sanctuary covers *ca.* 196 m^2.

38 <u>Aquincum</u>: *AE* (1994) 96 = *CIL* 3. 10605a; <u>Bedaium</u>: *ILS* 664 = *CIL* 3. 5565.

supporting various usurpers in previous generations (it was at Carnuntum that Septimius Severus was acclaimed emperor). Indeed, the conference at Carnuntum had been arranged to deal with the issues that had arisen around the question of succession in the Tetrarchic system: both Constantine and Maxentius, following the death and retirement of their fathers respectively, had set themselves up in opposition to those officially chosen as the new Caesars, while Maximian had emerged from his enforced retirement with the backing of troops on the Danube frontier. By referring to Mithras in such a fashion during this conference, the Tetrarchs were making a statement: the god you view so highly supports our rule and you should do the same.

Unfortunately, we do not know if soldiers stationed at the forts located at Aquincum and Ad Enum from the late 3rd c. onwards frequented their local mithraea. At Ad Enum this would seem likely, given the close proximity of the temple to the nearby fort at Pons Aeni. In contrast, at Aquincum the fact that the only mithraeum still in use at the turn of the 4th c. (Mithraeum IV, known as that 'of Symphorus') was located in the civilian town, may be indicative of a more civilian-orientated Mithraic congregation. That being said, the aforementioned examples from Carnuntum and Poetovio were also located within the civilian towns and were still attended by soldiers, so this should not be ruled out in the case of the mithraeum at Aquincum.

Alongside the aforementioned inscriptions from North Africa indicating support for the cult amongst the imperial government, we also have an inscription from the Lambaesis Mithraeum which refers to the governor of Numidia in AD 303, Valerius Florus. Given that this mithraeum was set next to a large fort, and earlier dedications indicate a close connection with soldiers stationed here, Florus' dedication might also be seen in a similar light to those by the imperial government on the Danube, in an effort to maintain the loyalty of the soldiers stationed here.[39]

Now we return to Rome, where the epigraphic evidence contrasts significantly with what has been outlined elsewhere thus far. The 4th c. marks the first time when we see evidence for a notable number of men of senatorial status in Rome becoming involved with the cult. However, there is a distinct chronological gap in the evidence, with two of the inscriptions dating to the early 4th c. and the rest from the AD 360s–80s. Beginning with the two earlier inscriptions, as mentioned a *vir perfectissimus* by the name of Fl. Septimius Zosimus installed a mithraeum in his house. Yet, while he states he was a priest of Brontis and Hecate, no mention is made of a Mithraic title, which perhaps indicates

the mithraeum was provided for adherents in his household rather than serving as his own place of worship. The other inscription from the early 4th c. was erected in AD 313 at a *Phrygianum* located on the Vatican Hill by C. Magius Donatus Severianus, who held the Mithraic title *pater sacrorum*. Severianus informs us in the inscription that he also served as a priest Liber, while he had also partaken of a *taurobolium* in honour of Magna Mater.[40]

The later inscriptions, from the mid to late 4th c., were uncovered at two find spots. The first, where the aforementioned inscription of Severianus was also discovered, was at a *Phrygianum* located on the Vatican Hill, where around a dozen inscriptions were found, which predominantly speak of one family: the Caeonii. Among them is the city prefect of AD 365, Caeonius Rufius Volusianus Lampadius, who served as a *pater*. His son, Ceionius Rufius Volusianus, is also mentioned in one of the later inscriptions, erected in AD 390, as a *pater*. Other members of this group, nearly all of whom are listed as *patrēs* include: Alfenius Caeionius Iulianus Kamenius, whose inscription was erected in AD 374 and who served as governor of Numidia in the AD 370s (he is called both a *pater* and *hieroceryx sacrorum*); Rufius Caeionius Sabinus in AD 377; and Petronius Apollodorus and his wife, the daughter of Lampadius, Rufia Volusiana. However, Volusiana is not referred to via a Mithraic title, and so there is no reason to assume she was an initiate. Other initiates who are listed but were not part of the family include: Caelius Hilarianus, Ulpius Egnatius Faventinus, and Iunius Postumianus. While Postumianus was a *pater patrum*, the other two held the grade of *hieroceryx* (an amended version of *corax*) in tandem with the title of *pater*. All of these men were of senatorial rank, although one inscription bears the name Sextilius Agesilaus Aedesius, who was not of noble birth, but was mentioned by Ammianus as a friend of Volusianus Lampadius. Finally, the famous aristocrat Vettius Agorius Praetextaus is listed among these inscriptions as a member of a Mithraic community. Praetextatus is perhaps the most outstanding member of these later Mithraic adherents, having served governor of Lusitana, proconsul of Achaea and praetorian prefect, as well as being a consul elect at the time of his death in AD 384. Like Severianus, each of these individuals held more than a single priesthood, including those of Liber and Hecate, and most had partaken in a *taurobolium*.[41]

A second group consists of seven Mithraic inscriptions discovered on the Campus Martius. These also refer to a Mithraic group based around one family, in this case the Olympii. Most of the inscriptions are dated, covering the period of the late AD 350s–80s. The men

---

39 Clauss (1992) 248–49.

40 *CIMRM* 1. 523.

41 *CIMRM* 1. 420, 466, 513–15, 521, 520, 522, 544.

listed are: Nonius Victor Olympius and his sons, Aurelius Victor Olympius and Aurelius Victor Augentius, and in a dedication of AD 376, the latter's son, Aemilianus Corfo Olympius. Initially, Nonius Victor Olympius is referred to as a *pater patrum* while his sons held the grade of *pater*, but by AD 376, the latter two had both been elevated to the role of *pater patrum*. Another grandson of Nonius Victor Olympius was Tamesius Augentius Olympius, who is recorded as building a mithraeum in AD 382, although he provides no Mithraic title. These men held the rank of *vir clarissimi*, except for Aemilianus who is listed as a *clarissimus puero*, indicating he was only a child when he was initiated. Aemilianus also holds the unusual title of *hierocoracica*, which appears to be an alternative form of *corax*. Unlike their contemporary counterparts from the Phrygianum Mithraic group, these men made no reference to additional titles in these inscriptions, suggesting that having been situated on private property, as opposed to a major sanctuary, they were more private in nature.[42]

Contemporary to these dedications in Rome, senators also erected Mithraic inscriptions at Antium and Lavinium just outside of Rome. Both were on statue bases, with the example from Antium referring to the same Alfenius Ceionius Iulianus Kamenius from the *Phrygianum* inscriptions in Rome. At Lavinium, the senator Iunius Gallienus is named, but he does not appear in any surviving Mithraic inscription from Rome. Both men referred to themselves as *pater patrum*. Further down the coast at Neapolis, 1 m² marble relief depicting the bull-slaying scene which is the only certain example of a relief from the senatorial Mithraic congregations of the mid to late 4th c.—was paid for by an Appius Claudius Tarronius Dexter.[43]

In addition to these inscriptions from Rome and its hinterlands, an inscription found at Cirta in North Africa, which dates from the AD 360s, can be added to this corpus. This inscription states that Caeionius Caecina Albinus, governor of Numidia, repaired a mithraeum at Cirta. This man had almost certainly been initiated into the cult in Rome before arriving in North Africa, given that his father, the aforementioned Ceionius Rufius Volusianus, was an initiate, but the inscription makes no mention of a grade. Furthermore, fragments of another altar found at Satafis, which had been erected by a *vir clarissimus* who acted as a *pater patrum*, may also have come from one of the Mithraic communities in Rome.[44]

Statius' reference to the cult of Mithras in the *Thebaid* suggests the cult was widely known in Rome even in the 1st c. AD, yet there is little to indicate any elite involvement in the cult before the 4th c. Why did these aristocratic groups choose the 4th c. to establish Mithraic communities? To begin with, despite the upheavals of the 3rd c., the aristocracy in Rome had not changed a great deal from the Early Principate up to the Tetrarchic period. However, from the Tetrarchic period onwards the social landscape of the Roman elite underwent significant changes, particularly in regards to their numbers. Prior to the reign of Constantine, it is estimated that the senate of Rome had *ca.* 600 members; by the mid 4th c. it is believed to have been around 2,000. Despite attempts by Constantius II to curb this aristocratic inflation, under Valentinian I the senate continued to expand, with *duces, comites* and tribunes also now included in the group.

Status was absolutely fundamental to the identity of the traditional aristocracy, who thought of themselves as superior to the rest of the human race,[45] yet now they were faced with barriers that had previously separated them from their inferiors being removed. Naturally, this state of affairs led to friction between the older, established aristocratic families and the newly promoted men. For one, it led to the emergence of new terms, such as *spectabilis* and *illustres*, alongside the more traditional *clarissimus*, as a way for the major office holders to separate themselves from the more 'ordinary' senators.[46] Religious titles could also provide ways of differentiating the older families from the new. For generations, the holding of public priesthoods had been a feature of aristocratic life, and the close ties between the aristocracy and traditional polytheistic religions in Rome was still evident in the 4th c., as a letter from Paulinus to an aspiring *clarissimate* in AD 398 attests to.[47] As a result, it appears some members of long established families sought to enhance their status by obtaining a number of priesthoods, including Mithraic titles, to separate themselves from these 'new men'.

Of course, in holding various priesthoods, one wonders how committed these men were to each of these cults: did they separate their time between them equally? Did they have any particular preference among them? Furthermore, it is unclear how this would relate to the wider Mithraic community: did these men set themselves up as the leaders of the entire Mithraic community in Rome, or were they a community apart? Furthermore, if there were large numbers of slaves

---

42   *CIMRM* 1. 400–406, 751b.

43   Antium: *CIMRM* 1. 206; Lavinium: *CIL* 14. 2082; Neapolis: *CIMRM* 1. 175.

44   Diana: *CIMRM* 1. 140; Cirta: *IlAlg* 2. 541; Satafis: *CIL* 8. 8397 = *CIL* 8. 20241.

45   Symm. *Ep.* 1.52.

46   Salzman (2002) 14.

47   Paul. *Ep.* 8.3.

and ordinary citizens partaking in the cult, why would the elites look to add to their prestige by holding titles relating to a cult predominantly consisting of men of a lower status, given that their adoption of Mithraic titles was intended to distinguish them from lesser men entering the Senate? Indeed, the extant evidence for Mithraic initiates in the epigraphic record from late 3rd c. Ostia, refers predominantly to men who appear to have been slaves, while contemporary evidence from the mithraeum at the *Foro Boario* in Rome records the presence of ordinary citizens.[48] However, with no extant epigraphy dating to the 4th c. emerging from any other Mithraic contexts beyond these senatorial circles, we cannot know what other social groups were attending mithraea in Rome at this time, and how they relate to these aristocratic initiates, aside from what we might discern from the topographical context of the mithraea. As Jonas Bjørnebye has observed:

> The only evidences for senatorial membership are found in Mithraic shrines in other temples, such as is the case with the Phrygianum inscriptions, or in very small mithraea located within the urban households of one or two senators. The majority of the mithraea, especially very large and possibly semi-public mithraea of the Crypta Balbi and the Terme di Caracalla, suggests that most mithraea were still associated with its traditional social segment of the urban population—petty bureaucrats and junior officials, shopkeepers, well-to-do freedmen, and so forth ...[49]

Finally, a word might be said about the supposed relationship between Julian (AD 361–63) and the Mithras cult. At the end of his work *The Caesars*, Julian has Hermes tell him that he has revealed the secrets of Mithras to him, while in another work, *To King Helios*, he mentions his reverence for Mithras.[50] Other passages by Gregory Nazianzen and Libanius also infer Julian's initiation into the cult, with Gregory referring to Julian entering a cave to perform secret rites, while Libanius says that Julian built a temple to an unspecified deity in his palace at Constantinople where he "partook of the Mysteries, being initiated and in turn initiating".[51] Whether Julian was actually initiated into the 'Mysteries' has often been debated. Robert Turcan

dismissed the interpretation that this passage indicates Julian was an initiate, but a more recent reappraisal by Rowland Smith was far more accepting. Smith believes that the references in Julian's own works prove that he was initiated into the Mysteries of Mithras, although he questions the validity of the other passages, and believes that Julian's belief in Mithras was a personal affair that he avoided publicising.[52] Regardless, there is no extant epigraphic evidence that testifies to Julian making any dedications to Mithras or supplying any mithraea with significant investment. However, Julian's religious beliefs were a myriad of philosophies and deities, and what he believed to be 'Mithraic' was not necessarily the same as other Mithraic initiates in different times and places. It is possible that Julian saw Mithras as another form of Helios-Apollo, and that his Mithraic adherence was part of his general association with the cult of the Sun. This, in my view, does not make Julian's worship of Mithras (if this was the case) any less Mithraic though, only that this was another variant of the cult.

Mithraic Hierarchies

Given the lack of epigraphic evidence from this period, how Mithraic communities were structured in the 4th c. remains unclear. However, there are indications that in some cases a grade structure was still in place in at least the early decades of the 4th c. On one side of the central relief from the Konjic Mithraeum is a depiction of what appears to be a Mithraic feast, with two figures assuming the central places of Mithras and Sol in the centre while being attended to by other characters, two of whom appear to be wearing lion and raven masks. If this is indeed an image of a Mithraic ritual, rather than from the Mithraic narrative, then it is likely that the central figures are a *pater* and a *heliodromus*, who are being served by men from the grades, including those of *leo* and *corax*.[53]

At Ostia, the mosaic which decorated the floor of the Mithraeum of Felicissimus depicts the seven grades of the Mithraic hierarchy. Given that this mithraeum likely dates to the late 3rd c., one may assume the grade system was still being implemented here, and probably in other contemporary Ostian mithraea. Indeed, there was a *pater* who led the Mithraic community that met in the

---

48   <u>Ostia</u>: *CIMRM* 1.299 (the Mithraeum of Felicissimus); *CIMRM* 1. 218, 220, 222–23 (the Mithraeum in the House of Diana); <u>*Foro Boario*</u>: *CIMRM* 1. 436, 449–52.

49   Bjørnebye (2016) 200.

50   Julian, *The Caesars* 336c and Julian, *Or.* 4.155b.

51   Greg. Naz. *Or.* 4.55; Lib. *Or.* 18.127.

52   Two works which argue unequivocally that Julian was initiated are Bidez (1930) and Athanassiadi (1981) 88, 140, 160. Against this view, see Turcan (1975) 105–28. For a balanced recent synthesis, see Smith (1995).

53   *CIMRM* 1. 1896.

House of Diana, although no other grades are mentioned here.[54] This is perhaps to be expected, however, as there is a general trend in Mithraic evidence across all periods that the title *pater* is the most frequently referred to grade, which was probably due to the fact this was the most acclaimed position within the Mithraic hierarchy. The aforementioned Eutactus at Venetonimagus also served as a *pater patrum*, while Martius Martialis at Trier led this community as a *pater*, indicating these Mithraic cells were arranged via something akin to the standard Mithraic hierarchy. Surprisingly, a scrap of 4th c. papyrus from Egypt, a province otherwise unforthcoming concerning Mithraic evidence, appears to contain lines from a Mithraic initiation, and refers to the title of *pater* and *leo* (with the *pater* appearing to oversee the initiation of the *leo*), indicating that traditional hierarchies were also still being implemented here.

Elsewhere, however, the evidence regarding the structure of Mithraic communities is more complex. An altar from the Gimmeldingen Mithraeum (as with the rest of the assemblage dating to AD 325) provides us with an interesting problem regarding this Mithraic community's structure. In this case, it is striking that a certain Materninius Faustinus paid for the mithraeum to be constructed, as well as the main relief and altars, yet his grade is listed as *carax* (one assumes this was a version of *corax*). For the donor of all of this to hold the lowest grade appears rather bizarre, given that Mithraic hierarchies would have almost certainly mimicked those of the secular world. How do we explain this? It is unlikely that this man was humble enough to pay for these things and then take on a servile role during rituals, while it is also improbable that, despite his financial status, he was of a lower social status then his fellow initiates, and thus limited to obtaining only the lower grades. The most plausible explanation seems to be that the *corax* grade was not seen, at least in this congregation, as the lowest grade but as one of the highest, thus inverting the traditional hierarchy.

A similar oddity is to be found amongst the senatorial dedications in Rome, where Caelius Hilarianus and Ulpius Egnatius Faventinus held the title of *hieroceryx* while at the same time serving as *patrēs*, thus holding both the highest and lowest grades simultaneously. Alfenius Caeionius Iulianus Kamenius also held the titles of both *pater* and *hieroceryx sacrorum*. What did the role of a *corax* mean in these communities? Was it not considered the lowest grade, but in fact one of the highest? Did the alteration of the title to *hieroceryx* signify this role was different to what it previously involved? Once again, the answers to these questions remain uncertain, but evidently these groups did not feel confined to using the Mithraic terminology found elsewhere, or assigning each individual a single role.

These references from Rome, plus the aforementioned iconographic evidence referring to the grades at Hawarte, are the only extant examples we have of a Mithraic grade system being implemented from the mid 4th c. or later. Of course, absence of evidence does not necessitate evidence of absence, and just because we have nothing to indicate a grade structure does not mean Mithraic communities did not continue to utilise one. However, as we turn to ritual practice, it becomes clear that a lack of evidence for grades amongst many Mithraic communities went hand-in-hand with other alterations, which add credence to the notion that the such a hierarchy ceased to be implemented in some instances.

Ritual Practice

Initiation Rituals

As outlined in the introduction, the mithraea abandoned in Germania Superior in the 3rd c. were found to contain the remains of various items, such as swords and crowns, which were likely to have been used in Mithraic initiation rites. Among the mithraea abandoned from the later 3rd c. onwards around the north and north-western provinces, however, such evidence is almost completely absent. A sword was found in one of the pits containing refuse from the Tienen mithraeum, but this can only be dated to the latter half of the 3rd c.[55] An alternative way of demonstrating that initiations were still enacted would be to utilise the epigraphic evidence, but as we have seen, the last reference to a Mithraic grade in the north/north-western provinces dates from AD 325. There is the aforementioned initiation script from Egypt, which uses the terms 'lion-place', 'lion', and 'father', with the father asking the lion questions. However, the precise dating of this remains unclear, beyond a 4th c. origin, and it may only originate from the opening decades of this period.[56]Another papyrus fragment from Egypt, dated to *ca.* AD 300, records an initiation prayer in which Helios-Mithras is mentioned as the recipient. This has become known as the 'Mithras Liturgy', but to what degree it is a Mithraic document has been debated. It consists of seven prayers, through which the initiand ascends the planetary spheres before reaching the sun and coming face-to-face with Helios-Mithras himself. This is interspersed with periods of

---

54   *CIMRM* 1. 220–24.

55   Martens (2004) 38.

56   Brashear (1992).

silence, along with whistling and tongue-clicking, a mighty crash of thunder (possibly using cymbals) and the Mithraic adherent bellowing until he is on the verge of collapse.[57]

At Hawarte though, the archaeological evidence suggests that initiations may have still taken place well into the 4th c. The central relief looks to have stood in a niche that was bordered by two pilasters on either side with a vaulted lintel above it, with two grooves running the length of the niche on either side, suggesting that a frame was erected around it in order to conceal the cult image.[58] We may infer from this that the cult relief was dramatically unveiled and bathed in light at the height of the initiation ceremony. Furthermore, as discussed above, below the niche were found symbols of the Mithraic grades, and if this system was still utilised to its full extent here, one assumes initiations to access a new grade would have been required.

Rome is the only location where we have definite evidence for Mithraic initiations continuing into the latter half of the 4th c., with inscriptions attesting to them being conducted amongst senatorial groups. Furthermore, we have an account dating to the latter half of the 4th c. that describes Mithraic initiations, which probably originates from Rome. This source, attributed to the anonymous Christian writer known as 'Ambrosiaster', describes Mithraic initiations as involving the initiate being blind-folded and having to jump into or across pools of water, while other initiates would flap their arms, make bird noises, and roar like lions. He also states that the initiates may be pushed across ditches filled with water and their hands tied with chicken intestines.[59] Despite the questionable nature of the source, the description does fit with various aspects of the Mithras cult that we know to be real: the blind-folding of the initiate, other members filling the roles of the raven and lion, the prominent role of chicken remains. As such, it is reasonable to conclude that Ambrosiaster's account is reliable to an extent. However, there is no reference here to swords or torches being waved in the face of prospective initiates, or them having to undergo such trials naked.

It is likely that senatorial groups in Rome were not particularly keen on engaging in intense rites, and so undertook less strenuous forms of Mithraic initiations.

Indeed, it is worth remembering that a child was inducted into the Olympii group, leading one to wonder whether he would have been expected to undergo the intensive trials usually undertaken by grown men. Additionally, contemporary events infer that the activities conducted by these senatorial Mithraic communities were not particularly secret affairs. During the reign of Valentinian I, there was a rise in accusations of sorcery among the elite of Rome. Those leading the investigations were 'new men', such as the *praefectus annonae* Maximinus, while those under suspicion were members of the established aristocracy, just like those who attended these Mithraic congregations. However, while one can see a how a small group of elites gathering in private to worship Mithras might be easily (or deliberately) 'confused' by those outside of the group as meetings that were nefarious in nature, it is striking that neither the cult of Mithras, nor any of the aforementioned individuals, are mentioned in relation to this.[60] The most plausible explanation for this is that these senatorial groups simply adopted Mithraic titles via relatively public and less intensive initiation rituals.

Sacrifices

Alongside a lack of evidence for initiation rituals, there is almost no evidence for individual sacrificial deposits being made in mithraea after the early 4th c. The only clear exception to this is from the mithraeum at Trier, although the circumstances surrounding this are particularly unusual. Here, within the entrance to the mithraeum the remains of a bird were found in a pit alongside 329 coins and a large amount of ash. The coin sequence ran to the reign of Honorius, indicating that this deposit was made in the late 4th or early 5th c. This deposit also shows that the mithraeum was still being used at this time, but it might be that that this act was conducted as part of the ritual abandonment of the temple, or at least shortly before its doors were closed for the final time.[61]

Feasts

In contrast to the lack of evidence regarding initiations, evidence for feasts have been found in several mithraea

---

57   Meyer (1976).

58   Gawlikowski (2007) 348.

59   Ambrosiaster, *Quaestiones veteris et novi testamenti* 114.11 (ed. Souter (1908) 308). This source was originally attributed to Augustine but has now been identified as the work of Ambrosiaster, see Hunter (2004) 307–309. For identifying the time and place Ambrosiaster composed his work, see Lunn-Rockliffe (2007) 12–17.

60   Amm. Marc. 28.1.1–56; Brown (1970).

61   Trier: Walters (1974) 25. It is possible that sacrifices occurred at the mithraea located in Dalmatia, Hawarte and Septeuil in the 4th c., given the remains of cult feasts uncovered at these locations. But it is difficult to establish whether these animals were killed on site or brought here, having already been prepared to eat. Additionally, the evidence for sacrifices held in other mithraea may have been deposited elsewhere after the completion of the ritual, thus leaving no trace in the mithraeum.

active in the 4th c., although they are still not particularly common. At Septeuil, which was only in use for a short period in the mid to late 4th c., 8,612 animal bones were found among the ashes of a hearth, 74% of which came from chickens, suggesting the traditional Mithraic focus on fowl. Animal remains were also found in the rural mithraea at St Urban and Schachadorf in Noricum, as well as those at Konjic and Jajce in Dalmatia. The presence of the aforementioned 'Mithraic feast' relief at Konjic, also suggests that such rituals may have been conducted here well into the 4th c., although the relief itself only dates to the late 3rd c. Unfortunately, the ratio of chicken bones to other animal remains in these examples is unclear. The latest evidence for a cult meal comes from Hawarte, where a deposition, including culinary pottery and animal bones (mostly of chicken and goat), was made at the turn of the 5th c. What is notable about the evidence for Mithraic feasts is that many of the sites in question were located in rural settings, or at least a notable distance from the nearest urban centre. In contrast, urban mithraea are far less forthcoming when it comes to such materials in the 4th c. Strikingly, the mithraeum in Lentia, which included a kitchen in its layout, produced no evidence of animal remains, but instead contained a significant quantity of fruit and nuts, perhaps suggesting a change to an untraditional format of the ritual.[62]

Votive Practices

One of the most intriguing aspects of the Mithras cult in the 4th c. is the emergence of what appears to have been new forms of ritual practice. The distribution of different forms of votive offerings across the late 3rd to 4th c. are illustrated in figs. 17–20. To begin with, the dedication of votive altars in Mithraic contexts diminishes during this period, although given the general decline in the epigraphic habit evident at this time this is to be expected.[63] The votive altars included in these figures consist of: three altars from North Africa (one from Diana and two from Lambaesis); one in Dalmatia at

Konjic; and on the Danube frontier, examples were erected at Lentia, Poetovio, Ulcisia Castra and Virunum. On the Rhine frontier, a set of sandstone altars was erected in AD 325 when the mithraeum at Gimmeldingen was founded. Among these is the latest Mithraic votive altar erected north of the Alps. Notably, one of the altars from Gimmeldingen was dedicated to Luna, although this is not surprising given the goddess' regular appearance in the tauroctony scene, and references to her have been found on other altars from mithraea, albeit not in great numbers.[64] In addition to this, the dedication of Mithraic reliefs as votives also looks to die out in the early 4th c.[65]

Some of the Gallic mithraea have produced votives that are unusual in Mithraic contexts, although the dating of these materials is often unclear. The mithraeum at Les Bolards was found to contain *ex votos* in the form of various body parts, including a marble hand and two legs,[66] adding further credence to the argument that the cult of Mithras in this region had become increasingly associated with healing powers. The Martigny Mithraeum also provided an interesting corpus of ceramic vessels (*ca.* 99 in total), a number of which have votive formula written on them and are dedicated to DIM (*Deo Invicto Mithrae*). These vessels were manufactured until the late 3rd c., thus the deposition of them may have stretched into the 4th c.[67] Whether such numbers of ceramic votives were common among other mithraea is unclear, as much of the pottery from earlier excavations was not afforded the importance it has now.

However, the declining evidence for these types of votives did not mean that offerings ceased to be made in mithraea; rather, it appears new forms of votive practice emerged in certain areas. Large numbers of low denomination coins, often numbering in the hundreds, but in some cases over a thousand, have been found in the later occupation levels of various mithraea located in eastern Gaul, Germany, Pannonia and Noricum. Unfortunately, in many cases, the excavation of these sites was undertaken in the 19th and early 20th c., so little information regarding the context of the coins is available, but the prevalence of such coins dating to the mid to late 4th c. is clear. However, excavations at certain sites have provided indications as to how these coins may have been deposited, and it is clear the intention behind their deposition was votive in nature.

This can be most clearly seen at Martigny (figs. 21–24), where the exact location of each coin found in this

---

62   Totalling 4.2 kg, this consisted of vines, prunes, berries, apple-pips, walnuts and millets, see *CIMRM* 2. 1421 and Karnitsch (1956) 252.

63   The decline in the epigraphic habit has been looked at in various articles, including Mrozek (1973); MacMullen (1982) and Meyer (1990). Derks (1998) 238 suggests that Caracalla's extension of Roman citizenship brought to an end the desire to demonstrate one's citizenship via inscriptions. A search of the Heidelberg database (http://edh-www.adw.uni-heidelberg.de/inschrift/erweiterteSuche, accessed on 10.12.16) using the search terms 'altar' and 'votive', yielded the following results from across the entire Roman empire: AD 150–99, 263 examples; AD 200–49, 486 examples; AD 250–99, 53 examples; AD 300–49, 10 examples.

64   Luna on Mithraic altars: *CIMRM* 1. 324, 799, 800, 2. 1484.

65   *Foro Boario*: *CIMRM* 1. 435–6; Pregrade: *CIMRM* 2. 1468–71, Clauss (1992) 171; Sitifis *CIMRM* 1. 148–49, Clauss (1992) 251–52.

66   Walters (1974) 10, 14.

67   Wiblé and Cusanelli Bressenel (2012).

mithraeum was recorded. The resulting distributions demonstrate that during the 4th c. the deposition of coins took on a crescent shape around the main cult relief, as well as next to the termini of the benches close to the *cella* door.[68] At Les Bolards, a concentration of coins was found next to where the relief had stood, while another was deposited at the base of a lion statue halfway down the nave.[69] At Trier, the deposition of the coins differs from the other examples in that, while 49 coins were found on the floor of the temple, there were also another 329 deposited in the aforementioned pit located at the entrance to the mithraeum. Given that these coins were of negligible value, this was unlikely to be a hoard, while one doubts whether the person responsible saved these coins over decades before burying them. A more likely scenario is that the coins were deposited on the floor of the mithraeum, alongside the other 49, as votives, but were removed from their initial context and redeposited in the pit.[70]

In addition to this example, at Poetovio a number of mid 4th c. coins were found in a water-basin of Mithraeum II, while a similar occurrence was found at Septeuil. Coins running until AD 351, uncovered on the floor of the Mackwiller Mithraeum, were concentrated in area of *ca.* 0.50 m² alongside sherds of broken ceramic, indicating they were contained in the vessel.[71] In contrast to the large quantities of coins found in the above mithraea, in some only a relatively small number of coins were deposited, but their location suggests they were not left accidentally either. At Bornheim-Sechtem, a small concentration of coins was found at the foot of the cult relief, while at the mithraea of Arupium and Epidaurum in Dalmatia, a small number of coins (just three in the case of the latter) were deposited in small niches situated around the central reliefs, in the first half of the 4th c.[72] Given that many of these coin finds originated from locations around where the cult-relief had stood, this might be taken as a further indication that little was now done to hide the image, as in previous periods, and that initiation ceremonies were either no longer carried out, or no longer consisted of an initiate kneeling before the cult image and being subjected to various tests.

Why did the deposition of coins become more common in mithraea in Late Antiquity? Eberhard Sauer has suggested, and I am in agreement with him, that given the evident parallels with similar rituals at non-Mithraic sites, such evidence could be taken as indicative of a more open form of Mithraic practice, with accessibility to the mithraeum no longer strictly controlled.[73] Certainly, the act of dropping a coin can require little education in the workings of a cult, a fact attested to at the mithraeum beneath *San Clemente* in Rome and at Brocolitia, where many modern visitors still throw coins into the remains of the mithraea.[74] Perhaps such offerings are meaningful, but it is unlikely that many of these people have an in-depth knowledge regarding the Mithras cult. If mithraea were accessible to a more casual form of worshipper from the mid 4th c. onwards, this advances the argument that initiation rituals (and perhaps the cult hierarchy) had become marginalised or this was completely abandoned during this period, at least in some mithraea, given the 'deregulation' such activity implies. It also raises questions as to how this affected any rituals that were linked with the topography of mithraea, for, if the space inside these structures was being used in a different way, then was the traditional layout of a mithraeum still a necessity: indeed, was the mithraeum *itself* still a necessity?

It is important to highlight that this coin phenomenon is not to be found in every mithraeum. At Hawarte, there is no indication of any such activity, while none of the mithraea found at Rome or Ostia have produced such numismatic evidence. Certainly, in the case of Rome and Ostia this may be due to the lacklustre recording of finds and contexts in pre-modern excavations, but that no such evidence has emerged in *any* of the mithraea at these three locations, does suggests that this practice was largely restricted to the north/north-west provinces.[75] It is perhaps no coincidence that it is at Rome and Hawarte where we find evidence of Mithraic communities still engaging in some form of initiation process.

The Ritual Fragmentation of Objects

Of all the ritual practices that Mithraic worshippers engaged in during the 4th c. (and most likely in earlier periods), the least understood is the fragmentation of their own cult objects. At first it might seem odd to suggest that Mithraic initiates would intentionally break their own cult objects, yet there are valid

---

68   Wiblé (2004) 140–43.

69   Planson *et al.* (1973) 57; Thévot (1948) 309, 325.

70   No remains of a container for the coins were found.

71   Trier: Walters (1974) 25; Poetovio II: Sauer (2004) 347; Mackwiller: Hatt (1957) 58–62.

72   Bornheim-Sechtem: Ulbert (2004) 86; Arupium I and II: *CIMRM* 2. 1851–52; Epidaurum: *CIMRM* 2. 1883. The mithraeum at Timavo also produced *ca.* 300 coins, although their chronological distribution has not been published, see Pross Gabrielli (1975).

---

73   Sauer (2004) 336.

74   Perhaps the most bizarre modern 'offering' was a model of the Brocolitia mithraeum left within its remains: Richard Hingley, *pers. comm.* 30.3.17.

75   One explanation for the lack of such evidence at Ostia is that none of the mithraea remained in use long enough to see this practice utilised, as was the case in Britain where no extant mithraeum appears to have remained use after the early 4th c.

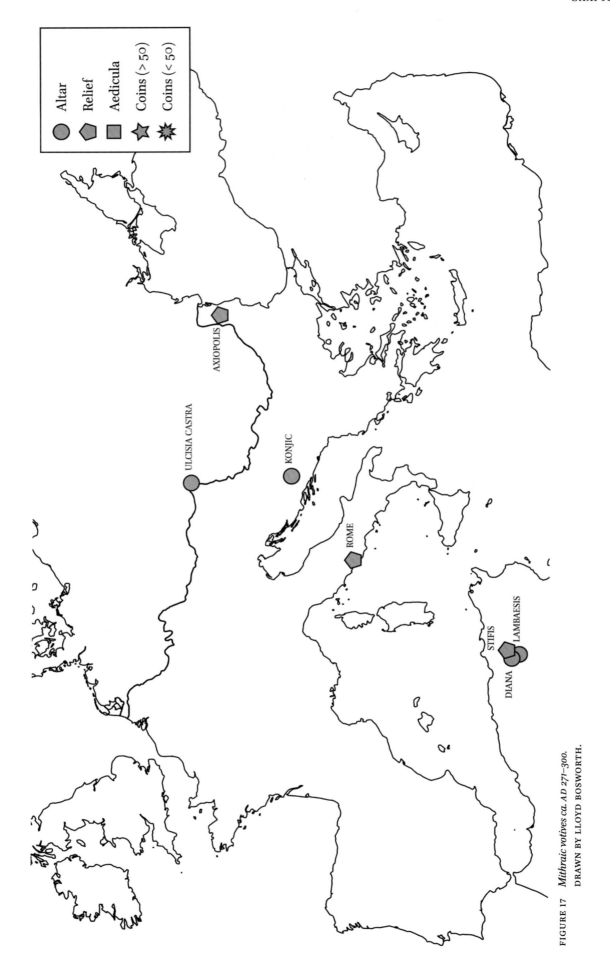

FIGURE 17 *Mithraic votives ca. AD 271–300.*
DRAWN BY LLOYD BOSWORTH.

THE DEVELOPMENT OF THE CULT OF MITHRAS IN LATE ANTIQUITY 35

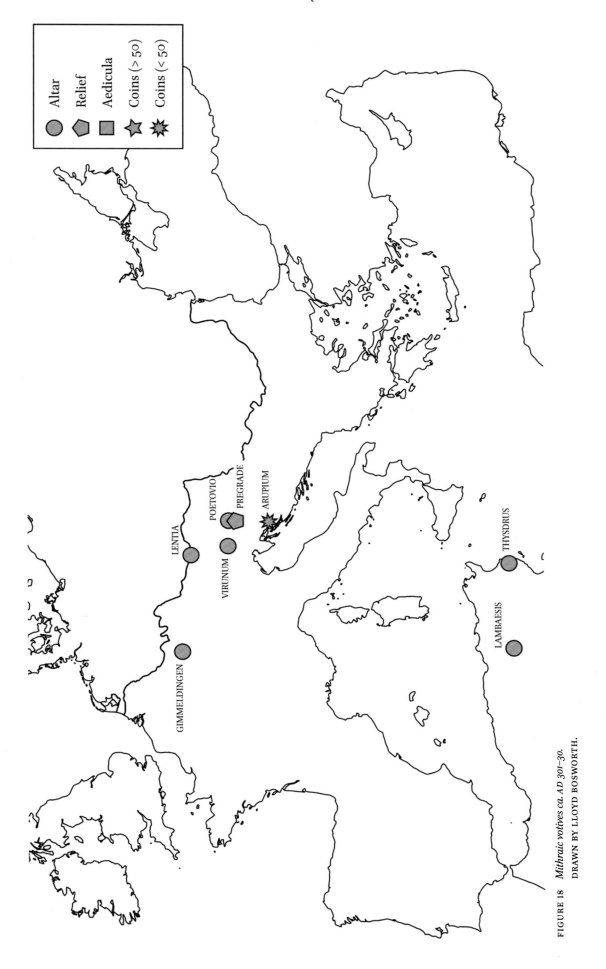

FIGURE 18 *Mithraic votives ca. AD 301–30.*
DRAWN BY LLOYD BOSWORTH.

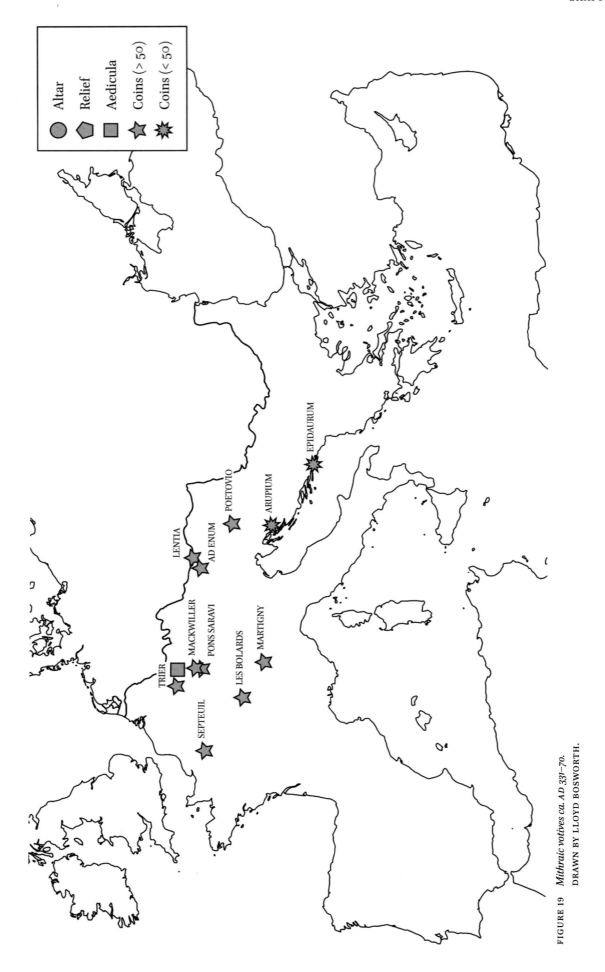

FIGURE 19 *Mithraic votives ca. AD 331–70.*
DRAWN BY LLOYD BOSWORTH.

THE DEVELOPMENT OF THE CULT OF MITHRAS IN LATE ANTIQUITY 37

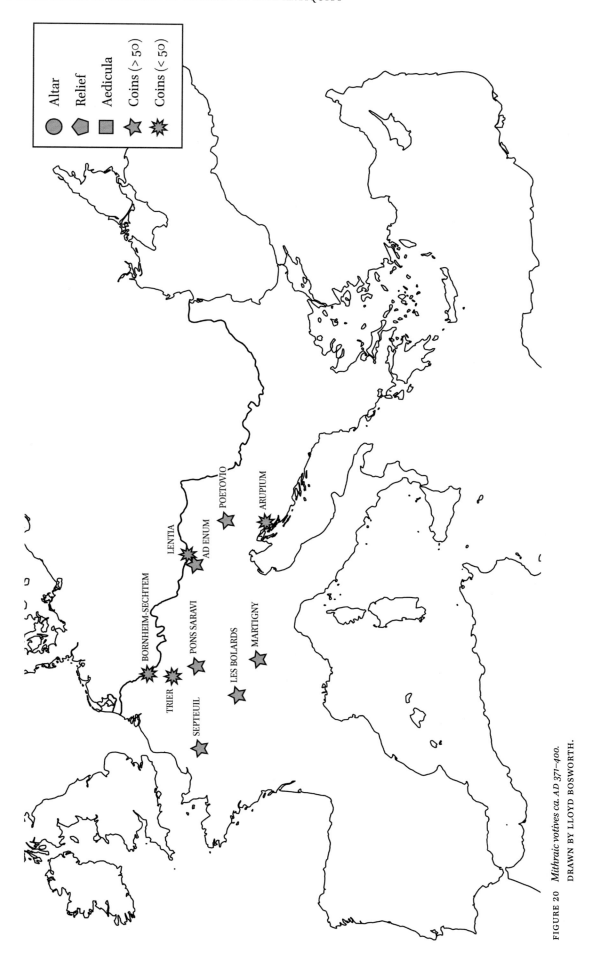

FIGURE 20 *Mithraic votives ca. AD 371–400.*
DRAWN BY LLOYD BOSWORTH.

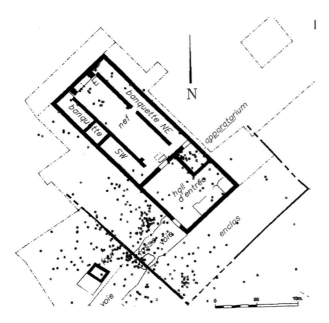

FIGURE 21   *Distribution of coin finds at the Martigny Mithraeum ca. AD 268–94. Wiblé (2004) 140.*

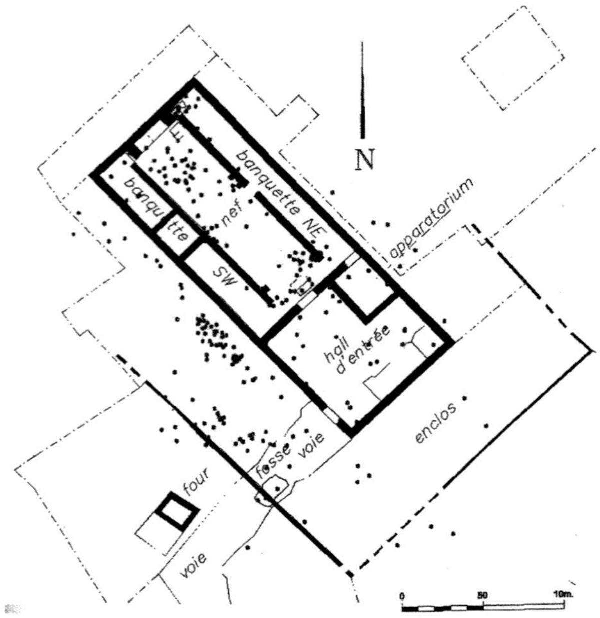

FIGURE 22   *Distribution of coin finds at the Martigny Mithraeum ca. AD 330–48. Wiblé (2004) 141.*

reasons to believe that the breaking of images and the retention of individual parts was practised in Mithraic circles, at least in the 4th c. Recent excavations of the Bornheim-Sechtem Mithraeum have produced substantial evidence that the Mithraic initiates here did indeed retain 'broken' items, which evidently continued to have some form of ritual significance. At this mithraeum, various elements of statuary had been deposited in two distinct locations: a niche in the north-east wall of the temple, and down a shaft in the centre of the nave (along with a scorched coin of Valentinian I). What was particularly striking about the statuary was that all the pieces bore traces of fire damage, yet the mithraeum itself showed no signs of this. The most likely explanation is that these items were recovered from another mithraeum which had been burnt down in the late 4th c. (with the date based on the presence of the scorched coin), but even in such a state they were deemed valuable by the Mithraic community at Bornheim-Sechtem. In addition to this was the deposition of fragments from the same lead-glazed cult vessel in three different contexts in two different building phases: one amongst the statuary fragments in the niche, one down the shaft in the centre of the aisle, and another in an earlier shaft that had been covered over during the second phase. In all three cases, the ceramics bore a complete image (Cautes, a snake and a lion, see fig. 24), which suggests that the vessel had not been broken randomly, but with precision. The conclusion here is that the cult vessel had been broken and certain fragments were

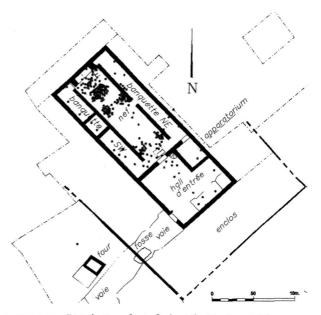

FIGURE 23   *Distribution of coin finds at the Martigny Mithraeum ca. AD 378–402. Wiblé (2004) 142.*

deposited over time, possibly to mark different phases of occupation.[76]

Evidence from other mithraea suggests the ritual breaking of images was not uncommon in Mithraic communities, although unfortunately elsewhere the context

---

76   Ulbert, Wulfmeier and Huld-Zetsche (2004); Wulfmeier (2004). Alternatively, the Mithraic community at Bornheim-Sechtem might have fragmented and burnt the statuary themselves.

FIGURE 24 *Fragments of a Mithraic ceramic vessel from the Bornheim-Sechtem Mithraeum. Ulbert, Wulfmeier and Huld-Zetsch (2004) fig. 6.*

of this material is less clear than at Bornheim-Sechtem. At Mainz, the so-called 'Mainz Vessel' was found to be missing certain elements that carried depictions of animals from Mithraic lore: a snake, a lion and a raven. That the container was broken with such precision makes it highly unlikely that it was victim of an accident. It is possible that these pieces were ritually deposited somewhere in the mithraeum, but as the mithraeum was only partially excavated the opportunity to uncover them was missed. Other Mithraic sites have produced individual ceramic sherds bearing images of animals, such as at Tienen (a lion and a snake), Nida-Heddernheim (a snake) and Aquincum IV (a lion and a snake). Huld-Zetsche has postulated that these images were saved and deposited separately because of their identification with the Lion, Nymph (snake) and Raven grades.[77]

Additionally, there was the deposition of multiple statue fragments found in the Londinium Mithraeum. These included the heads of Mithras (fig. 25), the dagger-hand of the same statue, and the heads of Minerva and Sarapis. Whether these were buried by the Mithraic worshippers or those who subsequently took over the temple is unclear, but based on the aforementioned evidence it is possible that former were responsible for this. It might be that the burial of these statue pieces—which were all in an incredibly well-preserved condition—was an act of ritual closure, just as the sacrificial deposit at Trier appears to have been. Unfortunately, thus far Londinium is the only site to have produced such a deposit, although as this chapter has highlighted, this may be because this was a unique, regionally specific act. One may draw attention to the main relief from Mithraeum 'III' at Carnuntum, from which the head survived remarkably intact, although the details of its discovery remain obscure (fig. 26). It is hoped that future excavations will yield further, more secure evidence of such a practice in Mithraic communities that will allow us to gain a greater insight into what this act was intended to achieve.

Variations of the Name 'Mithras'

Finally, it is worth highlighting how Mithras' name took on different variations across the Roman world. Alongside the unusual terminology used in the inscriptions found at Gimmeldingen mentioned above, we should add here that these dedications were made to a 'Midre', as opposed to Mithras. Given the aforementioned uses of the terms *carax* and *fanum*, it seems unlikely (unless we are dealing with a truly incompetent inscriber) that this was a mistake. Rather, we may assume that the Mithraic congregation at Gimmeldingen did indeed meet to worship Midre instead of Mithras. In addition to this, at Konjic in Dalmatia, the main relief of the mithraeum bears the inscription *Deo Soli inv[ict]o Meter[ae]*, with Meterae replacing 'Mithras'. Given the well-worked images apparent on the relief, it is difficult to believe this was a mistake, and instead perhaps is another variation of Mithras' name in a particular community. One of the aforementioned reliefs from Pregade also refers to Mithras in a usual fashion, calling him *I(nvicto) D(eo) O(rienti) O(mnipotenti)*. The only other example of this title is to be found on an undated relief from Dražinovići (Moesia Superior).[78] Additionally, in the 'Mithras Liturgy' from Egypt discussed above, Mithras is combined with his fellow sun-god Helios. Such an amalgamation of Mithras with Helios (somewhat surprisingly) has not been found elsewhere, to my knowledge.

Conclusion

So, if our Mithraic initiate set off on his trip around the Roman empire, would he encounter the same cult throughout his voyage, or would he have been perplexed by what he came across? Let us imagine that a Mithraic

---

77 Ulbert, Wulfmeier and Huld-Zetsche (2004).

78 Dražinovići: *CIMRM* 2. 2213.

FIGURE 25 *The head of Mithras from the Londinium Mithraeum.*
© MUSEUM OF LONDON.

adherent departed from Hawarte to the western provinces. He would be leaving what appeared to be a very isolated rural mithraeum, with its own unique iconography and a *cella* with an 'L' shaped bench. He might pass through Dalmatia, where some Mithraic communities called Mithras 'Meterae'. Here, devotees met in mithraea with just a single bench and a tauroctony carved into a rock-face. Coming to Rome he would have found again a quite different Mithraic community, one that was built around senators who adopted Mithraic titles, amongst other priesthoods, as they sought to differentiate themselves from the 'new men' entering the Senate. If he visited the mithraeum of *Via Giovanni Lanza* 128, he would find a bizarre situation of a mithraeum with no benches at all. Moving to Gaul, he might have encountered a Mithraic community which worshipped Mithras as a healing deity, with mithraea situated alongside temples devoted to such practices; he would also have found *ex votos* left in mithraea in the hope of curing ailments, and a doctor as the head of a congregation. All the mithraea here would contain two benches running in parallel to each other, unlike those in Hawarte, Dalmatia and *Via Giovanni Lanza* 128 in Rome. From Gaul, he could have headed north to Lentia, where a mithraeum took pride of place alongside a temple to *Dea Roma* and the *Genius Augusta*, whilst other mithraea in the

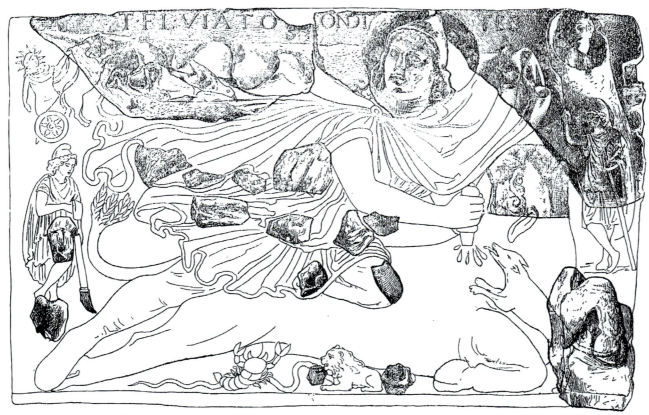

FIGURE 26 *The main relief (shaded areas indicate extant fragments) from Carnuntum III. Cumont (1899) fig. 431.*

surrounding area received the benefaction of the imperial government. This suggests that the cult of Mithras was still very popular amongst the military in this region and was seen as tool by which to keep the army in the check. In North Africa, a similar situation was to be found at Lambaesis. If he then passed into Germany, at Gimmeldingen he would have found a mithraeum referred to as a *fanum* with the words for Mithras and *corax* spelt differently.

This is a broad sketch, but the evidence outlined over the course of this chapter indicates that the Mithraic cult, although initially appearing to be relatively uniform, had come to mean different things to a range of people in a variety of places by the 4th c. As I have suggested throughout, however, regardless of the differences exhibited among these Mithraic communities, we should not disregard one as any less 'authentic' than the other, as some scholars have done when describing aristocratic groups in Rome, or Julian's understanding of the cult. Different groups of people still engaged in Mithraic worship, and their motivations for doing so were just as valid as someone on the Danube frontier or in the Syrian Desert.

On a more macro level, one may divide the extant evidence for the cult of Mithras in the latter half of the 4th c. into three geographic spheres: the north/north-west provinces, Rome, and Hawarte. In the case of the north/north-west provinces, it is among these Mithraic communities that we see the possible marginalisation or complete disregard of the initiation rites, in favour of a more open form of Mithraic worship. In contrast, in Rome, the senatorial elites were unlikely to leave their mithraea accessible to anyone to visit; indeed, if anything, these men formed Mithraic communities to separate themselves from others. Even so, if the mithraeum at *Via Giovanni Lanza* 128 is anything to go by, their mithraea did not adhere to the typical format. Additionally, unlike their western provincial counterparts, these Mithraic worshippers still conducted initiation ceremonies, although based on their composition and the account of Ambrosiaster, it is likely these were not of the same level of intensity as they had been in other Mithraic communities in the past. Far away on the eastern fringe of the empire, the fittings of the Hawarte Mithraeum suggest initiations also continued here, but, due to its location, one would imagine the composition of this Mithraic community was considerably different from that at Rome. Indeed, the Mithraic worshippers of Hawarte almost appear to have gone full circle, with its worshippers absorbing influences from the East as well as the cult in the West.

Evidently, a Mithraic initiate moving from one side of the empire to the other would have been confused by these developments. Furthermore, should an initiate from the turn of the 3rd c. been brought forward in time to a 4th c. Mithraic community then he too would have been faced with aspects alien to him. This would have included: the marginalisation of initiations and sacrifices; the rise in coin depositions and apparent openness of mithraea; the influence of Roman society's highest strata on some Mithraic communities; and adaptions to Mithras' name. All these developments were substantial changes in how the cult operated. Furthermore, that certain new mithraea failed to adhere to the traditional *cella* arrangement infers that the ritual(s) this design was intended to facilitate (such as Beck's 'passage of the soul') might have become redundant. If this was the case, then one might begin to question whether mithraea were actually needed any more. In any case, that the cult could grow and adapt should not surprise us, for all religious movements must do this as time progresses. The question is whether such developments served to help the cult thrive or decline in the circumstances it found itself. In the case of the cult of Mithras, it was the latter.

CHAPTER 2

The Decline of the Cult 1: The Evidence

Introduction

In a recent study on the religious transformation of the Late Roman world, the opening chapter begins with the remark that "[T]he Roman Empire was full of gods in 310. Their temples, statues, and images filled its cities, towns, farms, and wilderness." Over the course of the next few pages, Alexandria is provided as an example of the sheer number of temples that could co-exist within a city during the early 4th c., while the author goes onto describe how the number of temples recorded here (almost 2,500) seems insignificant when compared with the many sites found in rural areas of the Roman world.[1]

That the Roman empire in the opening decade of the 4th c. contained a multitude of temples is undeniable. However, this scholar simply accepted the fact, like so many before him, that the status of Roman temples had remained largely uniform up until the accession of Constantine, and that it was only subsequent to AD 312 that dramatic changes in the fortunes of these structures occurred. Yet, was this really the case? What evidence is this actually based on? Even if the Roman empire was full of temples, where they even in a usable condition or largely in a state of decay? In claiming that the 4th c. saw unprecedented changes in the status of temples, it would seem relatively straightforward to prove this by utilising quantitative data on the construction and restoration of these buildings. Yet it is striking how rarely such an approach has been undertaken by scholars when discussing non-Christian cults—Mithras or otherwise—in Late Antiquity.[2]

This is of course symptomatic of the traditional narratives which take the textual evidence as accurate descriptions of events, for the temples attacked by 4th c. bishops and holy men were always described in the historical accounts as being active sites. Certainly, some temples did incur the ire of Christians because they still attracted significant numbers, such as the Alexandrian Serapeum, but we must also consider that many stood almost derelict, and that the suppression of religious activity at these locations was simply hammering the final nail into their coffin rather than a titanic clash between religious ideologies. To acknowledge that a bishop's victory was over a dying or long deceased cult makes the achievement sound rather hollow, while active and popular temples play far better in such narratives. A good example of this is the supposed fate of the Temple of Isis at Philae, which, according to Procopius, was destroyed by Justinian in the 6th c. with the intention of suppressing the worship of this false god and erecting a church on the site. In reality, the temple was never destroyed, a small church was installed in one of its rooms, and the epigraphic evidence suggests a gradual decline in non-Christian activity some time before the temple was abandoned, after which it was later used as a church.[3]

Alongside these historical narratives of violent closure, one may also point to the various laws that were issued throughout the 4th and early 5th c. that placed increasing restrictions on temples, with this seen as a major factor in the declining status of temples in the 4th c. Initially, this began with the confiscation of temple lands under Constantine, although to what extent this was widespread, is unclear.[4] Subsequently, several laws ordered their closure (AD 346/54/56) and then later their destruction (AD 435).[5] Perhaps these rulings made an impact in some locations, but that the former had to be reissued several times suggests they were not particularly effective. Furthermore, what were they attempting to deal with: widespread continuing support for temples or just a handful of popular sites?

Fortunately, recent years have seen the emergence of a number of studies that have sought to add to our understanding of the status of temples in Late Antiquity by going beyond the texts and utilising the archaeological and epigraphic evidence. What these have shown is that the construction and restoration of temples in various regions went into decline long before the reign of Constantine, suggesting that any popular appeal they had held was now diminished. For example, Fauduet has shown that building activity associated with Gallo-Roman temples in Gaul lessened significantly across the 3rd c., while Sears has observed that (aside from a brief

---

1 Watts (2015) 17–24.
2 Lavan (2011).

---

3 Dijkstra (2011) 421–29.
4 *Cod. Theod.* 10.10.24. Chastagnol (1986) has argued that rather than Constantine, it was Constantius II who promulgated this law, while Delmaire (1989) 643, places the responsibility with Gratian. Goddard (2006) 284 and Tantillo (1997) 387 n.260 both believe that no one actually promulgated such laws.
5 *Cod. Theod.* 16.10.4, 25.

© KONINKLIJKE BRILL NV, LEIDEN, 2019 | DOI 10.1163/9789004383067_004

resurgence under the Tetrarchs) investment in temples in North Africa declined rapidly from the early 3rd c. onwards. In Egypt, Bagnall has argued that temple construction began to decline from as early as the 1st c. AD (in clear contrast to the image presented of Alexandria above).[6] However, one should also note that in some areas this decline was so gradual that investment did continue across the 4th c., and occasionally into the 5th c., with building work being undertaken on temples *after* the laws ordering their closure were issued. For example, in Britain, a temple at Caerwent was repaired during the Valentinianic era, while the temple in Insula XVI at Verulamium shows evidence of building work until the turn of the 5th c.[7] Further examples of restorations in later periods from Italy, Rome, and Gaul also exist, and will be discussed below.

Despite the aforementioned edicts, even Christian emperors were not above pursuing the preservation of temples. In AD 341, Constans ordered that those connected with plays and spectacles held in the circus should be left untouched.[8] Even the emperor Theodosius I, one of the most ardent supporters of Christianity's religious supremacy in the Roman empire, stated that statues placed within temples had to be measured by their artistic value as opposed to their religious significance, and left alone accordingly.[9] The emperors were more concerned, it would appear, with stopping cult practices than tearing down the buildings that these took place within; if a temple was left for largely secular use, then there was little reason for it to be closed permanently or destroyed. As Theodosius' ruling indicates, many still saw temples and their contents for their architectural and artistic value, which added to the urban fabric of their town. It was better to find an alternative use for such buildings than leave them as a dilapidated eyesore. As such, a word of caution should be given here in assuming that all later restorations were necessarily connected with continuing religious activity at these sites. In many cases, temples did not serve a religious role alone, thus their continued use or abandonment need not always reflect the maintenance or abandonment of religious rites. One need only look at the temples in the Roman Forum to see the array of uses a temple could fulfil: the Temple of Concordia Augusta was also used as an art gallery and to house meetings of the Senate; the Temple of Saturn served as a treasury; the Temple of Castor and Pollux housed the *fiscus* (the

imperial purse) and the office of weights and measures.[10] There is no reason to assume that temples could not continue to be utilised in such fashion, without any religious connotations, in Late Antiquity.

It is also important to note that changes in building patterns do not give us the whole story, for they give us no information regarding when structures were abandoned or what became of them subsequently (this will be discussed in the final chapter). Yet, construction/restoration patterns can still provide a valuable insight into the status of religious buildings and the cults that occupied them. It is reasonable to assume that periods that saw increasing construction/restoration of a particular type of temple mark a time when the cult associated with these buildings was in an ascendency. Arguably, one might expect to see fluctuations set in at some point subsequent to this, with cycles of repair to pre-existing temples and the erecting of new ones as old temples collapsed or were no longer deemed suitable for use. However, when we see an irreversible decline set in it is clear we are seeing the twilight of these structures. What should be stressed, however, is that this does not indicate a decline or end to the worship of a deity; indeed, what the evidence might be indicating is a move away from worship associated with a particular structure to an alternative form that is not necessarily evident in the archaeological record.

As for the Mithras cult, a quantitative approach towards the construction and restoration of mithraea has, at least to my knowledge, never been undertaken. Regardless, this has not stopped scholars from making (often contradictory) observations about the status of the cult in the 4th c. Cameron dismissed it as already in decline when the Tetrarchs honoured Mithras at Carnuntum, while conversely, others such as Griffiths and Clauss have argued that the cult was at the apex of its fortunes at this time.[11] Not only are such statements problematic as they are made without the support of any substantial evidence, but they also ignore the possibility of regional variation. As we have seen, the cult of Mithras was by no means uniform across the Roman world, and it may be the case that the cult entered into a decline at a variety of times and rates in different regions. Indeed, this will be demonstrated in this chapter, with mithraea experiencing an earlier decline in Gaul and along the Rhine than in the Danube provinces or in Rome.

---

6 Fauduet (1993) 132–33; Sears (2011) 231–33.

7 <u>Carwent</u>: Brewer (1990) 79, (1993) 59; <u>Verulamium</u>: Kenyon (1935) 241, Lowther (1937) 33–34.

8 *Cod. Theod.* 16.10.3.

9 *Cod. Theod.* 16.10.8.

10 On the use of temples in the Forum for purposes beyond the religious, see Gorski and Packer (2015) 168, 227, 289.

11 See Cameron (2011) 149, *contra* Griffith (2000) and Clauss (2012) 32.

It is vital, however, that we do not look at these patterns for the construction/restoration of temples or mithraea in isolation, for these did not occur in a vacuum. In archaeology context is everything, and we must look at these changes in relation to the wider world in order to draw reasonable conclusions. For example, if the evidence for the construction/restoration of temples rises and falls in correlation with the data regarding public building in general, then we can reasonably surmise that investment in these structures does not reflect religious adherence but rather the economic circumstances at the time. Yet, if a particular type of temple follows a significantly different pattern to that of other temples and structures, then arguably this will allow us to trace the changing status and support for these buildings in their communities. If other forms of building are being neglected while these particular temples continue to be constructed/restored, then this shows a genuine dedication among the cult's adherents. If the opposite occurs, with these particular temples failing to demonstrate any notable levels of construction/restoration while other structures were subject to investment, then it would appear that the cult in question has lost much of its appeal. Arguably, this is even more the case when dealing with structures such as mithraea, which could be relatively small, had a basic set-ground plan, required no windows, and (if deemed necessary) could be installed in pre-existing buildings or caves. Certainly, for a group of able-bodied soldiers, constructing a mithraeum—and certainly repairing one—would not have proven a tremendous challenge.[12]

As will be illustrated here, mithraea rarely follow the patterns exhibited by temples in general or other buildings, thus the changes we observe in relation to mithraea are specific to the cult, and provide an insight into the levels of commitment among Mithraic communities to their maintenance in the 4th c. This is not to say that external factors did not always play a role in this, such as a severe decline in the population. Such a factor would undoubtedly limit the expansion, and perhaps negatively impact on, any cult regardless of its status; if there is no-one to initiate, how do you keep the cult going?

In this chapter, I will begin by outlining how the quantitative data for the construction/restoration of mithraea alter across the 3rd and 4th c. on an empire-wide level as well as discussing what regional differences can be observed among this data. I will then turn to look at the construction/restoration of mithraea in particular regions (Italy, Noricum and Pannonia), and how these patterns compare to general building work in these provinces. What will be demonstrated is that the construction/restoration of mithraea in general began to decline at the turn of the 4th c., and that this cannot be attributed to external factors alone, given that it does not correlate with the building patterns exhibited by secular and other religious structures.

The Decline in Construction/Restoration of Mithraea

In fig. 27, all the quantitative data regarding the construction and repair of mithraea from the turn of the 3rd c. onwards have been combined. Evidently, the overall number of mithraea constructed or repaired had already begun to decline in the late 3rd c., although the early 4th c. saw more restoration work undertaken on mithraea than at any other time. Notably, there is also no indication of any sudden reduction of such activities in the 4th c., which is what one might have expected to see should the cult have been enjoying significant popularity and then been brought low via persecution. Rather the cult gradually lost the support required to continue building new mithraea and restoring pre-existing ones.

The distribution of this evidence from the late 3rd to mid 4th c. is shown in figs. 28–30.[13] In the late 3rd c., there was a notable concentration of mithraea being worked on in Rome/Ostia, while on the Danube frontier various examples were built, and in Gaul several mithraea exhibit construction or repair. Two new mithraea were also created in Dalmatia, while two in Britain (Brocolitia and Londinium) were the subject of restoration. Strikingly, despite the popularity of the cult in the Rhine region in earlier periods, this frontier has produced little evidence for such activity at this time.

The extant remains of mithraea constructed in the early 4th c. have been found across the West at Rome, Jajce, Rockenhausen, and Spoletium, while the date of construction for the 4th c. mithraeum at Gimmeldingen is known from inscriptions. Along the Danube, there is no further evidence for the construction of mithraea at this time, but there are several examples of mithraea being restored in major towns. Such data provide a strong contrast to the neighbouring Rhine area, where the sites

---

12 An interesting modern parallel is to be found with the Kingdom Halls of Jehovah Witnesses. These structures, often relatively small, tend to follow the same plan, and rarely have windows. As a result, they can often be constructed in just three days, usually by groups consisting mostly of volunteers from among Jehovah's Witness congregations: see Stark and Iannacone (1997) 148.

13 Given that in the late 4th and early 5th c. only two mithraea were built and renovated, respectively, there is little need for distribution maps for these later periods. For references for this data, see Appendix B.

THE DECLINE OF THE CULT I: THE EVIDENCE

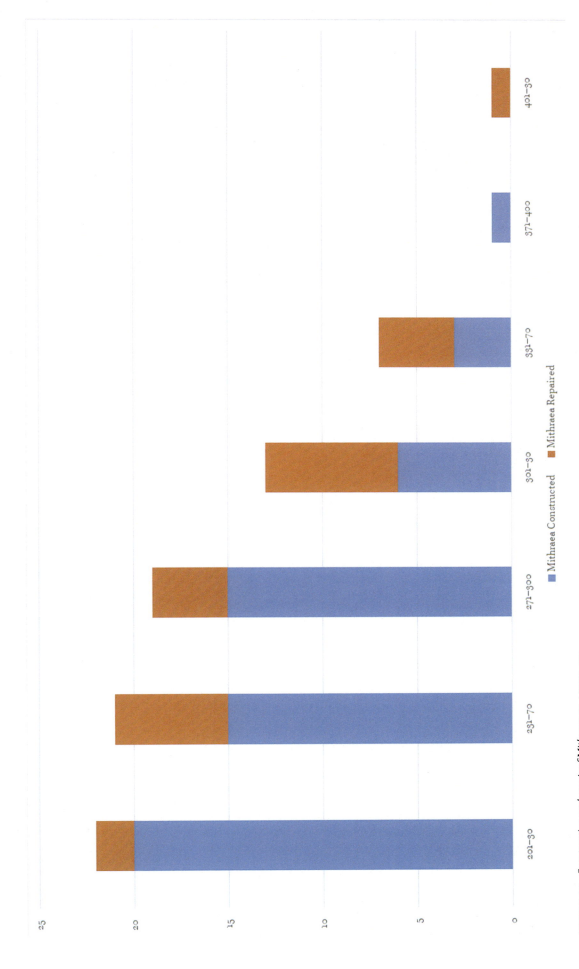

FIGURE 27 *Construction and repair of Mithraea ca. AD 201–400.*

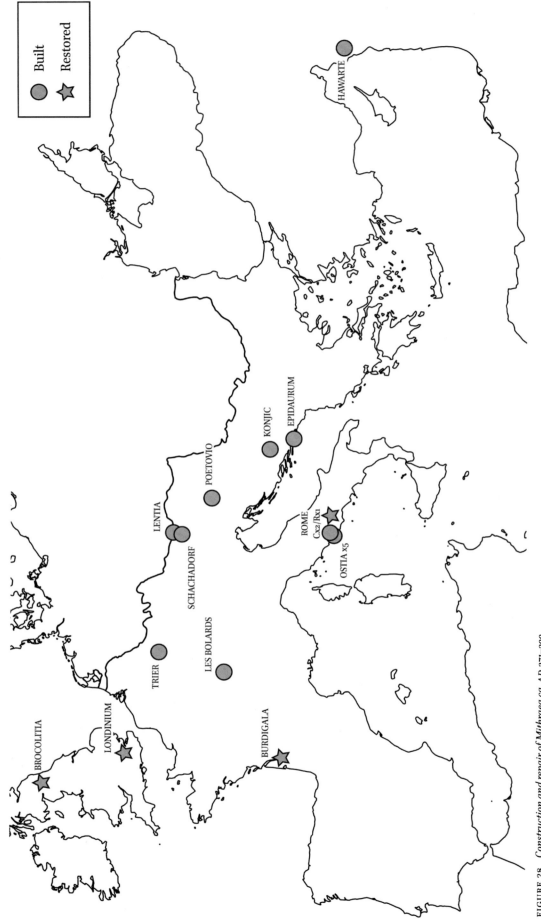

FIGURE 28 *Construction and repair of Mithraea ca. AD 271–300.*
DRAWN BY LLOYD BOSWORTH.

THE DECLINE OF THE CULT I: THE EVIDENCE

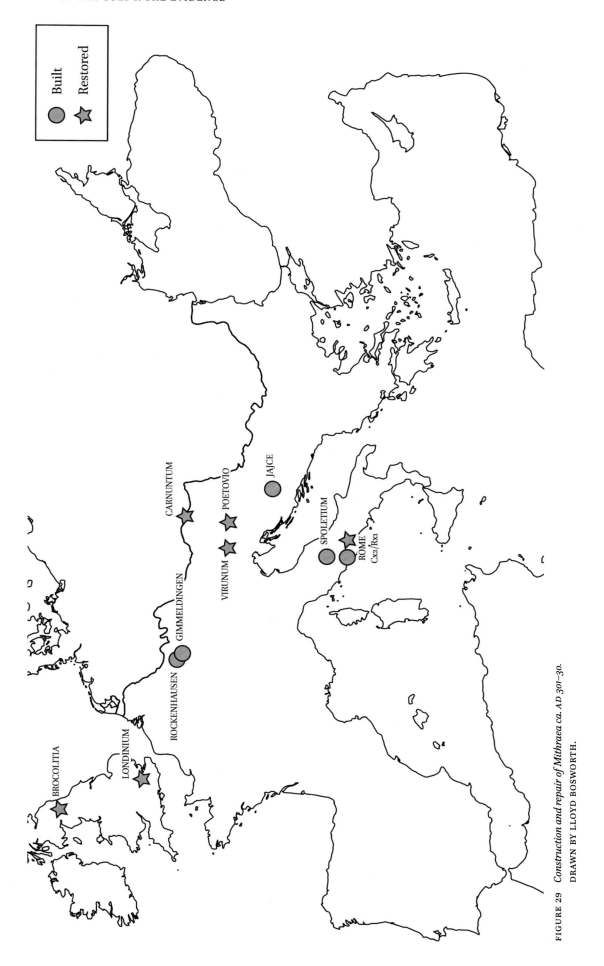

FIGURE 29 *Construction and repair of Mithraea ca. AD 301–30.*
DRAWN BY LLOYD BOSWORTH.

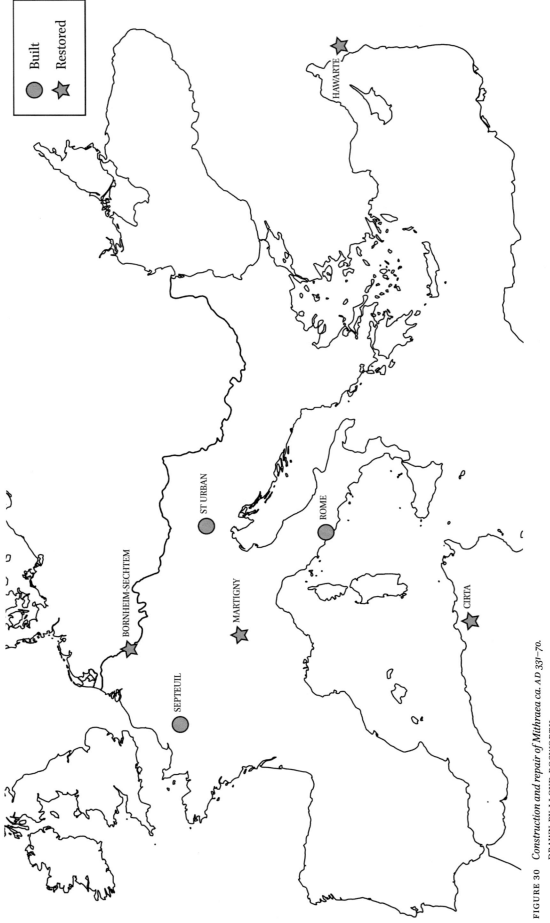

FIGURE 30 *Construction and repair of Mithraea ca. AD 331–70.*
DRAWN BY LLOYD BOSWORTH.

of Rockenhausen and Gimmeldingen were situated in rural locations. Judging by the lack of Rhineland-based evidence in the late 3rd c., it would seem that the status of the cult had already largely diminished in this region by that time.

In Britain, the mithraeum at Brocolitia was again restored after suffering serious damage in the late 3rd c., while the Londinium Mithraeum was frequently provided with new floors due to the unstable ground on which it was built. In Rome, the mithraea at the *Foro Boario* and *Crypta Balbi* were subject to renovations in the early 4th c., while the mithraea at *Via Giovanni Lanza* 128 and in the *Phrygianum* on the Vatican Hill were created at this time. Unfortunately, we have no further information from Ostia, although given the number of mithraea constructed there in the late 3rd c., and the continuing evidence for Mithraic activity in Rome, it would be surprising if no further work had been undertaken on any mithraea in the town. Notable by its absence at this time is any such evidence from Gaul, a surprising fact given the 3rd c. appears to have marked the heyday for the cult in this region.

By the mid 4th c., both the construction and restoration of mithraea had diminished substantially in all regions. The only extant mithraea known to have been constructed at this time are those found at Septeuil and St Urban. Neither required any significant construction work, with Septeuil installed in a pre-existing building and the St Urban Mithraeum in a natural cave; some time during the mid 4th c. a mithraeum was also created at the house of the Olympii on the Campus Martius, but this does not survive. Of the mithraea that were restored, these include those at Hawarte (where a new podium was installed in the *cella*), Martigny (where a new mortar floor was laid), and Cirta in North Africa, although this is only known to us via an inscription. At Bornheim-Sechtem a mithraeum looks to have been largely rebuilt at this time, although it was almost half the size in length to the previous phase, suggesting a diminishing congregation size.[14]

At the end of the 4th c., construction work associated with mithraea had all but ceased, with the only exception being an epigraphic reference from Rome attesting to the construction of a mithraeum by Tamesius Augentius

Olympius. However, in the East, the Hawarte Mithraeum has provided evidence for repair work into the early 5th c. in the form of new wall paintings and a pedestal installed in the *cella*. This mithraeum's construction at the end of the 3rd c., with alterations made at least once in the 4th and again in the 5th c., alongside its five levels of wall paintings, provides a strong contrast to its western counterparts.

Overall, it is clear that by the 4th c. many mithraea could no longer rely on the support that the cult had once enjoyed in the preceding century, however, such a decline was not uniform across the Roman world. There is little evidence for the construction and repair of mithraea in Italy (outside of Rome and its hinterlands), Gaul and (perhaps most surprisingly) the Rhine in the early 4th c., yet such a decline does not become apparent along the Danube or in Rome until the mid 4th c., at which time support appears to have diminished significantly across the empire. Even those mithraea that were built or repaired in the mid 4th c. or later do not exhibit any more notable investment, with new mithraea now only installed in old structures or natural caves some distance from urban centres. The only location in which the consistent care of a mithraeum took place throughout this period looks to have been at Hawarte, located far from any declining interest in the West.

Mithraea and Wider Patterns of Construction and Repair in Late Antiquity

As outlined above, it is important to see how the patterns of construction/restoration for mithraea relate to those for other structures. Fortunately, scholars have already undertaken an analysis of these broader patterns in certain areas of the Roman empire. Beginning with Italy, Jouffroy has shown that building activity associated with temples and shrines was already in decline by the 2nd c. AD, with only 61 temples providing such evidence from this period, as opposed to the 129 from the 1st c. In the 3rd c., there is a significant reduction again in this evidence, with only 11 temples exhibiting building activity, followed by just eight after the turn of the 4th c. However, Jouffroy also demonstrated that this decline in temple construction and restoration was part of a wider lack of investment in public building from the 1st to 3rd c.: only 17 utility buildings (baths, basilicas and markets) were constructed in the 3rd c., as opposed to 54 in the 2nd c., while only 11 entertainment buildings (theatres, circuses and amphitheatres) were erected in the 3rd c., following 38 in the 2nd c.

If we break this information down into smaller chronological periods covering the late 2nd c. to the turn of

---

14   An altar found in the Martigny Mithraeum, commissioned by the governor of the province Publius Acilius Theodoras, was dedicated to 'All the Gods' (*AE* (1998) 872). The upper part of the inscription is missing, and some have postulated that this may have referred to Mithras. However, the idea that the mithraeum was now being used for the worship of multiple gods is worth considering, and also that the renovation of the floor did not constitute the repair of a mithraeum *per se*.

the 5th c. (fig. 31), we can see that there is a gradual decrease in overall building activity from the mid 3rd c. to the early 4th. Thereafter, in the mid 4th c., there is a considerable resurgence in construction activity, including among temples at Ostia (Temple of Herculius), Herodina (Temple of Diana) and the Capitolium at Verona,[15] although this again reduces towards the end of the century. Perhaps the most notable example of a temple being restored in the late 4th c. is that of Isis at Ostia, which was ordered by the emperors Valens, Gratian and Valentinian II. All three were Christian, but Gratian in particular has been seen as adopting an overtly anti-'pagan' stance, given his decision to relinquish the title of *Pontifex Maximus* and remove the Altar of Victory from the Senate House.[16] In this case, it is reasonable to assume that this support was determined by the continuing popularity of the cult amongst the sailors who travelled with grain shipments to Rome. Indeed, the *Isidis Navigium* festival (which marked the opening of the sailing season) continued to be celebrated throughout this period. That Gratian was willing to condone such a project demonstrates that even the most ardent of Christian emperors were not necessarily completely opposed to supporting building work on a 'pagan' temple if it served a purpose, in this case perhaps as a symbol of generosity to those upon whom Rome was reliant for its grain supply.[17]

The patterns relating to Italian mithraea do not adhere to those of civic buildings or temples in general. As with most types of structure, there was a reduction in building activity relating to mithraea in the mid 3rd c., although mithraea still exhibit as much building activity as basilicas, markets and baths combined, while also providing more evidence for this than either temples in general or all forms of entertainment buildings. Furthermore, in contrast to the rest of the data, building work on mithraea was relatively stable into the final decades of the 3rd c. This differentiation continues into the following period, for, while other structures start to see some resurgence in the early 4th c., evidence for the construction/restoration of mithraea drops significantly, and after this there is no further evidence for mithraea being built or repaired in Italy outside Rome. Once again, this differs from the rest of the data, which indicate a significant amount of other building work in this period. Thus, the patterns of construction/resto-

ration of mithraea in Italy do not appear to have been tied to the economic situation, or linked to social factors such as euergetism,[18] but rather to factors particular to the cult.

In the city of Rome, a decline in the fortunes of temples can be traced across the 3rd and 4th c. Only two new temples were built under Severus Alexander, with another under Aurelian, while the Temple of the Divine Romulus (which was possibly completed by Constantine) on the *Sacra Via* was the only new temple erected in the early 4th c., during the reign of Maxentius. There are only a few examples of the restoration of temples during this period: the Temple of Jupiter Ultor on the Palatine was restored under Alexander Severus; the Temple of Venus and Roma was restored by Maxentius in AD 307; the Temple of the 'Harmonious Gods' was repaired by Praetextatus while he was serving as City Prefect in AD 367; the Senate and people of Rome paid for the repair of the Temple of Saturn in AD 350; and a temple to Flora or Venus may have been restored by a private individual in the late 4th/early 5th c.[19]

As for other civic buildings, these follow much the same pattern as temples. Between the death of Alexander Severus and the accession of Diocletian, only one bathhouse (the Baths of Decius) was constructed in the city, while only one other was restored (the Baths of Nero). It also took more than 30 years to complete the restoration of the Colosseum after it was struck by lightning in AD 217, over three times as long as its initial construction took. However, in the 4th c. there was, as across the rest of Italy, an increase in civic building in Rome, and again this mainly consisted of the construction and repair of utility buildings, particularly baths. This consisted of: the construction of the Baths of Diocletian, Constantine and Naeratius Cerialis; and the restoration of the Baths of Helena, Domus Augustiana and Agrippa; other forms of building, including temples, received far less attention.[20] In contrast, the mithraea in Rome follow a different pattern to other buildings, for they continued to be constructed and repaired into the latter half of the 4th c., although there was a notable decline in this after the early 4th c.[21] Not only does this put the data regarding the mithraea in Rome at odds with the construction patterns across the rest of the city, but the data also

---

15   Ostia: *AE* (1941) 66 = *AE* (1948) 127; Herodina: *CIL* 9. 688; Verona: *CIL* 5. 3332 = *ILS* 5368.

16   Sheridan (1966).

17   Alföldi (1937) remains an invaluable, if dated, discussion of the Isiaic festivals in 4th c. Rome. For a more recent assessment, see Salzman (1990) 239–40.

18   For the impact of the decline of euergetism on public building in Late Antiquity, see Ward-Perkins (1984).

19   Richardson (1992) 456–57. For the temple of Flora or Venus, see Mulryan (2011b).

20   Richardson (1992) 456–57.

21   For a summary of the construction and repair of mithraea in Rome, see Bjørnebye (2007) 28–51.

THE DECLINE OF THE CULT I: THE EVIDENCE

suggest that the cult persevered to a greater extent in Rome during the 4th c. than elsewhere in Italy.

In Gaul, the aforementioned quantitative analysis of the construction of Romano-Celtic temples undertaken by Fauduet, found that the number of newly constructed temples declined considerably after the 1st c. During the 1st c., 98 temples were constructed, yet there are only 38 known examples from the 2nd c. Only eight temples were built in the 3rd c. and none were constructed in the 4th.[22] Occasional evidence for the renovation of certain temples is known from the 4th c., with examples from Champallement, Matagne-la-Grande and Matagne-la-Petite, with some recorded even as late as the 6th c.: Caesarius of Arles recalled admonishing his congregation in southern Gaul for rebuilding a temple.[23] Evidence for civic building in Gaul is also far less common in the 3rd c., with just one amphitheatre erected (at Metz) after the Severan period,[24] while the construction of public baths became far less common as well.[25] Once again, the mithraea in Gaul differ from the general patterns. Most Gallic mithraea were built from the turn of the 3rd c. onwards. However, as we have seen, by the 4th c. investment in mithraea in this region had become relatively uncommon, with just one example of construction (Septeuil) and one of restoration (Martigny) known.

What then of the Danubian provinces that are a particularly fertile area for Mithraic evidence? In fig. 32, chronological changes in the construction/restoration of public buildings and temples in Noricum and Pannonia are illustrated.[26] Most notable is the immense amount of evidence for building activity associated with temples in the 2nd to early 3rd c., which far outweighs all the other evidence for public building. However, by the mid 3rd c. the data present a marked shift, as from this point onwards only five instances of temple building work are known: the reconstruction of the temple of *Dea Roma* and the *Genius Augusti* at Lentia; a temple to Silvanus was built at Cirpi by a veteran; the restoration of temples to Jupiter and Victory by the Tetrarchs at Aquincum and Bedaium respectively; and the restoration of a temple to Bona Eventus at Sirmium by an imperial freedman in the reign of Constantius II, which is the last known example of building activity relating to a temple in this region.[27] At the same time, evidence relating to civic building is relatively low, but this does not differ considerably from the level of the 2nd c. Indeed, much of the extant evidence for urbanisation in this region originates from the 1st and early 2nd c., and additions to this process are rarer in subsequent periods.[28]

How priorities had changed in this region by the later periods is demonstrated well by the evidence from Gorsium. At some point in the 3rd c., Gorsium was largely destroyed, with its sizeable temple precinct—which had possibly served as the centre for the imperial cult in this region—left in ruins. Under the Tetrarchs a large reconstruction program in the town was undertaken, yet both temples and civic buildings were conspicuously absent in this, with the main focus now on buildings of a military or administrative nature.[29] As discussed previously, the Tetrarchs evident priority in this region was a stable, loyal military, and the building work undertaken at Gorsium was emblematic of that. Many of the known

---

22   Fauduet (1993) 119–20. This is from a total of 223 temples recorded in Gaul.

23   Caesarius, *Serm* 53.3; Goodman (2011) 168.

24   Bedon, Chevallier and Pinon (1988) 257.

25   Bedon, Chevallier and Pinon (1988) 290–303; Laurence, Esmonde Cleary and Sears (2011) 229. To my knowledge, no complete quantitative survey of all temples and/or public buildings in Gaul has ever been undertaken.

26   Data regarding temples in this graph is taken from Walsh (2016). For other forms of building: <u>Acumincum</u>: for a basilica, see *CIL* 3.13358; <u>Andautonia</u>: for baths, see Lolić and Wiewegh (2012) 219 and Nemeth-Ehrlich and Špalj (2003) 123; <u>Auguntum</u>: for a macellum, see Cristilli (2015) 83; <u>Aquae Iasae</u>: for the forum see Lolić and Wiewegh (2012) 219, for baths see Ragolič (2014) 335–36 and *CIL* 3. 4121; <u>Aquincum</u>: for the forum see *CIL* 3. 10495, for amphitheatres see Fitz (1980) 173 and Márity (1992) 69, for a basilica and macellum see Márity (1992) 69, for baths see Márity (1992) 69, *CIL* 3.3525, 10489; <u>Carnuntum</u>: for the amphitheatres see Fitz (1980) 173, on baths see Mráv (2013) 216, on a macellum see Mráv (2013) 216; <u>Celeia</u>: on baths see Lazar (2002) 83; <u>Cetium</u>: on baths see Scherrer (2002) 226; <u>Cibalae</u>: on baths see Lolić and Wiewegh (2012) 213; <u>Flavia Solva</u>: on the amphitheatre see Alföldy (1974)

181; on baths see Hudeczek (2002) 210; <u>Lauriacum</u>: for the forum see Alföldy (1974) 183 and Kandler and Vetters (1986) 103, on baths see Kandler and Vetters (1986) 103; <u>Municipium Iasorum</u>: Schejbal (2004) 115; <u>Pannonhalma</u>: for the forum see *CIL* 3.4380; <u>Savaria</u>: on the forum see Póczy (1980) 265, on baths see Scherrer (2003) 64, on a macellum see Póczy (1980) 265; <u>Scarbantia</u>: on the amphitheatre and baths see Gömöri (2003) 85; <u>Sirmium</u>: on the hippodrome see Jeremić (1995) 142, on the baths see Poulter (1992) 107–108; <u>Sisica</u>: Faber (1973) 143, Cristilli (2015) 133; <u>Teurnia</u>: Glaser (2002) 140; <u>Vindobonda</u>: on baths see Mader (2004) 73; <u>Virunum</u>: on the amphitheatre see Groh (2005) 90, *AE* (1936) 85, (1999) 1197 = (2002) 1094, (2001) 1587, (2004) 1070–72, *CIL* 3.4826.

27   <u>Aquincum</u>: *AE* (1994) 96 = *CIL* 3. 10605a; <u>Bedaium</u>: *ILS* 664 = *CIL* 3. 5565; <u>Cirpi</u>: *AE* (1971) 323; <u>Lentia</u>: Karnitsch (1956); <u>Sirmium</u>: *AE* (1998) 1051 = *AE* (2001) 1661. When writing Walsh (2016) I included a small temple to Diana at Carnuntum, but was subsequently informed that recent research on this structure suggests it served a secular, rather than religious, function: Marion Großmann *pers. comm.* 24.9.15.

28   Šašel-Kos (2010).

29   Poulter (1992) 110–11.

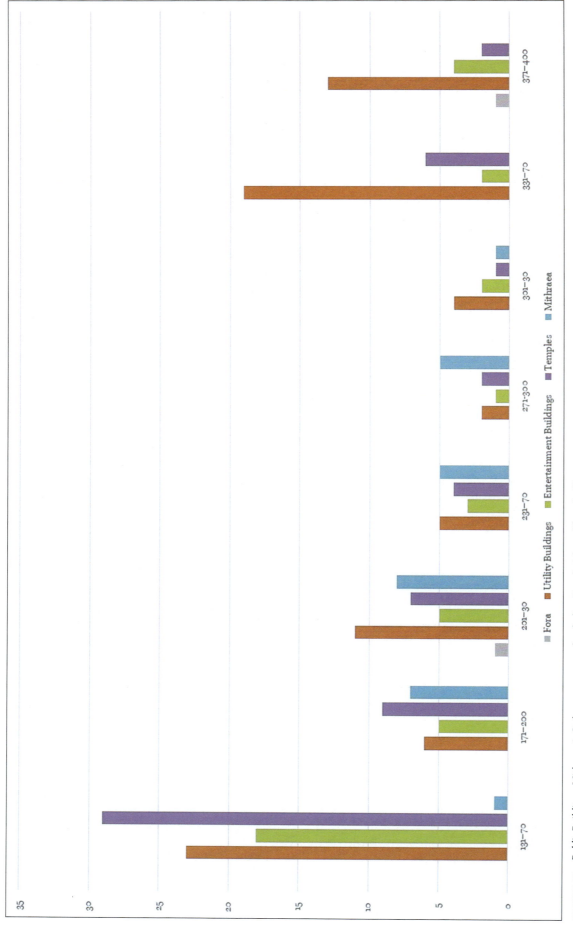

FIGURE 31 *Public Building v Mithraea in Italy ca. AD 131–400 (excluding Rome). Adapted from Jouffroy (1986), with the amendments and additions made to Ostian mithraea based on White (2012).*

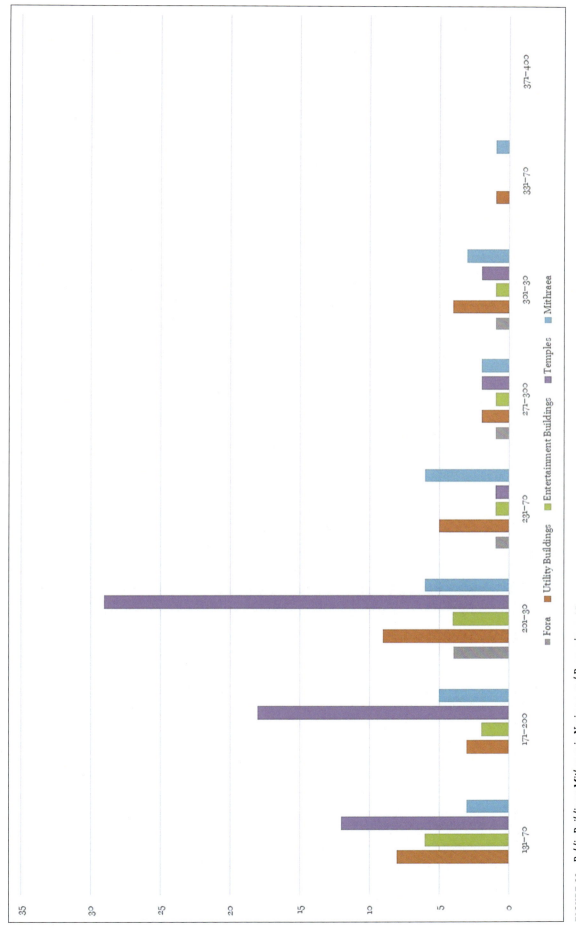

FIGURE 32 *Public Building v Mithraea in Noricum and Pannonia ca. AD 131–400.*
ADAPTED FROM WALSH (2016).

civic buildings that were erected in early 4th c. Pannonia were to be found at Sirmium; this can be explained by the fact it was made an imperial capital in the Tetrarchic period, and as a result held an unusual status in comparison to many other Danubian towns.[30]

The quantitative data relating to mithraea in these provinces once again follow a peculiar pattern. Like temples in general, the number of mithraea that were the subject of building activity increased until the turn of the 3rd c., but while there was a large reduction in the construction/restoration of other temples between AD 231–70, as well as across other forms of building work, the evidence for such work on mithraea remains relatively stable. Indeed, the type of building most likely to be subject to construction or restoration in this period were mithraea. In the late 3rd c., the evidence for the construction/restoration of mithraea does decline, although remains around the same level as entertainment buildings and temples in general. However, there is an increase in the construction/restoration of mithraea in the early 4th c., with only utility buildings (mainly baths) the subject of greater attention. Yet, by the mid 4th c. the picture shifts again, as evidence for the construction/restoration of mithraea significantly decreases, as it does for all forms of civic building by this time. By the final decades of the 5th c., civic building in Noricum and Pannonia had ceased entirely, in stark contrast to neighbouring Italy. It may be the case then that along the Danube, limited resources did have some impact on support for mithraea in the 4th c., given that all other building types also exhibit an irreversible decline.

In summary, it is clear that in many locations across the Roman West building activity associated with temples declined notably in the 3rd c. However, there is a degree of regional variation evident: in Italy, this decline begins in the late 2nd c., at which time the construction and repair of temples in the Danube region was still increasing; indeed, a decline here is not evident until the mid 3rd c. A further regional difference is that temples in Italy and Gaul continue to exhibit evidence of repair into the 5th c., while in Noricum and Pannonia there is no extant evidence of such activity: it ceases a century before. In some cases, we also find a close relationship between the fortunes of civic buildings and temples, such as in Italy and Gaul where the building patterns of temples fall and rise in correlation with those of other buildings. In contrast, in Noricum and Pannonia this is not the case, with civic building already at a minimum in the 2nd c., when temples were increasingly being repaired and constructed. Therefore, while temple construction and repair did generally decrease in the 3rd c., when this decline began, the rate at which it occurred, and how it relates to the wider context of building investment, varied from region to region.

Mithraea rarely appear to have followed the wider patterns of construction/restoration. Where they do, such as in Noricum and Pannonia—where there is a correlation between the data for mithraea and other temples between AD 131 and 230—this does not remain the case through subsequent periods, for mithraea entered into a decline at a later stage compared to temples, and mithraea still exhibit extraordinary support in the early 4th c. In Italy, we find the reverse: there is a rise in building activity associated with temples in general in the 4th c., while such investment in mithraea had ceased by the early 4th c. As outlined, similar patterns appear in Rome and Gaul, with the construction/restoration of mithraea often a phenomenon unto itself. Thus, we can say that the patterns of investment in mithraea were not, for the most part, linked to wider trends in temple or civic building, and so when construction work on mithraea began to decline it was not necessarily due to resources, but rather based on a desire on the part of Mithraic worshippers to build or repair these structures.

Charting the Declining Use of Individual Mithraea

The patterns of construction and repair of mithraea clearly indicate that the cult gradually lost the support it once had, but can we trace the declining use of individual mithraea through extant finds? Unfortunately, this proves difficult in most cases, as the evidence we are reliant on to demonstrate this is the numismatic data, and from the late 4th c. coin circulation north of the Alps declined significantly, thus a decline in coin deposition need not indicate a mithraeum with declining attendance numbers. As Sauer demonstrated in the case of Poetovio, the reduction in coin deposition in Mithraea II and III declines in tandem with the overall coin circulation in the town, suggesting a decrease in the former was due to supply rather than the use of these mithraea.[31]

There are some cases, however, where the rate of coin deposition in a mithraeum differs from the wider patterns of coin circulation, suggesting there was indeed a drop in the number of people frequenting the temple. At Trier, the coins deposited in the mithraeum largely date from 330–48, with a significant decline thereafter.[32] A similar decline in deposition also occured at Pons

---

30 Poulter (1992) 107–109.

31 Sauer (2004) 341.

32 Sauer (2004) 348.

Saravi and Rockenhausen, although in these cases there was a resurgence in depositions between 363–78. This pattern is reflected in wider coin finds from Gaul, including those from Trier, with coin circulation having dramatically reduced in 348–63 and then become more common again in 363–378.[33] The mithraeum at Trier, however, fails to adhere to this pattern, and instead its coin deposition continues to show a decline. Thus, it would seem that although coins were available to offer to Mithras, there were no longer people willing to do so. Notably, as discussed in the previous chapter, this mithraeum is unusual in that it yielded a sacrificial deposit that looks to have been made as part of a ritual closure of the site by the Mithraic adherents. If this were the case, then the declining evidence for votives would correlate with this image of a mithraeum with diminishing support, as opposed to a vibrant active cult being suddenly expelled.

Additionally, the reduction in size of the mithraeum at Bornheim-Sechtem in the mid 4th c. is relevant. Originally measuring up to *ca.* 13.5 m in length, it was reduced in its final phase (seemingly during the reign of Valentinian I) to just *ca.* 7.2 m in length. Such a reduction would suggest that the size of the Mithraic community here had dwindled by the 4th c., albeit not to a degree where they were unable to restore the temple.

Conclusion

The patterns of construction and repair for mithraea indicate that throughout the 3rd c. the cult of Mithras enjoyed relatively stable support, better than for other pagan temples. The cult did not rely on public funds to sustain itself, so we can assume that building work associated with mithraea was paid for, or undertaken by, the Mithraic communities themselves. That they were willing to do so in a period rocked by civil war and economic instability, that saw a dramatic fall in the

construction and repair of other buildings, infers that the commitment of Mithraic initiates to maintain the cult community at this time was relatively high.

Yet from around the turn of the 4th c., the desire amongst Mithraic adherents to support the upkeep of their temples began to dissipate, as had that for other temples somewhat earlier. This decline was not uniform, with the construction and repair of mithraea in Gaul, along the Rhine and Italy (outside of Rome) having already become a rarity in the late 3rd c. The surge in support the cult enjoyed in Dalmatia in the late 3rd c. also looks to have quickly disappeared, for no more mithraea were built here, and existing ones exhibit no further evidence of restoration. In contrast, in the Danubian provinces, Rome and close to the Rhine frontier, mithraea were still being constructed and repaired. Yet this did not last long either, for, by the mid 4th c., the construction and repair of mithraea had become a rarity in these areas too.

Although the urban decline evident in the Danubian regions would undoubtedly have negatively affected the construction and/or repair of mithraea, the decline in building activity cannot be ascribed to purely external factors. In the 3rd c., when economic problems and changing attitudes towards euergetism negatively impacted on the general construction and repair of buildings, including temples, mithraea prospered in spite of this. It is not difficult to see why this was, given that mithraea were not particularly difficult buildings to erect or repair, and it was almost certainly within the ability of Mithraic communities to cover such expenses, or even undertake the work themselves, even in times of economic hardship. As such, even if mithraea exhibited a dip in construction and repair, one would expect to see to see such activity pick up again subsequently, as other buildings experienced a resurgence of support in the 4th c. That we do not see this can only be seen as indicative of a declining interest among the worshippers of Mithras to support these temples. This is not to claim that they ceased worshipping Mithras, but perhaps did so away from the traditional environment.

---

33   Wigg-Wolf (2016) table 1.

CHAPTER 3

The Decline of the Cult II: Explaining the Decline

Introduction

By the mid 4th c. the cult of Mithras had evidently entered into a decline, but why? As will be shown here, there were various factors that contributed to this. First among these was the significant decrease in the size of the populations of the settlements where many mithraea were situated. As people fled to interior areas, as Roman hegemony became harder to maintain on the frontiers, the Mithraic cult found itself with an increasingly limited number of recruits upon which it could draw. Secondly, the concentration of the remaining populations inside small fortified settlements, perhaps often alongside *foederati*, impacted significantly on the social networks of possible Mithraic worshippers, reorienting them so that they were attracted to other forms of religious worship at the expense of their support for the Mithraic community. Thirdly, the changes in ritual practice (outlined in chapter one) led to the cult no longer generating significant commitment amongst its followers, for the rituals they now practised were not as demanding as they once were, and thus those who felt far less committed to the cult could now access it. Additionally, Mithraic rituals were no longer as distinct as they had previously been, meaning that there was little to prevent Mithraic worshippers transferring their focus to other religious groups or locations with similar rituals. Finally, although unlikely to have been the case in many instances, the mithraeum at Trier provides a rare example where declining activity can be charted against the transformation of the surrounding area and town into a more overtly Christian city, suggesting perhaps an indirect form of coercion by the Christian authorities.

During the course of this chapter, I will refer to modern sociological studies regarding how commitment to religious movements is fostered, and how this might help us understand how the changing circumstances of the Mithras cult saw diminishing support for mithraea during the 4th c. Regarding such a methodology, I am well aware of the difficulties posed by utilising modern studies of largely monotheistic movements to understand the workings of the polytheistic past. However, in some regards, little has changed in human nature in the last 1,500 years, and much of this evidence is simply referring to amassed quantitative data that support some logical observations, such as that people's religious choices are largely tied to their social networks, or that by not strictly controlling admission into a community

you risk involving those with far less regard for its maintenance. Naturally, such approaches are never definitive however, and some factors might be more important in certain contexts than others, yet the fact remains that, based on modern studies of religion, the trends we see in the Mithraic evidence in the 4th c. would be expected to have led to a declining commitment amongst worshippers to maintaining the cult community. This is exactly what we see with the declining support for mithraea in this period.

To be clear on what I mean by 'commitment' regarding the Mithras cult, I refer to the desire to maintain the mithraeum as the space in which Mithraic worshippers met and undertook their rituals. As there is no evidence for Mithraic activity beyond mithraea, these were emblematic of Mithraic communities: without them the cult of Mithras, as we understand it, could not exist. If people no longer wished to build or maintain mithraea, but instead let them slide into decay and ruin, as was the case in the 4th c., then this must be taken as indicative that people no longer felt committed to this form of Mithras worship. This is, however, *not* the same as the belief in, or desire to worship, Mithras declining. Indeed, as shall be argued in the following chapter, it is entirely possible that the worship of Mithras continued beyond the final demise of mithraea, in perhaps a more individualised form. Here in this chapter, we are contending with the end of the long-established, highly organised Mithras cult, not the end of the worship of Mithras itself.

Declining Populations

Perhaps the most obvious reason behind the declining support for mithraea in the 4th c., was the change in settlement patterns that was occurring across much of the Roman West in this period. As the grip of the empire loosened across the frontier regions, in many locations where the cult of Mithras was active there appears to have been a notable decrease in the population, as large numbers of buildings in towns and *vici* were abandoned. The people that remained in the area often sought refuge either inside pre-existing forts or erected new ones at defendable locations, such as on hilltops and near rivers. In a number of a cases mithraea continued to be used, but they would have seemed like isolated islands of activity in a sea of dilapidation.

© KONINKLIJKE BRILL NV, LEIDEN, 2019 | DOI 10.1163/9789004383067_005

THE DECLINE OF THE CULT II: EXPLAINING THE DECLINE

At some sites, the decline of *vici* began in the 3rd c., and we see a decline in support for the cult at these places accordingly. At Borcovicium on Hadrian's Wall, where the mithraeum ceased to be used at the turn of the 4th c., the *vicus* looks to have been abandoned in the late 3rd c. and subsequently demolished for building material. The shrine to Mars Thincus, located alongside the mithraeum in the *vicus*, was also abandoned sometime in the early 4th c. At Tienen in Gaul, a similar situation was to be found, whereby the mithraeum ceased to be used in the late 3rd c., around the time the *vicus* it was situated in was abandoned.[1]

In most other locations where Mithraic communities were to be found, such changes are not evident until later in the 4th c. Along the Danube, at Poetovio, most of the evidence for occupation in the late 4th c. comes from a fortified hill overlooking the Drava River. The buildings next to Mithraeum II look to have been abandoned in the second quarter of the 4th c. and were subsequently used to house inhumations, while a similar case was to found in the structures next to Mithraeum III. The industrial area in which Mithraeum V was located also appears to have been abandoned in the mid 4th c.[2] At Aquincum, during the course of the 4th c., the side of the town containing the last active mithraeum was abandoned.[3] Carnuntum is now generally accepted to have been a victim of a powerful earthquake in the mid 4th c., which significantly damaged many buildings across the settlement. Despite reconstruction work under Constantius II, the town never appears to have recovered significantly, and was described (as was much of the region) by Ammianus as a deserted ruin by the late 4th c., the time when the mithraea ceased to be used.[4] Similarly in neighbouring Noricum, at Lentia both the temple to *Dea Roma* and the mithraeum continued to be used until the end of the 4th c., but by this time the occupation of Lentia had shrunk significantly in size down to a fortified position on Castle Hill, while the fort at Pons Aeni, which was situated across the River Inn

from the mithraeum at Ad Enum, was abandoned sometime in the early 5th c.[5]

Even among interior areas such as Gaul, evidence of declining populations is also to be found. At Pons Saravi, evidence for activity in the *vicus* declines after the mid 3rd c., and it was abandoned entirely by the mid 5th c.[6] At Martigny, a number of structures in the town appear to have gone out of use in the mid to late 4th c., including the amphitheatre, the houses of Minerva and *Génie domestique*, and the Gallo-Roman temple to the south of the mithraeum. As such, it appears that by the turn of the 5th c. the town was in a significant state of disrepair.[7]

At Lambaesis in North Africa, a mithraeum was situated outside a military camp next to the large Asklepieion. Lambaesis had served as the capital of Numidia from the reign of Septimius Severus until Constantine, when the administration was moved to Cirta. The archaeological evidence for occupation does not provide a clear indication of the state of the site in the 4th c., but the epigraphic record suggests activity had dwindled significantly by this time. The presence of the *legio III Augusta* in the neighbouring camp is known until the mid 3rd c., at which time inscriptions attesting to them cease. No inscriptions dating to later than the Tetrarchic period have been found in the 'Grand Camp', which is the same time the last dedication was made in the mithraeum. The last evidence for the use of the neighbouring Asklepieion comes in the form of an inscription erected by the governor Domitius Zenofilus in the early 4th c.[8]

Evidently, by the second half of the 4th c. many mithraea found themselves low on possible recruits. In particular, the military and *portoria* staff that had once been spread across these regions in significant numbers were now few and far between. Large and important towns such as Aquincum, Carnuntum and Poetovio, which were major hubs of Mithraic activity, now stood largely empty and dilapidated. Where once large numbers had walked the streets and pathways of these settlements, now only a few (if any) footsteps were to be heard. From a simple numbers perspective, how was the cult of Mithras to maintain (or expand on) the recruits it had gained in the preceding centuries in such circumstances? Even if some mithraea continued to be used, it is hard to see why, at Poetovio for example, three or four

---

1 Borcovicium: Christie (2011) 88, 91. Unfortunately, the forts at Brocolitia and Vindobala remain largely unexcavated, but other sites on Hadrian's Wall show similar trends, such as Birdoswald and Wallsend: see Rushworth (2009) 296–312. Tienen: Martens (2004) 26–28.

2 Poetovio II: Horvat *et al.* (2003) 175; Poetovio V: Horvat *et al.* (2003) 170.

3 Láng (2012), Póczy (1997) 49. Ammianus describes how Valentinian did not wish to linger at Aquincum as it did not provide suitable winter quarters, see Amm. Marc. 30.5.14.

4 For the earthquake at Carnuntum, see Kandler (1989) and Decker *et al.* (2006). Amm. Marc. 30.5.2.

---

5 Lentia: Karnitsch (1956); Ruprechtsberger (2005) 14; Ad Enum: Kellner (1995) 498.

6 Pons Saravi: Rorison (2001) 223.

7 Wiblé (2008) 82, 117, 123, 175.

8 *AE* (2003) 2022. For the fate of Lambaesis in the 4th c., see Groslambert (2011) 22–24.

mithraea would be needed to service a small community living in the hill-fort.

Changing Social Networks

The alterations that occurred in settlement patterns from the late 3rd c. onwards not only indicate that there were fewer possible adherents for Mithraic communities to draw on, but also that prospective initiates were now living in a considerably different social context to those who had come before them. Especially in areas such as Hadrian's Wall, the Danube frontier, and Lambaesis in North Africa, the cult of Mithras had long been closely associated with the military. Indeed, during certain periods at Mithraeum v at Aquincum, as well as at the mithraea in Brocolitia and Lambaesis, when a new commander took over he appears to have followed a tradition of making a dedication to Mithras.[9] As discussed, the support from the upper echelons of the Roman government for the cult along the Danube during the Tetrarchic period was almost certainly designed to earn the loyalty of soldiers on this frontier. Yet, from the late 3rd c., the changes in settlement patterns outlined above led to considerable shifts in the social networks of those living along the frontiers, which significantly undermined the cult of Mithras' ability to foster commitment among these people.

First, however, it is important to outline how social networks play a role in the religious choices people make. Traditionally, the most common model for explaining why people make the religious choices they do is 'deprivation theory', which assumes that people seek a religion that will provide them with something they feel they are lacking (e.g. people who join healing cults are predominantly sick and wish to be cured). However, studies of membership in religious movements have shown no evidence of this phenomenon. Instead, what has been discovered is that religious affiliation is largely based on a desire (either consciously or subconsciously) to conform to those with whom we are closest. Stark and Lofland's study of the Unification Church was one such case that demonstrated this:

> ... all the people the Unificationists encountered in their efforts to spread the faith, the only ones who joined were those *whose interpersonal attachments to members overbalanced their attachments to non-members*. In part this is because ... social networks make religious beliefs plausible and *new* social net-

works thereby make *new* religious beliefs plausible. In addition, social networks also reward people for conforming. [I]n effect, conversion is seldom about seeking or embracing an ideology; it is about bringing one's religious behaviour into alignment with that of one's friends and family members.[10]

In another modern example, despite being one of the fastest growing religious movements in the modern world, the records of the Mormon mission president from 1981–82 indicate that on average only around one in a thousand attempts to convert a stranger result in success, while in contrast there is a 50% chance of a friend or relative converting. Many other studies have found this pattern repeated elsewhere.[11] Thus, it would appear the primary driving force behind joining a religious movement is the desire to maximise 'social capital', that is, interpersonal attachments.[12] If the majority of people a person knows are part of certain religious movement, then they are likely to join that movement too.[13]

As a result, this means that major shifts in social networks can lead people to making religious choices they or their predecessors might not previously have done. Marriage and migration are the two such situations where this is most likely to occur, as they can result in significant exposure to new social networks. A major crisis, such as a plague or famine, may also lead to people adopting new religious affiliations, as these events can rapidly remove many members of one's existing social circle. For example, if one has ten friends, seven of which belong to one cult ('X') and three to another ('Y'), in terms of religious affiliation there is a ratio of 7:3 between cults X and cult Y. As such, one would be more likely to be a member of cult X than Y. However, should a crisis remove five of those members of cult X, one would be left with a ratio of 2:3 in favour of cult Y, thus there is now more to be gained in terms of social capital by shifting allegiance to cult Y.[14] Of course in the polytheistic Roman world one would not necessarily be limited in such a situation to having to choose one cult

---

9   <u>Aquincum v</u>: Clauss (1992) 183–84. <u>Brocolitia</u>: Clauss (1992) 79; <u>Lambaesis</u>: Clauss (1992) 248–49.

10   Stark and Finke (2000) 117.

11   For 25 empirical studies that came to the same conclusion, see Knox, Meeus and t'Hart (1991).

12   I use terms here such as 'capital' and 'costs' which is taken from the 'religious economy' model that has become the common approach in explaining religious activity in a relatively straight-forward way. In should be noted that this is not the same as North's (1992) 'market-place of religions' metaphor, which implies people have free-choice of religions. Indeed, referring to religious activity via economic terms demonstrates the choice was not 'free'.

13   Stark and Finke (2000) 118.

14   Iannacone (1990); Stark and Bainbridge (1997).

THE DECLINE OF THE CULT II: EXPLAINING THE DECLINE

over another, but people only have a finite amount of time and energy, and if one is free to worship cults A, B, C, D, E, F etc., how does one choose which of these to devote the most time to? Based on this model, it would most likely be determined by one's interpersonal relationships with the members of these cults.

Traditionally, the social networks from which the cult of Mithras drew adherents, particularly the army, had allowed it to maintain a steady following, for these were men who lived and worked side-by-side for many years. Certainly, they would have families and other social connections, but primarily their lives revolved around largely male-orientated and highly structured bodies. However, from the late 3rd c. the situation in the northern provinces brought about major changes in social networks, particularly in militarised areas such as on the Danube frontier and Hadrian's Wall. Whereas once soldiers had been housed in forts alongside their comrades-in-arms, while the civilian populations predominantly operated in the neighbouring *vici* and towns, these two spheres were now largely integrated into one, as those inhabiting the latter abandoned these in favour of taking shelter within the forts. For example, along Hadrian's Wall the restructuring of barrack blocks into less uniform patterns, along with the presence of child burials inside forts, has been suggested as indicating family groups now occupied these spaces. At Lentia, Late Roman inhumations found in the Castle Hill area indicate a significant number of females were now living in the hill fort.[15]

The 4th c. also saw the settling of large numbers of *foederati* along the frontier regions of the Roman empire, which may also have impacted on the social networks of those living in these areas. During the reigns of both Constantius II and Valens, we are told various barbarian groups were allowed to cross the Danube and settle within the Roman empire, on the basis that they would provide recruits for the Roman army. Up to 200,000 'barbarians' apparently relocated on Roman soil, including Goths and Alans being settled in Pannonia. Under the command of Alatheus and Saphrac, these forces would go onto contribute to the sizable numbers of non-Roman troops utilised by Theodosius in his conflict with Eugenius.[16]

Of course, attempting to trace in the archaeological record where such groups settled is immensely difficult. At Poetovio, a small cemetery found near the Late Roman fortress on Castle Hill dates to the late 4th and early 5th c., and consisted of burials that contained "barbaric elements", suggesting that they may have acted as the garrison.[17] A similar situation might have been found at Lentia, where artefacts originating from across the Danube have been found in the aforementioned late 4th c. graves.[18] At the site of Krefeld-Gellep on the Rhine, burials dating to between AD 400 and 425 were situated within an existing cemetery but broke from previous norms, with weapons and Germanic jewellery appearing alongside the deceased. At the fort of Vermand in Gaul, a particularly large burial dating to *ca.* AD 400 was found to contain expensive weapons and apparel, indicating that a Frankish chief perhaps served as the site's commander.[19] At Birdoswald, the construction of a timber hall and assorted other timber buildings near the west gate were suggested by the excavators to indicate that the fort was now manned by *foederati* troops.[20]

Evidently, such changes along the frontiers would have significantly reoriented the social networks of the inhabitants there. With mixed populations now living in much closer quarters, and the distinction between military and civilian becoming increasingly blurred, it is not difficult to see why a male-only cult that had become bound up with Roman military identity might find itself decreasing in popularity. That increasing numbers of settlers from across the frontier were beginning to inhabit these regions may also have been detrimental to the cult's continued success, for these people brought with them their own beliefs and traditions to which the local populations were now exposed. Whereas in the early 3rd c. a soldier in these areas would have spent much of his time alongside his fellow Mithraic initiates, circumstances now dictated that social contact with a range of others was now more frequent.

What then of Rome, where aristocratic Mithraic communities survived into the late 4th c.; can the decline of the cult be explained in a similar way here? Indeed, it can. The membership of these groups had been based largely on family relationships, but as time progressed and the older members of the congregation passed away, the social ties of the surviving younger members would likely shift through marriage and career postings, resulting in an increased exposure to other cults that would serve them better than investing time and energy in supporting a Mithraic community. There is no reason to assume that it was to Christianity that these adherents turned, for the likes of Symmachus or Nicomachus

---

15   Hadrian's Wall: Collins (2012) 50; Lentia: Ruprechtsberger (1999) 88.

16   Amm. Marc. 31.4–16; Christie (2011) 65–66.

17   Horvat *et al.* (2003) 164.

18   Ruprechtsberger (1999) 67–69. On the difficulties of identifying ethnicity via finds on the Late Roman frontiers, see Swift (2000).

19   Christie (2011) 64.

20   Christie (2011) 91.

Flavianus the Elder never joined a Mithraic community, nor the many other senators that came from long established families. Michele Salzman has identified through a quantitative study that a large proportion of the aristocracy in Italy remained non-Christian into the last decades of the 4th c., and that this persistence was to be found strongest in Rome, meaning there was still an array of religious practices for aristocrats to be exposed to.[21] Furthermore, while much of the North African aristocracy did not show any eagerness to covert from polytheism to Christianity either, there is also no evidence for any of them joining a Mithraic community.[22] Indeed, given the long list of priesthoods many of these aristocratic Mithraic initiates held, it is difficult to see how they could provide strong support for their Mithraic communities in the long-term, given that by having such an array of social contacts it meant they were constantly exposed to other religious movements where their social capital would be better served.

Incidentally, there does appear to be a trend among mithraea that those linked to or situated on the property of a patron, exhibit a shorter period of use. The Londinium Mithraeum, built in a residential area by the veteran Ulpius Silvanus, was only active for only around 50–60 years, in contrast to those on Hadrian's Wall which remained in use for around twice this length of time. The same may also be said of the Mithraeum II ('of Victorinus') at Aquincum which, like the Londinium Mithraeum, was only in use for around half a century, from the late 2nd to early 3rd c.[23] Given that so many mithraea have been found in Ostia and Rome without any accurate dating material having been recorded, it is possible that these sites were contemporaneously active. In actuality, this may be a reflection of different Mithraic groups rising and falling over time, with their continuing use of a mithraeum depending on who owned the property in which it was situated. Much like the aforementioned aristocrats, those who controlled access to these mithraea may have found their social capital better invested elsewhere in other forms of cult practice, or it might be that they simply moved away or the male line of the family came to end. In any case, the frequent reorienting of social networks that would occur in urban settings, and which drove senatorial Mithraic worshippers to abandon the cult, were likely to have had a similar effect on Mithraic groups elsewhere that relied on a particular person or family to host them.[24]

Finally, it is worth briefly highlighting how the social networks of the elites in late antique Gaul were different to those networks in Rome or North Africa. In Gaul, Salzman has revealed a much more rapid conversion to Christianity, something she believes was driven by their much closer proximity and more frequent interaction with the imperial court based in Trier.[25] Although we cannot be certain, but one wonders if the mithraea located on private estates in the north-western provinces, such as at Bornheim-Sechtem and Mackwiller, found themselves also losing support for this reason, as their owners began to find greater opportunities to earn social capital by converting to Christianity. Additionally, one may venture that such a relatively rapid Christianisation of the aristocracy in Gaul may have led to a stricter enforcement of the anti-'pagan' legislation in this region.

Changes in Mithraic Rituals

As outlined in chapter one, one of the major alterations that occurred in various north-west Mithraic communities was the apparent abandonment (or at least marginalisation) of certain rituals, in particular initiation rites, and the turning to new forms of votive practice, such as the deposition of coins. Furthermore, in places where Mithraic initiations did continue, such as amongst senatorial groups in Rome, there is reason to believe that these lacked the emotional intensity of those from earlier times. That we see such changes in Mithraic rituals around the same time that support for mithraea was declining cannot be a coincidence. Indeed, by utilising sociological studies into how religions foster commitment among their congregations, it becomes apparent these transformations in Mithraic ritual practice would have only served to lessen commitment amongst Mithraic worshippers towards the maintenance of their community.

Let us begin with why having less demanding rituals would be detrimental to such commitment. In order to participate in any religious movement, members of a cult will have to pay certain 'costs'. Such costs may be material, social, physical or psychological, and can take a variety forms, such as: regulations surrounding dress, diet and sexual practice, or rituals in which members must participate. Thus, the higher the costs the greater commitment among members as "potential members are forced to choose whether to participate fully or

---

21 Salzman (2002) 77.

22 Salzman (2002) 94.

23 Tóth (1988) 41–45; Zsidi (1995) 367.

24 Some mithraea installed in houses could become the main focus of the building, such as at Lucus Augusti in Spain, where

the mithraeum continued in use after the construction of the town wall destroyed part of the wider building: see Alvar, Gordon and Rodriguez (2006).

25 Salzman (2002) 89.

not".[26] Simply put, the more expensive something is, the more we value it. By forcing its members to engage in intensive initiation ceremonies, most likely repeatedly as they moved from one grade to another, the cult of Mithras made membership more valuable. By 'vetting' its members in such a fashion, Mithraic communities could be sure to maintain a relatively high level of commitment among its members, as those who felt little commitment to the cult would be prevented from joining or maintaining their membership.

However, when a religious community allows itself to become more accessible and places less demands on its followers, as was the case amongst various Mithraic communities in the 4th c., this creates a situation whereby a greater number of people with little sense of commitment to the cult can participate. Such people, who feel they can reap the rewards of a cult (e.g. help from the deity or access to the afterlife) without having to contribute much to it, are known as 'free-riders'. A common modern example of this is people who only attend a church at Christmas. They hope for the same rewards as those who attend all year round, while they also expect the churches to be operating without having made a contribution to them in the previous 364 days. If these 'free-riders' are perceived to be reaping the same benefits as other members who often attend and help maintain the upkeep of the church, then the latter will naturally begin to question why they are exerting themselves to such an extent, and thus may become laxer in their own participation. Let us imagine commitment on a scale of one to ten, with the commitment of a congregation being the average of its members' total commitment. In a congregation of 50 who all have a commitment rating of ten out of ten, then the average commitment will be ten. If they are joined by 20 more adherents, who are all at a three on our scale, then average commitment for the whole congregation will fall to eight. Essentially, free-riders dilute the commitment of congregations.[27] Amongst many Mithraic communities in the 4th c., the absence or marginalisation of initiations, and the implementation of more accessible rituals, would have opened the door (quite literally) to free-riders participating in the cult. As such, one would expect the overall commitment of Mithraic adherents to drop.

Furthermore, these changes to Mithraic rituals meant that the bonds forged between the cult members would no longer be as strong. To undertake an intensive initiation ritual in which one is blind-folded and stripped, a significant amount of trust must be placed in those conducting these rituals by the initiate, that is they will not take advantage of his helpless state. Not only through joining the cult did someone invest in the support of Mithras, but also that of their co-worshippers. Indeed, in his cognitive study of Mithraic rituals, Luther Martin highlighted the importance of 'rites of terror' in forming a strong group mentality, arguably a feature of more importance than any other form of bonding exercise.[28] In contrast, by the mid 4th c. simply being able to drop a coin at the foot of the Mithraic relief and partake in a meal, rather than undergo an intensive initiation ceremony, was unlikely to foster the same degree of camaraderie amongst Mithraic communities as those ceremonies of the past. If Mithraic worshippers felt less indebted to each other, they were less likely to pull together to maintain their community during times of hardship.

Perhaps the most important issue here was the declining uniqueness of Mithraic rituals. As people participate in cult rituals, they accrue what has been termed 'religious capital'. Religious capital "consists of the degree of mastery of and attachment to a particular religious culture".[29] Thus, the more unique a cult is, the greater the level of religious capital obtained through participating in rituals and following the cult's regulations. Alternatively, if a cult is not especially unique, there is a greater risk of its followers becoming more attracted to other forms of similar worship, as the religious capital gained from participating in this cult could be equally gained from joining other cults. This is not to say one might entirely abandon the first cult, but there is only a finite amount of time, effort, and funds that people have: if the same costs are applied across a range of cults, why would one necessarily value one any more than another? Or if two cults require similar types of rituals to be performed, why not practise them in the same location?

As outlined in the introduction, there were elements of Mithraic ritual practice that had been specific to the cult, first and foremost of which were the initiation rites. Initiation ceremonies did play a role in a number of cults in the Roman world besides that of Mithras, most notably those of Isis/Sarapis, Magna Mater/Attis, and the Eleusinian Mysteries.[30] As to what these rituals involved in other cults is unclear.[31] It is those of the Isis/

---

26   Iannacone (1994) 1188.

27   Stark and Finke (2000) 147–50.

28   Martin (2015) 34.

29   Stark and Finke (2000) 121.

30   For a discussion of religious initiation rites in the Graeco-Roman world, see Bremmer (2014).

31   It was long thought that the *taurobolium* was part of the initiation process into the cult of Magna Mater, but this has been shown to be incorrect: see Cameron (2011) 160–63; McLynn (1996). Some priests of the cult (*galli*) did practise eviration,

Sarapis cult that we have the most information about, although the accuracy of this evidence is debatable as it is transmitted to us via Apuleius' fictional narrative in the *Metamorphoses* (late 2nd c. AD). In this account, the protagonist Lucius is purified with water and fasts for ten days, before undertaking a night-time ritual within the inner chambers of the temple. Few details are provided on what this involved, but Lucius does state that he came close to death before the goddess appeared to him bathed in light,[32] an experience which sounds similar to the climax of Mithraic initiations. Regarding initiations into the Eleusinian Mysteries, it has been suggested that a passage of Plutarch relates to this, where once again we find the protagonist experiencing panic and desperation in the dark, before a holy light appears.[33]

Yet, as argued in the introduction, we should be wary of overstating the similarities here at the expense of understanding the differences. Certainly, such rituals were all likely to have involved an intense emotional experience that was designed to act as the metaphorical death and resurrection of the initiate, but how this was acted out may have been significantly different among these cults. Indeed, there is no indication an initiate into the Mysteries at Eleusis or Isis would be stripped naked and have a bow and arrow or swords pointed in their face. The aforementioned papyri from Egypt also suggest a script had to be followed in Mithraic initiations. One would presume a similar practice was applied in the initiations into other cults, but in having scripts this infers there were specific things that needed to be uttered and given the significant differences amongst these cults they were unlikely to have translated easily from one to another. Furthermore, it must be borne in mind that many of the gods and cults that operated in the Roman world, including the central Roman pantheon, the imperial cult, and many local deities, do not appear to have demanded such things from their followers, or at least not to the extent of these cults.[34] Just

having secret intensive initiation rituals made the cult of Mithras almost unique, and placed demands upon all its followers that few other cults could match.

The deposition of coins, however, is another matter entirely, for such a practice was common at religious sites throughout the Roman empire. Indeed, the deposition of coins as votives had long been performed at various sites in Rome itself; Suetonius relates how equestrians would throw a coin into the *Lacus Curtius* in the Forum for the welfare of Augustus.[35] During the late 3rd to early 4th c. we find the Christian author Lactantius bemoaning the worship of false idols and the deposition of coins at statue bases, thus suggesting such a practice was, at least in his experience, commonplace, while Sozomen also makes reference to this practice.[36]

Archaeological excavation has yielded further evidence of coins being offered at votives at various sites in Late Antiquity. In Gaul, such activity is recorded in the non-Mithraic cave sanctuary of Pennes-Mirabeau and at a rural shrine at Lioux. In Italy, various sites have produced coins dating to the 4th and 5th c, including examples found at Marina Piranomonte, Pertosa, Celle Civita, and Grotta Bella. Much like in mithraea, at these sites this activity also centred on the main cult statue/relief.[37] There is also evidence from Britain of coins being deposited in temples that appear to have been left to decay, such as at Hayling Island where coins ran to the end of the 4th c., while in Temple V at Springhead small concentrations of coins, the latest of which dates to AD 375, were found against the west wall.[38] In the late 3rd c., the mithraeum at Biesheim appears to have been converted into a temple dedicated to a different god, given that at this time the Mithraic sculptures were buried under a raised floor that converted the standard tripartite division into an open-plan room.[39] This transformation was followed by the deposition of *ca.* 200 coins dating from the late 3rd c. until AD 395 on the floor of the building. At Martigny, the Gallo-Roman temple that lay close to the mithraeum, was the recipient of a high number of coins as votives in the 4th c., with the spatial pattern of their deposition concentrated on the centre of the temple. Furthermore, not far from

---

    which may be seen as an initiation rite, but this is unlikely to have been common among Roman citizens who joined the cult. This is partly because one needed to be exceptionally dedicated to the cult in order to suffer the physical and mental toll this resulted in (thus atypical of general society), but also because this practice was banned under Roman law. Contravening this law could result in the culprit being banished or being discounted from inheritances: see Bowden (2010) 101. For initiation rituals in the cult of Magna Mater in general, see Alvar (2008) 276–82.

32   Apul. *Met.* 11.23.

33   Plut. *Mor.* 15. 178 ('On the Soul').

34   This is unsurprising, given that civic priesthoods were often bestowed as political rewards rather than taken up out of religious adherence.

35   Suet. *Aug.* 57.

36   Lactant. *Div. inst.* 2.2.14–15.; Sozom. *Hist. eccl.* 2.4.

37   On cave sanctuaries, see Brenot (1990) 206–10. On sites in Italy, see Goddard (2006) 296–97.

38   King (2008) 37. Given that this phenomenon has only recently been established in mithraea, despite large amounts of coins appearing in many early excavations, it is likely that there were other (perhaps many other) examples of such coin depositions in temples that were not recorded.

39   It would seem the benches now only stood 0.10m above the nave: see Kern (1991) 64.

THE DECLINE OF THE CULT II: EXPLAINING THE DECLINE

Martigny, a sanctuary of Jupiter at Furlenboden has produced evidence of coin offerings into the 6th c.[40]

It is not only temple sites that have yielded such evidence: spring sites also attracted such offerings in the 4th c. Eight such sites have yielded over 1000 coins: Conventina's Well and Bath in Britain; Bourbonne-les-Bains and Nîmes in Gaul; Bornheim-Roisdorf in Germany; Vicarello in Italy; Burgaski Bani in Bulgaria; and Zichron Ja-akov in Israel.[41] Of these, the most notable in the context of this study is Coventina's Well, which lay in close proximity to the mithraeum of Brocolitia. The mithraeum of Brocolitia, like its fellow British Mithraic temples, did not produce a large body of coins, as it went out of use prior to such depositions becoming frequent occurences in mithraea, but in Coventina's Well one of the highest concentrations of coins as votive offerings from across the whole Roman world was found. Over 16,000 coins had been deposited in the well, with reliefs and altars from the associated temple placed on top of them intact and unmolested.[42] The spring site at Bornheim-Roisdorf was also situated less than two hours walk from the Bornheim-Sechtem mithraeum, while Bourbonne-les-Bains is another site which is situated close to the Rhine frontier. At Bornheim-Roisdorf, the nature of the deposition matches that of mithraea: falling in the mid to late 4th c., before ending at the turn of the 5th. At Bourbonne-les-Bains, the pattern is different, as the height of coin deposition occurred between the 1st c. AD and AD 299, after which a smaller number of coin deposits, which do seem to have been votive in nature, were made, up to the early 5th c. A final example of possible votive coin deposition at a spring site, although a smaller sample than the examples above, is to be found in the sanctuary which rose in the place of the Mackwiller mithraeum in AD 351. Here, 65 coins were found dispersed over the floor, the latest of which was minted in AD 388.[43]

A word should also be said on the large number of coins that have been found in structures at Königsbrunn (in Raetia), Mandelieu and Orbe (in southern Gaul). In all three cases the building had the ground-plan of a mithraeum, but no statues, reliefs or inscriptions remained to provide a definite identification. At Orbe and Königsbrunn a similar distribution pattern for the deposition of coins was found to that of Martigny: they lay in a semi-circle around where the cult relief might have stood. At Orbe, *ca.* 300 coins

were found, terminating in the late 4th c., while at Königsbrunn 96 coins were found, the latest of which was minted in AD 367.[44] The remaining uncertainty as to whether these structures were ever mithraea, or were perhaps mithraea converted for other uses, highlights how the distinction between the Mithras cult and other religious activities in this period was becoming blurred.

What of Mithraic feasts: how unique were these compared to other religious activity in the 4th c.? Unsurprisingly, such activities were popular across the religious spectrum. Indeed, it appears the imperial government was relatively accepting of them, and rather than ban them outright, it instead decided to try and secularise them. This is demonstrated in two laws dating from the late 4th and early 5th c. that refer to banquets. One, issued in AD 399, allowed people to continue engaging in banquets as long as they did not involve traditional rites, such as sacrifice. The second was issued in AD 407, which forbade feasts from taking place in the countryside, as they may be used to disguise non-Christian practices.[45] Yet realistically it was very difficult to police such activities, given their popularity.

Feasts were often part of larger celebrations, such as festivals, and were popular social events. As Goddard has argued, Christians and non-Christians alike could even partake in the same feasts, such as those that were held as part of the imperial cult celebrations, which were seen by Christians as purely traditional, rather than as religiously-charged, although others continued to engage in them as religious activities.[46] In some cases, it was simpler just to 'Christianise' such activities, such as at the shrine of St Felix at Nola in AD 406. Paulinus relates in three separate tales how, in this year, two pigs and a heifer were raised by local rustics so as to be brought to the shrine and sacrificed; this was done and after which their remains were cooked and given to the poor. This was carried out to fulfil vows made by the animal's owners. As Dennis Trout has observed, Paulinus "... was willing to create and promote a sanctioned Christian context for the enactment and reshaping of certain rituals rooted in the pre-Christian traditions of the Italian countryside".[47] If mithraea had become more accessible in Late Antiquity, the one type of ritual we may expect to see continuing then are feasts. Of course, one may argue that if Mithraic feasts continued to prioritise the consumption of bird and piglet, then they did retain their particularly Mithraic elements. However, this did not

---

40 Martigny: Wiblé (2008) 81–82; Furlenboden: Bielmann (2013) 160.

41 Sauer (2011).

42 Allason-Jones and McKay (1985).

43 Biesheim: Kern (1991) Mackwiller: Hatt (1957).

44 Orbe: Luginbühl, Monnier and Mühlemann (2004); Königsbrunn: Overbeck (1985) Mandeleiu: Brenot (1990).

45 *Cod. Theod.* 16.10.17, 19.

46 Goddard (2002).

47 Paul. *Carm.* 20; Trout (1995) 298.

necessarily mean that these people entirely understood *why* they ate such foods at mithraea. Just as tradition dictates that one eats turkey for Christmas dinner, did people now come to a mithraeum with chicken and pig meat to cook because that is what they had long done in these buildings at certain times of the year? The absence of individual sacrificial deposits of birds might indicate that while chicken was still consumed in Mithraic feasts, the overall importance attached to these animals, and the understanding people had of their meaning to the cult, had lessened.

The last known inscription attesting to the consecration of a mithraeum in the north-west provinces also implies that Mithraic ritual activity was now less distinct. As discussed in chapter one, the mithraeum at Gimmeldingen, dedicated in AD 325, was referred to as a *fanum*, which is a term previously unknown in a Mithraic context. It is an immense shame that the structure does not survive, but one might infer from the inscription that the dedicant did not see any considerable difference between a mithraeum and a Gallo-Roman temple. Furthermore, this forms an interesting parallel with the deposition of coins in the mithraeum and Gallo-Roman temple at Martigny mentioned above, which suggests the buildings were used for similar rituals.

This blurring in the distinction between Mithraic practices and those of other cults correlates with the declining support for mithraea, primarily along the frontier, in the 4th c. Notably, as we have seen, the mithraea in eastern Gaul were already struggling in the late 3rd c., and it is perhaps no coincidence that the cult had possibly become equated with healing springs here. Might the growing association between Mithras and healing in this region have led to the erosion of some of the cult's unique traits here at an earlier stage? This would explain the premature decline in support for mithraea in this region, for one could simply visit a spring site or the temple of another healing god to deposit *ex votos* if need be.

Thus, as the distinction between Mithraic rituals and other forms of religious practice became less apparent in Late Antiquity, there was little to stop Mithraic worshippers shifting their focus elsewhere: they could go to a spring and deposit a coin or engage in feasts at other major celebrations, with little to distinguish these activities from those now conducted in mithraea. Once again, it must be stated this is not to argue that these people necessarily 'converted' away from the cult of Mithras. Rather, by becoming less unique and demanding less of its followers, the cult of Mithras could no longer expect them to be more invested in it than in a spring site or neighbouring temple where similar rituals

were being performed in the hope of similar rewards. If people could just as easily undertake such practices in other locations, perhaps they now felt there was little need to maintain mithraea in the way their predecessors had. Perhaps Mithras, the 'eternal spring' and 'born of the rock', could be appeased just as well with coin deposits made at natural sites, such as at springs or in caves, rather than within mithraea. Indeed, if the rituals that were conducted in mithraea had altered considerably, then it was perhaps the case that whatever ritual the topography of a mithraeum was designed to facilitate, was also made defunct. Without this ritual to tie Mithraic worshippers to these structures, why would they want to maintain them?

Coercion by the Imperial Government

Another potential factor that began to drive Mithraic adherents away from mithraea were the actions of the imperial government. Naturally, some Mithraic initiates might have been put off frequenting their local mithraeum due to the various anti-'pagan' laws, although the application of such laws, as discussed, is difficult to chart. However, there were other, less direct ways of making Mithraic worshippers question their loyalty to the cult. At Trier, by the late 4th c. the mithraeum was one of the few temples still active in the *Altbachtal* precinct, but as discussed above, the reduction in coin deposits within it suggests that the use of the temple had rapidly declined after the mid 4th c. Incidentally, to the west of the mithraeum a temple (building 31, possibly to Hercules) was burned down, as were temples 14, 15, 16, 17, to make way for a new road during the reign of Gratian.[48] It seems unlikely that this was an act of anti-'pagan' feeling, for, as outlined previously, Gratian, despite his reputation as a devout Christian, was not above funding the repair of temples; rather, it is likely many of these buildings were no longer used regularly and the measure was more practical in nature. Yet, for Mithraic adherents visiting the mithraeum, the sight of these temples being torn down, while a Christian emperor sat in the nearby palace next to Constantine's massive Christian basilica, must have made them ponder whether their religious practices would be tolerated much longer.

---

48 Ghetta (2008) 24–25.

Conclusion

There was nothing miraculous or sudden about the decline of the cult of Mithras. Unfortunately for the cult, its dwindling support base was simply a product of the times, with a variety of factors determining why there was less desire to support and maintain mithraea. Firstly, there were simply fewer people to recruit from, in many areas. In particular, along the northern frontier regions, where the cult had enjoyed significant success, people were now emigrating to areas deemed safer, as Rome's influence waned. With cities declining around them, mithraea could no longer rely on access to the quantity of support it once had. In towns such as Poetovio or Aquincum, why would one need four or five active mithraea to serve such a small population? Part of the reason fewer mithraea were built or restored was likely to have been due to a simple question of supply and demand.

Not only did the number of possible initiates decline, but the social makeup changed around many mithraea. In areas where the cult had been reliant on the army for recruits, the social context of these regions changed considerably across the 4th c. Gone were the days when soldiers lived and worked alongside each other for the majority of the time; now their families and other civilians were also to be found occupying the remaining fortified locations. In addition to this, the increasing use of *foederati*, 'barbarian' groups employed not as Roman soldiers but as mercenaries working with the army, meant significant numbers mixed with the remaining Roman military; these new groups had their own forms of beliefs and rituals. From what sociological studies have shown, in previous generations commitment to the Mithras cult would have been fostered by the fact that initiates spent much of their time together outside Mithraic contexts: being part of the cult added to their social capital in these networks. However, with such networks increasingly disrupted from the late 3rd c. onwards, involvement in the cult of Mithras would no longer have produced the same social capital it once did, as those who worshipped Mithras found themselves more exposed to those who were not members.

Such issues were not limited to the frontier, as in Rome aristocratic Mithraic groups faced similar pressures, for among their social networks there was a great range of cults and gods they could be exposed to. Their desire to obtain Mithraic titles had been designed to preserve their status, in the face of increasing numbers of 'new men' being admitted to the Senate. Yet there would come a point where a channelling of their support into other religious movements would, and did, prove more

beneficial. When the patron of a Mithraic community or his family lost interest or was no longer able to support their mithraeum, this affected more than just those senatorial groups; other Mithraic communities elsewhere relied on such support, and, finding it removed, would be forced to vacate their mithraeum as a result. The relatively short-lived occupation of the Londinium Mithraeum is perhaps best explained by such a series of events.

Changes in Mithraic ritual practices also led to diminishing levels of commitment towards the maintenance of mithraea amongst Mithraic worshippers. By appearing to discard initiation rituals and instead have its followers deposit coins, the cult of Mithras no longer placed considerable demands on its adherents, and in doing so the value of worshipping Mithras decreased. The levels of trust needed amongst Mithraic worshippers in order to undergo demanding initiation processes needed to be high, but without such rituals that bond could no longer be formed, or at least could be made elsewhere outside of a Mithraic context. In contrast to initiations, Mithraic feasts look to have continued in a number of locations, but the absence of evidence for sacrifices might indicate that these had lost their unique qualities that made them specifically Mithraic in nature. Additionally, the deposition of coins had long been widely practised elsewhere and was by no means specifically Mithraic. In having rituals that were not overtly different to the practices of other cults in Late Antiquity, the religious capital earned through participation in the worship of Mithras could be easily transferred elsewhere, even in some cases to other nearby structures or natural features, such as springs. We cannot be sure, as it is unclear what it involved, but the ritual practice that was linked to the traditional mithraeum *cella* may also have ceased, given the evident changes in the use of space within these structures. Under such circumstances, why would adherents bother expending effort in maintaining mithraea?

As emphasised, this decline does not necessarily equate to people no longer worshipping Mithras, only that they moved away from the traditional model of a Mithraic community housed within a mithraeum to do so. We do not know what those who came to drop a coin in a mithraeum thought or felt, and it would be wrong to assume that their belief in Mithras was any less strong than their predecessors who underwent initiation rites. Yet, it is clear they felt less attached to the idea of worshipping Mithras in a mithraeum than previous generations of Mithraic worshippers, otherwise they would have expended effort on building or maintaining them. Why do we not see any new mithraea spring up among the fortified sites across Noricum and Pannonia in the 4th c.? Why instead do people continue to visit old, probably dilapidated mithraea located among the ruins of neighbouring *vici* and civilian towns? Mithraea were relatively easy to construct, and some of these same settlements would later feature churches, so such building was clearly within their means, they just evidently had no desire to do so.

Importantly though, as ever, this was not the case in every Mithraic community. The Hawarte Mithraeum, isolated as it was on the edge of the Syrian Desert, provides no indication of marked changes to ritual practice. No coins were deposited there, and the iconography depicting the grades, along with the cult image seemingly being hidden behind a curtain, suggest initiations were still enacted. Notably, evidence for numerous phases of restoration is evident in this mithraeum over the course of the 4th c. and into the 5th, unlike its contemporaries in the West.

Although it can rarely be proven, in places such as Trier it is possible that Mithraic communities did feel the weight of change as the urban landscape around them became increasingly Christianised. They may not have felt an immediate threat from this—with the redevelopment of the *Altbachtal* temple precinct coming during the reign of Gratian, an emperor who was largely benign in religious matters—but there may have been a sense that the clock was ticking.

CHAPTER 4

The Fate of Mithraea

Introduction

When the Tetrarchs erected the altar to Mithras at Carnuntum in the opening decade of the 4th c., few present at the time could have believed that within a hundred years the cult would be all but extinct. Yet, despite being one of the most widespread cults in the Roman world, and which retained a significant following in many areas into the early 4th c., we have seen how there was a general decline in the construction and repair of mithraea in the decades following the Carnuntum dedication, suggesting that the cult's following had significantly begun to wane. In this chapter, we will see how mithraea finally came to be abandoned during the 4th and early 5th c., and what factors might have laid behind this.

As highlighted, for many scholars past and present the demise of the cult was directly linked to the rise of Christianity, with Christians viewing the cult with a particular hatred that was expressed through the desecration, and occasionally the outright destruction, of mithraea. Certainly, there are some instances where this was the case, but for a cult so widespread it seems implausible that its fate can be prescribed to one reason alone. Here, I shall illustrate a more nuanced image of the end of the Mithras cult by reviewing the evidence for the fate of mithraea across the Roman world and assessing this within the context in which it occurred. How did the mithraea of the 4th c. come to meet their fate, and how did this vary regionally and chronologically? What forms of destruction and desecration are evident at Mithraic sites? What factors (e.g. Christian iconoclasm, barbarian incursion, pressure from the Roman government, civil war, Mithraic ritual practice, and natural disasters) might have led to this situation, and how common may each of these scenarios have been?

Before beginning this analysis, it is important to highlight that discerning what became of temples in the late antique period is unfortunately fraught with problems, from which mithraea are not exempt. This is due in part to when these structures were excavated. Many of the mithraea included here were uncovered in the 19th and early 20th c. during the course of excavations that often sought to clear everything down to levels dating to the 'High Empire' of the 1st and 2nd c., resulting in much of the late antique levels going unrecorded. On occasions where they have, rarely was this in detail and was often imbued with the preconceived notions of the excavators. For example, to an archaeologist of the late 1800s, objects found in a fragmentary condition were clearly the victims of violent destruction. In contrast, a modern excavator would be unlikely to judge so quickly, as we now know that the cultural biographies of objects and structures can vary greatly over time: what might seem to be worthless fragments to us could have had an entirely different meaning at the time of deposition. As such, we must be cautious in interpreting the fate of objects and structures without full consideration of the evidence and the context in which they were deposited.[1]

Further, it is often uncertain as to whether the latest date provided by the extant finds from a temple is close to that of its abandonment, or whether there was a period of continuing occupation not evident in the archaeological record. This is particularly difficult to ascertain in the case of earlier excavations where stratigraphy was not recorded. Concerning the end of mithraea, often we are reliant on the latest coin deposited in the structure, but rarely does any religious site in the north-western provinces produce evidence for the deposition of coins beyond the early 5th c. Why did the practice of offering coins cease? The answer is most likely the availability of coins: this period saw a significant decline in the minting of coins in the north-western provinces, meaning they would not have been readily available for people to give as offerings.[2] However, this does not mean that worship at these sites ceased. The grammarian Servius observed around the turn of the 5th c. that all springs were considered holy, suggesting that spring worship was still a widespread phenomenon that was conducted not only through the deposition of coins, but also by other means that are no longer extant in the archaeological record.[3] Indeed, the occasional finds dating to the Early Medieval period at some of the spring sites described above, suggest that the veneration of these sites continued after coins ceased to be deposited. There are instances in the historical texts that refer to prayers and other unspecified ways that rituals were undertaken at these natural features.[4] As such, we must bear in mind that there may have been alternative votives offered to Mithras that are no longer extant, with the coins perhaps only a part of a

---

1 For a lengthy account of the difficulties faced when establishing the fate of temples, see Ward-Perkins (2011).

2 Esmonde Cleary (2013) 348–49; Kent (1994); Moorhead (2012).

3 Serv. *In Vergilii Carmina Commentarii* 7.84.

4 Sauer (2011) 539–40.

© KONINKLIJKE BRILL NV, LEIDEN, 2019 | DOI 10.1163/9789004383067_006

larger picture, and not necessarily the last objects ritually deposited in these temples.

Such issues with dating can also affect our interpretations of how temples relate to later buildings, which is especially problematic when the buildings in question are churches. Indeed, the construction of churches over or within temples has often led to the assumption that this must relate to the closure of the latter, yet without adequate dating evidence these events could have occurred decades, or even centuries, apart.[5]

However, while earlier archaeological reports may be less than ideal by modern standards, with various issues surrounding the dating of the abandonment of various sites, data obtained from more recent archaeological investigations do provide us with the opportunity to revisit some of this older work and re-evaluate their original conclusions. We cannot necessarily prove new theories without any doubt, but we can at least provide new perspectives on the material, just as has been done via coin depositions in mithraea using the recent work at Martigny and other sites. When such evidence is taken into consideration alongside recent work that has provided context for the mithraea—such as the clear evidence for urban decline surrounding these temples, and the evident lack of Christian material—we are provided with an opportunity to produce a more nuanced understanding of what brought the worship of Mithras inside mithraea to a close.

Geographical and Chronological Variation in the Fate of Mithraea

In figs. 33–37, the geographical distribution of the fate of extant mithraea across our period is shown.[6] As fig. 32 indicates, just two mithraea, located at opposite ends of the empire, appear to have gone out of use in the final decades of the 3rd c.[7] On the Rhine frontier, a mithraeum at Biesheim was partially burnt down and had its images broken. Given the state of the statues and reliefs it is unlikely that this was an accidental event, but as this looks to have been an isolated incident there is little to suggest any significant widespread threat to the cult in this region at this time. The structure was subsequently reused, although the statues and reliefs were covered over and the floor level raised to that of the side benches, creating an open plan. As such, whether this building continued to be used by Mithraic worshippers is unclear, but this would seem unlikely. In the East, the mithraeum at Caesarea Maritima met a more passive fate, reverting to its pre-Mithraic use as a storehouse (fig. 38). As noted, the scarcity of Mithraic finds from this region suggests that the transformation of the Caesarea Maritima mithraeum may have left the East entirely devoid of mithraea for a brief time, before the construction of the Hawarte Mithraeum at the turn of the 4th c.

In the first decades of the 4th c. (fig. 34), we find a much larger number of mithraea across the western half of the Roman empire being abandoned. In Rome, several mithraea (*Foro Boario, Castra Peregrinorum* and at *Via Giovanni Lanza* 128) provide no indication of continued use after the early 4th c. and were subsequently sealed up with most of their cult items left untouched therein. In contrast, various mithraea outside of Rome that were abandoned at this time were found with their statues and reliefs completely removed (Epidaurum, Lucus Augusti, Lambaesis and Tienen). Four other mithraea appear to have been left relatively intact, but contained broken or mutilated statues; of these, three lay close to the northern frontiers (Carnuntum III, Aquincum IV and Brocolitia), while the other was at Jajce in Dalmatia. The only mithraeum that was completely destroyed in the early 4th c. was located at Burdigala. The absence of much of the structural material suggests it might have been dismantled, perhaps indicating disuse at the time it was levelled. Fragments from the border of the main relief were found, although the main image itself had been removed, while most of the statuettes were beheaded, save for a relief of Aion that was untouched.[8]

During this period, the mithraeum in Londinium was also altered structurally in order to house a

---

5   A recent article by Schuddeboom (2016) concludes that the construction of churches over mithraea in Rome is a clear indication that Christians were responsible for the closure of these temples. Unfortunately, Schuddeboom does not take into account the fact that the construction of these churches often post-dates the evidence for occupation of the mithraea by at least a few decades. The author also seems unaware of Bjørnebye's (2007) thesis (which is freely available online) and later article (2016) that argue strongly that there was little competition between the cult of Mithras and Christian communities in Rome.

6   It should also be mentioned that, of the many mithraea uncovered in Ostia, none are known to have been active into the 4th c. It is highly likely that some were, given that the cult continued to be active well into this century in Rome, but as there is no archaeological evidence that supports this for Ostia, they cannot be included here. See Boin (2013) 114.

---

7   Of course, various Mithraic temples had been abandoned before this time, such as those in Germania Superior at Dieburg and Stockstadt, following the retreat of the Roman frontier in the early 3rd c.

8   The details regarding the Burdigala Mithraeum are unclear, with much of the material unpublished. I have attempted to contact those who have published on it but have received no response.

THE FATE OF MITHRAEA 69

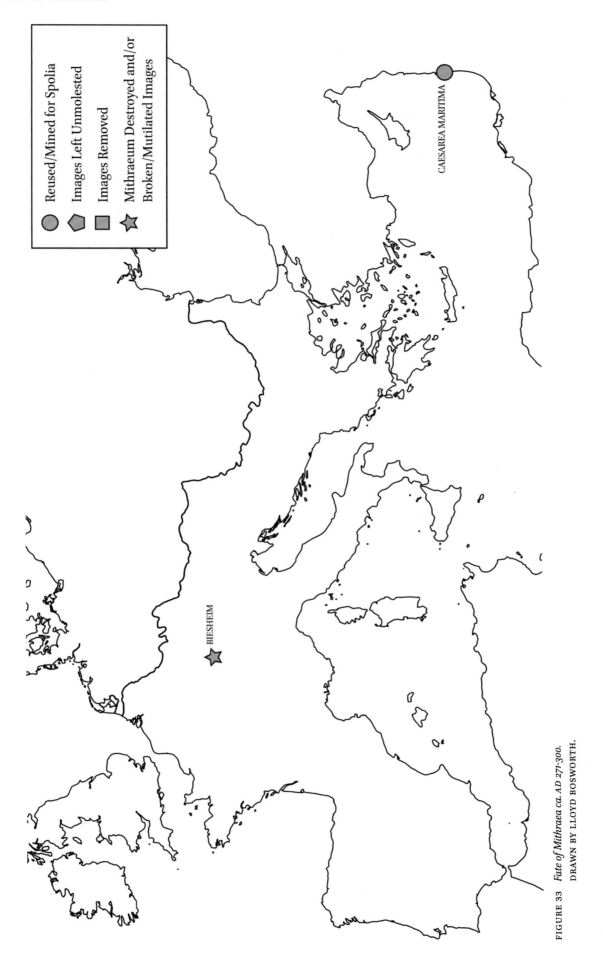

FIGURE 33 *Fate of Mithraea ca. AD 271-300.*
DRAWN BY LLOYD BOSWORTH.

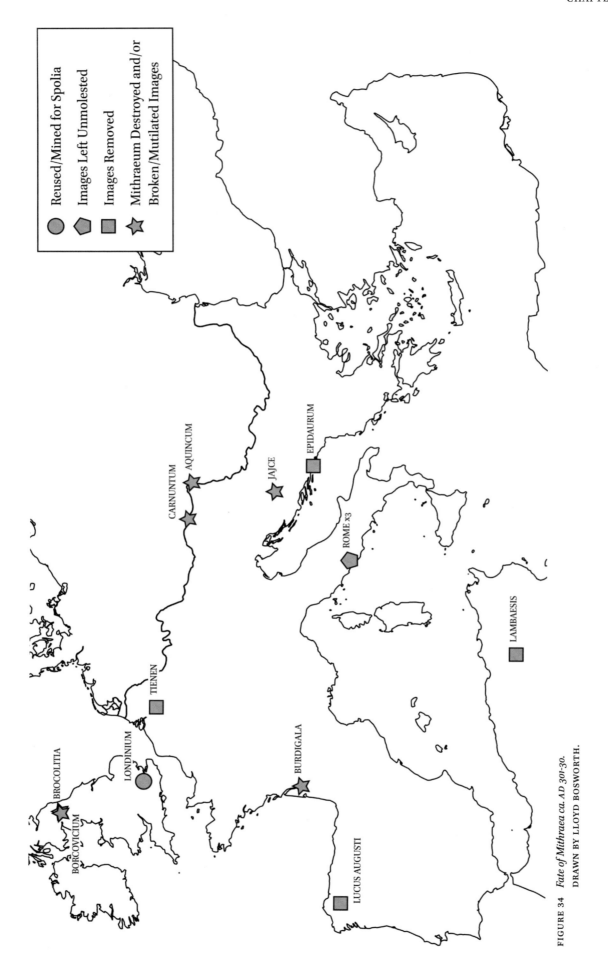

FIGURE 34 *Fate of Mithraea ca. AD 301-30.*
DRAWN BY LLOYD BOSWORTH.

THE FATE OF MITHRAEA

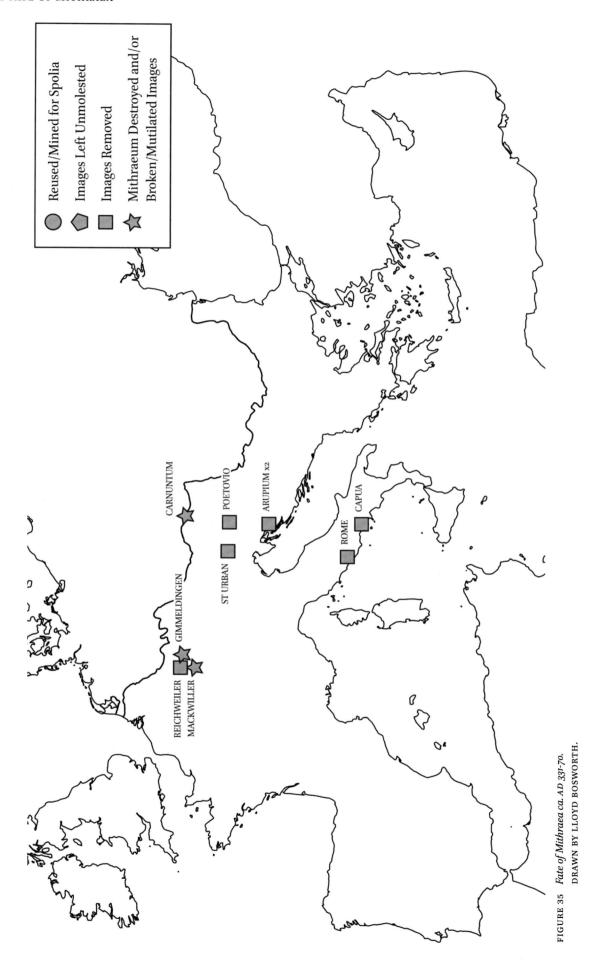

FIGURE 35 *Fate of Mithraea ca. AD 331-70.*
DRAWN BY LLOYD BOSWORTH.

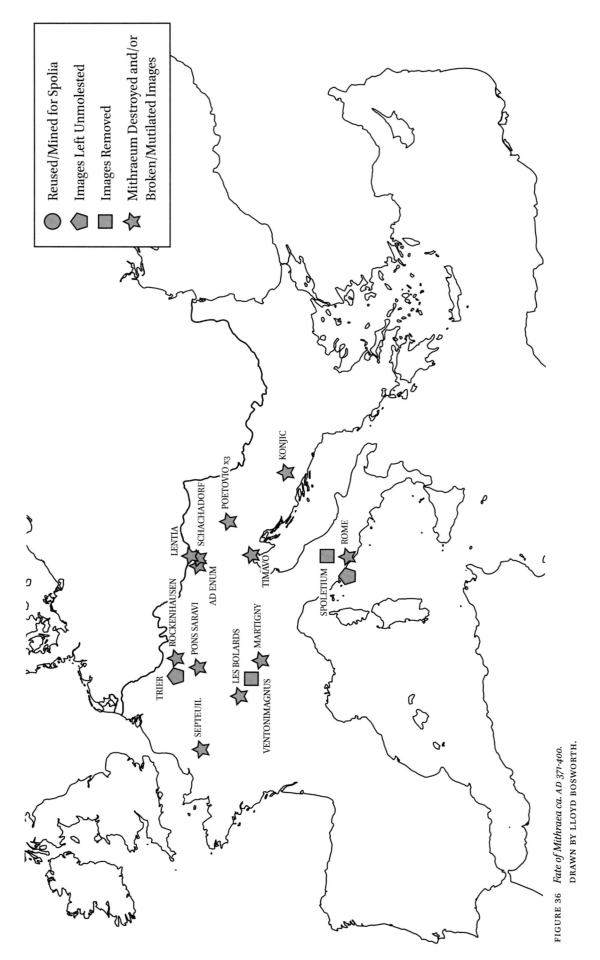

FIGURE 36 *Fate of Mithraea ca. AD 371-400.*
DRAWN BY LLOYD BOSWORTH.

THE FATE OF MITHRAEA

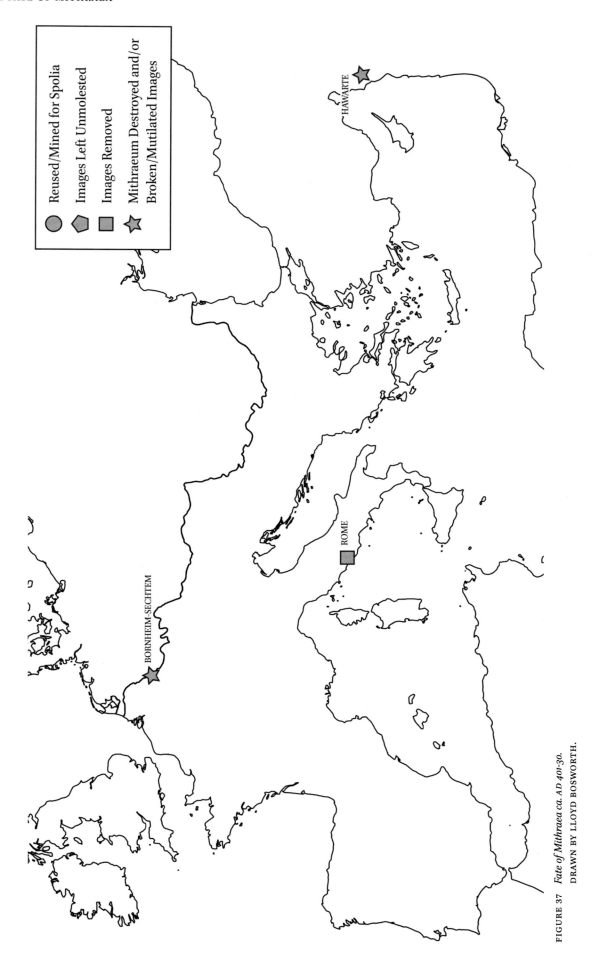

FIGURE 37 *Fate of Mithraea ca. AD 401-30.*
DRAWN BY LLOYD BOSWORTH.

FIGURE 38   *The Caesarea Maritima Mithraeum.*
PHOTO BY CAROLE RADDATO.

different cult group, possibly worshippers of Bacchus. This involved the colonnades in front of the benches being removed, the floor of the nave being raised to that of the benches, and the filling in of the well. Like at Biesheim, this created an open floor-plan, although tripartite timber partitioning running the length of the building remained in place. Given the raised height of the floor, one now had to ascend steps to enter the building, as opposed to descending. A pit was dug into its floor, into which various pieces of statuary were deposited: the head and right-hand (clutching a dagger-handle) of a large statue of Mithras; a piece of a Mithraic relief depicting a forearm of Mithras; heads from statues of the Roman goddess Minerva and Egyptian god Sarapis; and a statuette of the god Mercury.[9] Recent excavations have suggested that even if this mithraeum did not become a *bacchium*, the building continued to be utilised for some form of cult function, given that a contemporary well identified next to the mithraeum was found to contain a number of metal objects, four cattle skulls and around 40 coins deposited during the late 4th c.[10]

In the mid 4th c. (fig. 35), the number of mithraea being abandoned actually declined. Those that were destroyed or had their images mutilated were predominantly located on the northern frontiers, with a particular concentration along the Rhine, where one mithraeum was abandoned (the rural site at Reichweiler) and another two burnt down (Gimmeldingen and Mackwiller, the latter of which was rebuilt as a spring sanctuary). Although we cannot be certain, there may be a link between the fates of these three mithraea, given that they were situated in close proximity to each other. At Gimmeldingen, the main relief was found intact (albeit extremely weathered) and the upper half of a Cautes statue has been removed. A naked statue of Mercury found with these items had had its face and the *caduceus* damaged, suggesting it was specifically targeted. The destruction of the mithraeum at Mackwiller was more total, with all images found fragmented. On the Danube frontier, a mithraeum ('I') at Carnuntum was found with its images broken, and it contained a coin dating to AD 333; with such limited evidence though, we cannot be sure how accurate the dating for its occupation is. At Poetovio, the fate of Mithraeum IV is unclear, aside from the fact that various altars were taken and used for *spolia* sometime during the 4th c. In contrast, all mithraea located in the interior provinces at Arupium, Capua, and at *Ospedale San Giovanni* in Rome were found with their portable reliefs and statues removed, but no evidence for violent closure.

In the final decades of the 4th c. (fig. 36), the evidence for mithraea being destroyed and/or having their images mutilated is more widespread than in previous periods, with the two strongest concentrations of this found along the Rhine and Danube frontiers. These mithraea were located in a variety of contexts: in or around settlements (Ad Enum, Lentia, Poetovio II and III, and Pons Saravi); in a rural location at Schachadorf; and on a (possible) private estate at Rockenhausen. The form of the destruction at these locations was mixed. At Lentia, evidence for a fire was found inside the *cella* of the mithraeum and a small marble medallion depicting the bull-slaying was broken into two pieces, with the upper half missing. Similarly, the Schachadorf Mithraeum was also found to contain evidence of burning in the *cella*, but a statuette of the rock-birth was deposited in this completely intact. At Ad Enum, Poetovio and Pons Saravi (fig. 39), nearly all the internal fittings of these mithraea were completely fragmented, including their central reliefs which, when reconstructed, were all missing the head of Mithras. Strikingly, at Pons Saravi the remains of an adult male bound in chains was found lying on the base of the cult image in the mithraeum. Given that there was

---

9   We cannot be certain that this mithraeum was turned into a *bacchium*, but there are reasons to think this was the case. Firstly, a building in the forum at Cosa was remodelled in a similar fashion during the 4th c. to become a shrine to Liber Pater. Secondly, a marble statuette of Bacchus was found in the 4th c. levels, along with two torsos, which look to be from Bacchic statues: one found inside, the other outside the mithraeum, see: Henig (1998). A silver casket, found in a layer "directly associated with the temple but which cannot, because of documentation ambiguities, be placed in [a definite context]", has been dated to the late 3rd/early 4th c., and which depicts wild beasts, has also been suggested to be Bacchic, see: Shepherd (1998) 179–81.

10 Sadie Watson, *pers. comm.* (19/11/15); Bryan *et al* (2017) 105.

FIGURE 39   *Restored bull-slaying scene from the Pons Saraavi Mithraeum.*
PHOTO BY CAROLE RADDATO.

no sign of trauma on the skeleton, how the man met his fate is unclear, although it is apparent from the chains he had little choice in the matter.[11] It is also uncertain as to whether he was a Mithraic adherent or not; the location of the deposition makes it possible though, with this as a final act of desecration following the breaking of the cult images. Alternatively, however, this man may have been brought to an abandoned mithraeum outside the town gate to be executed or to hide the body. Given that Pons Saravi lay on a military road and occupied an important crossing point of the River Sarre, such acts of violence by members of the military community would not be unheard of. In this small *vicus*, which had been in decline since the 3rd c., there was little to guard against raiding parties.[12]

For the interior provinces, the fate of mithraea at the end of the 4th c. was more varied; in eastern Gaul, two

11   CIMRM 1. 983.

12   Human remains have also been found in mithraea located at Koenigshoffen and Doliche. At Koenigshoffen, a girl's skull and femur were found under fragments from the altar. As this mithraeum has provided no evidence of Mithraic activity after the first half of the 3rd c., and no subsequent activity is apparent until the 6th c., when this deposition occurred is difficult to establish, but it most probably post-dates our period: see Forrer (1915) 75–79. The same problem applies to the Doliche mithraeum which contained a burial; we cannot say when the body was deposited given the disturbed stratigraphy, but it is likely that it pre-dates the installation of the mithraeum in the mid 3rd c.: see Gordon (2007) 610.

FIGURE 40 *Relief of the rock-birth from the Trier Mithraeum.*
PHOTO BY CAROLE RADDATO.

mithraea (Martigny and Les Bolards) produced broken sculptures, while at Venetonimagus the mithraeum was abandoned and had all its fittings removed. Notably, at Martigny a bronze statuette of the bull-slaying scene was uncovered, which is highly unusual given that such metals were often removed given their value. In the case of Venetonimagus, it is possible that there is a link between the abandonment of its mithraeum and the desecration of those located at Les Bolards and Martigny, given the close proximity of these temples to each other.

At Trier, although the image of the rock birth that sat on the podium was left intact (fig. 40), a naked statue of Mercury was found decapitated (both head and body were present in the mithraeum). Additionally, only a few fragments of the central relief were left. It is possible that this apparent desecration occurred long after the abandonment of the temple, for a wall was later cut through the mithraeum during the Frankish period, while a pan used for lime-burning was found in strata dating to this time. Indeed, it is unlikely to be a coincidence that the fragments of the sculptures and reliefs found in a fragmentary condition were made of limestone, while the intact relief depicting the rock-birth was carved from plain stone.

In Italy, there is a mixture of desecration (one case in Rome and at Timavo) and abandonment (Spoletium, and *Santa Prisca* and *San Clemente* in Rome).[13] In the mithraeum under *Santa Prisca*, a number of figures in the wall paintings had been damaged, but overall this appears to have been quite random. As such, I am inclined to agree with Bjørnebye and Ward-Perkins that this was the result of the extensive filling of the mithraeum after it had been abandoned.[14] At Timavo, the fragments of two broken reliefs, both depicting the tauroctony, were found strewn across the floor of the mithraeum. In both cases, the majority of the images are missing, including the heads of both Mithras and the bull. At Konjic, the main relief from the mithraeum was found broken in two. This double-sided relief featured an image of the bull-slaying scene on one side that was flanked by depictions of Mithras wrestling with the bull, whilst on the other side there was shown a Mithraic feast attended by initiates of different grades. On the former side, the head of Mithras in all three images was missing, although on the latter side they remained intact.

There are only a few mithraea that were abandoned in the early 5th c., all of which are located at a considerable distance from each other (fig. 37). At Bornheim-Sechtem, the mithraeum was completely levelled. Only the foundations of the mithraeum were found *in situ*, with elements of its structure deposited in two nearby pits. This looks to have occurred in the early 5th c., as the last coin deposited in front of the cult image dates to AD 402. Other than the remains of the burnt statuary that seem to have been brought from

---

13 Frescoes were found damaged in the mithraeum at the *Castra Peregrinorum* under *Santo Stefano Rotondo*, although the precise dating for when this occurred is unknown, due to the church foundations displacing the original stratigraphy. The type of damage does not look to be as specific as at these other sites, and most artefacts from the mithraeum were found in excellent condition.

14 In a case of modern damage dealt to a Mithraic image, the face of Mithras in one relief from *Santa Prisca* was destroyed when it was removed in 1953 to be taken away for restoration, see Vermaseren and Van Essen (1965) 150. Concerning the axe blow visible on one relief, Sauer (2003) 134–36 argues that this is definitely an act of Christian iconoclasm. Both Bjørnebye (2007) 44–46 and Ward-Perkins (2011) 194 have highlighted the dubious nature of this interpretation,

THE FATE OF MITHRAEA

another mithraeum, no trace of the main relief or other items were found in the temple or in the nearby pits, suggesting it had been largely emptied prior to levelling. In Rome, only the mithraeum in the *Crypta Balbi* was apparently still active at this time, but this was soon transformed into a stable. The cult's almost complete disappearance from Rome by the early 5th c. is also indicated by the contemporary 'Speech of Praetextatus' by Macrobius. In this work, various deities are listed in relation to an almighty solar deity, but Mithras is not referred to once, quite a glaring omission given that Praetextatus was a *pater*.[15] At Hawarte, a cross with a loop at its head (presumably a chi-rho) was etched on a wall opposite the entrance to the mithraeum, and the eyes of demonic figures depicted in the wall-paintings throughout the temple were scratched out.[16] The mithraeum looks to have gone out of use at the end of the first decade of the 5th c., with the latest stratified coin dating from the reign of Arcadius (d. 408); a church, whose foundations cut into the mithraeum, was built over it shortly thereafter in AD 421.

What patterns emerge from this broad overview of the fate of mithraea? In terms of violent closure (based on either the destruction of the mithraeum or the mutilation of its images), the greatest chronological concentration is to be found in the late 4th c. However, the violent closure of mithraea is by no means unique to this period, as even a hundred years before this there is evidence of a mithraeum being destroyed at Biesheim. Furthermore, even decades before this took place, mithraea across the Rhine faced the wrath of invaders, as the Roman empire ceded this territory. Geographically speaking, it is on the frontiers of Britain, the Rhine and the Danube where we find the greatest abundance of mithraea in which evidence of violent closure are to be found. In contrast, there is less evidence for the violent closure of mithraea among the interior provinces. In Italy and Dalmatia, most mithraea had their fittings removed or left untouched, with only four sites across both provinces producing evidence of image destruction and/or vandalism in all periods, while the mithraea at both Lucus Augusti (Lugo) in Spain and Lambaesis in North Africa were also found devoid of any images. The only mithraeum located in the interior provinces that looks to have been destroyed was found at Burdiagala. However, the majority of mithraea still active in the interior provinces at the end of the 4th c. do appear to have

met a violent end, suggesting a change in circumstances at this time.

In some cases, it is notable that mithraea which have produced no evidence of violent closure were located near to others that did, and that the abandonment of both is roughly contemporary, suggesting a possible connection between their fates. We see this in eastern Gaul, where three mithraea were abandoned towards the end of the 4th c., two of which contained broken images (Martigny and Les Bolards), while another (Venetonimagus) had all its images removed. This may also have been the case at Reichweiler, which was abandoned around the same time as the nearby mithraea at Gimmeldingen and Mackwiller were destroyed. It is possible that some Mithraic congregations, upon hearing of a nearby mithraeum being destroyed, decided to remove the objects and abandon their temple in favour of a safer location.

Overall, the image presented here is that the majority of mithraea were abandoned in the late 4th c. and that a significant number have produced some form of evidence for violent closure. However, once again we are faced with a degree of regionalisation, as this abandonment varies in frequency in different areas, particularly when one compares interior regions to frontier zones. The question now is: why were they abandoned?

Factors Contributing to the Fate of Mithraea

When one looks beyond the traditional narrative of coercive Christianisation to explain the final fate of mithraea, one finds oneself faced with a range of possibilities. Outlined here are a number of factors that likely played a role in determining how mithraea came to be abandoned, and why in many cases their internal fittings were found in a mutilated state. Of course, many of these factors need not be exclusive, with two or more perhaps playing a role in the fate of a mithraeum and its fittings. What should be stressed is that the possible factors on which I am suggesting occur chronologically close to the date when mithraea appear to have been abandoned. As such, I will not be discussing the possibility of damage sustained in the Medieval or later periods. I do not doubt such incidents occurred, but what I am seeking to illustrate here is the end of the cult of Mithras in Late Antiquity, not its reception in later periods.[17]

---

15 For a commentary on this document, see Liebeschuetz (1999).

16 I have been unable to obtain an image of this cross, and have been told by the excavator that the whole image was badly preserved and thus it was difficult capture photographic evidence: Michal Gawlikowski, *pers. comm.* 19.1.18.

17 There have been several modern incidents where mithraea have been damaged for varying reasons, such as the mithraea at Arupium which were almost blown to pieces by dynamite when the area was mined for building material, see Beck (1984) 362.

Christian Iconoclasm

Christians have often provided the first port of call for scholars looking to establish why the Mithras cult came to an end in the late 4th and early 5th c. The evidence for the destruction and desecration of mithraea makes Christians seem an obvious choice, as who else would go to such thorough lengths to prevent these temples from ever being used again? The Bible is explicit in its condemnation of false idols and the wrath that should be brought upon them by the faithful:

> You shall not make for yourself a graven image, or any likeness of anything that is in heaven above, or that is in the earth beneath, or that is in the water under the earth; you shall not bow down to them or serve them; for I the Lord your God am a jealous God ...[18]

That late antique Christians held a special dislike for the cult of Mithras has been assumed by various scholars for good reason. Prior to the 4th c., the Christian authors Tertullian and Justin Martyr voiced their disdain for the cult,[19] while in the 4th c., Firmicus Maternus, a late convert to Christianity, was also critical of Mithraic communities:

> They name him Mithras. As for his rites, he reveals them in hidden caves: shrouded in the desolation of the darkness they shun the touch of the grace and glorious light. Truly an ill-omened exaltation of a deity! A hateful recognition of a barbarous ritual! You believe in one whose criminal acts you confess. When you repeat in these temples the liturgy of the Magi according to the Persian rite, why do you confine your approval to these Persian practices alone? If you think it not derogatory to the Roman name to enslave yourself to Persian liturgies and Persian laws.[20]

In addition to these writers, there are two recorded instances describing Christians desecrating mithraea in the 4th c. One comes from Jerome, who recalls how in AD 377/78 the Prefect of Rome, Gracchus, ordered the destruction of a mithraeum, and personally broke the images he found inside:

> ... did not your kinsman Gracchus, whose name recalls his patrician rank, destroy the cave of Mithras a few years ago when he was Prefect of Rome? Did he not break and burn all the monstrous images there by which worshippers were initiated as Raven, Bridegroom, Soldier, Lion, Perseus, Sun-runner, and Father? Did he not send them before him as hostages, and gain for himself baptism in Christ?[21]

The other incident involved an abandoned mithraeum in Alexandria. This mithraeum is described in various accounts as being handed over to the Christians of the city by Constantius II, so that a church could be built on the land. When the Christians began to demolish the mithraeum, they paraded the artefacts they found within the streets (although what these objects were is not revealed), provoking the anger of the local 'pagans'; this resulted in a bloody riot and the death of the bishop Georgios.[22]

However, to assume that these accounts demonstrate an active conflict between Christian communities and the cult of Mithras would be misleading. Firstly, there is no clear indication as to whether the mithraeum attacked by Gracchus in Rome was still in use, while in the case of Alexandria the historical accounts indicate that the temple had already been abandoned. Secondly, there are certain issues regarding the reliability of Jerome's account. For one, although many of the mithraea uncovered in Rome were not found in impeccable condition, none have produced evidence that correlates with Jerome's description (although it is possible that the mithraeum to which he refers has not been found). Additionally, Jerome's account does not come first-hand, for by the time Gracchus was Prefect of Rome, Jerome had long since departed the city. One must bear in mind that either Jerome's source, or Jerome himself, may have also embellished the account to make it more dramatic. Finally, while such accounts from Rome and Alexandria are important, they should not be taken as a general reflection of the view of Christians across the Roman world about the cult of Mithras, especially as the majority of contemporary mithraea lay far from these cities, in the northern areas of the empire.

If the literary sources fail to provide much evidence for violence directed at the Mithras cult by Christians, what can be discerned regarding Christian involvement

---

18   *Exodus* 20.4–5.

19   Tert. *De corona.* 15; *De Prae. Hae.* 40.3–4; Just. *dial.* 70.

20   Firm. Mat. *Err. prof. rel.* 5.2 (transl. by the author based on Turcan (1982) 86).

21   Jer. *Ep.* 107.2 (transl. Wright (1933) 341–43).

22   Ruf. *HE* 11.2; Sozom. *Hist. eccl.* 5.7; Socrates, *Hist. eccl.* 3.2.3. According to Socrates' account around 30 years later another mithraeum was discovered by the bishop Theophilus, who had his followers mockingly parade the items they found. The similarities in these accounts suggest that Socrates is actually relating the same event twice.

FIGURE 41 *Relief of the bull-slaying scene at the Doliche Mithraeum. After Schütte and Winter (2001) fig. 10.*
DRAWN BY THE AUTHOR.

in the fate of mithraea in the archaeological record? Certain evidence of Christian desecration has been found in four mithraea: the example at Hawarte, as well as at mithraea found at Ponza (Italy), Doliche (Turkey), and Ša'āra (Syria). At Ponza a cross was carved opposite the entrance, while at Ša'āra two crosses were incised onto a lintel that had been located above the entrance to the cave. At Doliche, a rock-cut tauroctony was defaced with a cross carved into Mithras' face (fig. 41). At Doliche, the mithraeum was abandoned in the AD 250s, but as to when the Ponza and Ša'āra mithraea were is unknown as all datable evidence had been removed. Both Greek (equal-armed) and Latin (longer vertical axis) crosses do not begin to appear until the early 5th c.,[23] so it would seem these carvings were created long after the abandonment of theses mithraea. The only example where such cross-carving is likely to have been contemporary to the closure of the mithraeum is at Hawarte. Here, the last evidence for activity in the mithraeum dates to less than 20 years before the construction of a church on the site.

Yet, the absence of sculptures or reliefs in these examples (save for Doliche where they were carved into the wall) may be just as important: when the Alexandrian mithraeum was converted into a church by Christians in the mid 4th c., the Christians are described as removing artefacts from the mithraeum and parading them around the street. This also concurs with various historical accounts of temple desecration collected by Trombley, which tend to follow a standard pattern: acclamations are made by a bishop against evil spirits, the statues were then smashed and removed, and finally Christian symbols were etched onto the structure.[24] Yet this does not mean that these mithraea were *initially* closed by Christian iconoclasts (although perhaps under pressure from them). The appearance of crosses next to doorways in temples and mithraea may have been, as Richard Bayliss has suggested, a more common occurrence at sites that had already abandoned: "[T]he position of crosses ... appears to highlight their apotropaic function for keeping banished demons re-entering the structure. Their use in this way may not therefore be part of the actual de-consecration, but subsequent activity in order to prevent re-consecration".[25]

Unfortunately, at other mithraea where the majority of artefacts were removed, such as at Capua, Lambaesis and Lucus Augusti, there is also no evidence of Christian graffiti, meaning their fate is completely unknown: was this removal a form of desecration by Christians? Were these items removed to be used as spolia? Were they sold on as artistic pieces? Were they moved to an undiscovered mithraeum? The lack of any indication of Christian desecration at the Lambaesis Mithraeum is worth highlighting, as the governor who erected an altar to Mithras here in AD 303, Valerius Florus, was a known persecutor of the Christians. As such, one would expect this mithraeum to have attracted the anger of Christian iconoclasts perhaps more so than any other, yet there is nothing to suggest that it did.[26]

Another methodology that scholars have used, to identify the work of Christian iconoclasts, is the mutilation or destruction of naked statues, such as those found in the baths at Perge, Aphrodisias, and Corinth.[27] Certainly, some Christian authors did make their disgust of naked statues plain: Mark the Deacon criticised a statue of Aphrodite at Gaza, while Theodoret remarked of a similar statue that it was 'more shameless than that of any prostitute standing in front of a brothel'.[28] However, generally speaking, mithraea were rarely filled with images of nudity, with Mithras and the torchbearers tending to be depicted fully-clothed. An occasional exception to this was in the image of the rock-birth, but even in this instance, Mithras is frequently portrayed

---

23 Thomas (1981) 91.
24 Trombley (1993–94) 1.245.
25 Bayliss (2004) 13.
26 On Valerius Florus' persecution of Christians, see *CIL* 8.6700 = *CIL* 8.19353.
27 On Perge, see Hannestad (2001); on Aphrodisias, see Smith (2012); on Corinth, where a herm was decapitated and marked with a cross over its genitals, see Saradi and Eliopoulos (2011). On such instances in Egypt, see Kristensen (2013) 186–90.
28 *V. Porph.* 59; Thdt. *affect.* 3.79 (transl. Kristensen (2013) 224).

FIGURE 42   *Rock-birth statuette from Carnuntum 'III'.*
PHOTO BY THE AUTHOR.

FIGURE 43   *Headless Rock-Birth statue from Mithraeum 'I' at Carnuntum.*
PHOTO BY THE AUTHOR.

only from the waist-up. Indeed, naked images are a rarity among the mithraea discussed here. The only examples are a relief of Mercury from Gimmeldingen, an altar from Poetovio III decorated with an image of Sol, and statuettes of the rock-births found in Carnuntum I and III. If Christians had smashed the fittings in Poetovio III, then it is very strange that the naked image of Sol was left intact: in fact, this could suggest that Christians were not responsible.

In the case of the rock-birth from Carnuntum III (fig. 42), only the right-hand of the statuette was missing, while the rest of it was left relatively intact, suggesting the damage had nothing to do with the deity's nudity. At the same mithraeum, the images of various gods that adorned the large altar were also left untouched despite not being clothed. It is the relief of Mercury from Gimmeldingen that gives us the strongest inference of an image being assaulted because of its nude state, with the head and *caduceus* in the god's right-hand having been struck off. Yet, if this was carried out by Christians, it is odd that the main relief of the mithraeum was left untouched by them; could it be that these Christians had little problem with Mithras himself, but simply sought to eradicate an image of indecency? If this was the case, then we are not dealing with anger directed at the cult of Mithras *per se*, but only selected images that were not even integral to the Mithras cult. The only example we have of mutilated nude depictions found alongside other fragmentary images is at Carnuntum I. Here, a statue of a naked Mithras being born from the rock was found with its head, arms and genitals missing (fig. 43), while most other images were also destroyed; only a statuette of a lion was left intact (fig. 44). Thus, based on the treatment of naked images, only at two sites (Carnuntum I and Gimmeldingen) do we see the possible involvement of Christians, although the fact that the Mithraic images were left unmolested at Gimmeldingen suggests that it was not the cult itself that invoked the ire of the assailants.

Occasions where images of animals and/or foliage have been found intact alongside other items that were destroyed is another criterion sometimes used to identify possible Christian involvement. This occurred at the Šaʿāra Mithraeum, where an arch decorated with signs of the zodiac and foliage was defaced: the former were chiselled out but the latter were left undamaged. However, like nude depictions, images of animals, outside of those featured in the main relief, are uncommon in mithraea. Of the mithraea discussed here, Carnuntum I and III, Poetovio II and III, and Les Bolards are the only examples to have produced images of animals separate from the main relief. However, at Poetovio III, a relief depicting a goat was found broken, with only the head remaining, thus lessening the possibility of Christian involvement. In contrast, at Poetovio II, a statuette of a lion was found intact, and the raven was all that

FIGURE 44 *Lion statuette from Mithraeum 'III' at Carnuntum.*
PHOTO BY THE AUTHOR.

remained of the central relief. At Carnuntum III a statuette of a lion was found complete, and at Carnuntum I a statue of a lion was found untouched, while various other images were found damaged. However, to complicate matters further, at both Poetovio II and Carnuntum III images relating the cult also survived: at Poetovio II a smaller tauroctony image was left untouched, while at Carnuntum III the main altar supported by depictions of various gods, was also largely undamaged (fig. 45).

If this was the selective work of Christian iconoclasts, why leave these images alone too? Once again, the evidence for Christian involvement is by no means conclusive. It is only at Les Bolards that a mithraeum has produced evidence strongly inferring Christian involvement in the mutilation of images. Here, a statue of Cautes was found with a damaged face, while his counterpart had been broken in two pieces (which are now lost). Various fragments of other images were also found, including some possible remains of the tauroctony; the only image found intact was a statue of a lion near the entrance.

Another site that is worth discussing in this regard is the mithraeum found at Vulci in Italy, although there is no dating evidence to indicate when the temple was abandoned. In this case, the statuette of a raven survived while two tauroctony statues and a statue of Cautes were found not only broken, but with blows evident all over their bodies. The evidence here strongly infers a violent attack on the mithraeum, and the fact that the raven was completely untouched suggests the perpetrators were selective about what images they targeted. As a result, in this instance, religiously motivated iconoclasts are the most plausible culprits. Thus, only three sites (Carnuntum I, Vulci and Les Bolards) provide a reasonable case from which to argue for the involvement of Christian iconoclasts, based on the survival of animal depictions, although at Vulci the lack of dating means this could have occurred post-abandonment.

As is evident, attempting to ascertain Christian involvement in the destruction and/or desecration of Mithraic temples based on the archaeological evidence is very difficult. It is therefore worth asking: is

FIGURE 45 *The altar decorated with the personifications of the winds and seasons from Carnuntum III. Cumont (1899) figs. 432–33.*

there actually any evidence of Christians living close to these Mithraic temples when they were abandoned or destroyed? By evidence, I am referring to textual records, evidence for nearby contemporary churches, burials of a clearly Christian nature, and nearby small finds with Christian symbols. This may also include so-called 'negative evidence', in other words the likely desecration or destruction of other 'pagan' buildings by Christians in the locale of mithraea, although, as with mithraea, this can be extremely difficult to prove.

In Gaul, Christian communities are known to have existed in Burdigala and Trier in the early 4th c., with their respective bishops attending the Council of Arles in 314.[29] A Christian basilica was erected in Trier under Constantine, although attempting to ascertain how reflective this is of the size of the Christian community is difficult, given the basilica's status as an imperial project.[30] As for the desecration of non-Christian sites, it is worth highlighting that inside the Trier Basilica, Christians etched various small inscriptions into the walls. It seems strange then that if the Christians in the town were willing to graffiti their own buildings, why did they not leave even a small cross inside the mithraeum, to indicate their triumph over a false god? In Trier's hinterland, there is no indication of any churches until the 5th c., but some early Christian gravestones have been found just outside the city walls.[31] In addition, from the literary texts, we know Gaul's most famous iconoclast Martin of Tours visited Trier in order to discuss the Priscillian controversy with Valentinian I, as did the equally anti-'pagan' Bishop of Milan, Ambrose. Yet, despite both men's apparent intolerant stance on non-Christian cults, in neither case is there any mention of Martin or Ambrose urging the closure of temples in the town.[32] This might have been due to a lack of overt 'pagan' activity in the town, but perhaps the most likely scenario is that the presence of the imperial court under the relatively tolerant Valentinian I and Valentinian II acted as a deterrent for any would-be iconoclasts, as

the accommodation of various high-ranking polytheists, such as Q. Aurelius Symmachus, was required. Furthermore, iconoclastic activities were often viewed, even by the most ardent Christian emperors, as a breach of the peace, rather than as acts of religious piety, thus one would be ill-advised to conduct them right under the emperor's nose.[33]

Elsewhere in Gaul, Martigny is known to have been a bishop's see by AD 381, with the incumbent attending the Council of Aquileia that year. It is perhaps only a coincidence, but the bishop's name was Theodorus, which was the same name as that found on a ceramic vessel buried at the entrance to the mithraeum. Alternatively, we may indeed be dealing with a man who occupied the role of bishop while attending non-Christian cults. A precedent for this may be found in Julian's visit to Ilion in 354, where he was met by the local bishop Pegasius who was also a worshipper of the Sun and utilised his position to protect temples from Christian iconoclasts.[34] Also in Martigny, archaeological excavation has uncovered what appears to be a Christian funerary chapel (9.5 m × 5.5 m). This looks to have been attached to a suburban villa erected in the mid 4th c. and enlarged before the turn of the 5th c, thus indicating a possible Christian presence in the town when the mithraeum was still in use.[35]

In relation to the so-called 'negative evidence' for a Christian presence in Gaul, one might expect to find many examples of this, given the reported attitude of Martin of Tours in such matters.[36] Yet only 2.4% (17/711) of the temples in Gaul are known to have been destroyed by violent means, and many of those included in this figure are the Mithraic sites discussed here.[37] Other examples that have been highlighted as possible cases of Christian iconoclasm include two hill-top sanctuaries at Tawern and Hochscheid. At Hochscheid, the temple was abandoned in the late 3rd c. and the statues were broken at a later date. Fragments of the legs and arms from a large statue of Apollo were found, while a statue of Sirona was found broken into three pieces, but with only the legs missing, and the rest showing no signs of intentional damage. Another statue of Apollo, this one

---

29   Wightman (1970) 227. According to a medieval inscription, Christians had already been present in Trier as early as the latter half of the 3rd c., and were already targeting false idols, with the bishop setting up a torso from a statue of Venus to be ridiculed by the Christian population, but this story is likely to have been a later fabrication, see Wightman (1970) 229.

30   The construction of the basilica is usually assumed to be that mentioned by Eusebius (Euseb. *Vit. Const.* 4.17), but it is not certain whether this building is the one he is referring to. The foundation layers of the basilica were found to contain coins from AD 312–18: see Kempf (1979) 8–9.

31   Wightman (1970) 232.

32   On Martin's visit to Trier, see Sulp. Sev. *Dial.* 2.5.7–9. On Ambrose's visit, see Amb. *Ep.* 30.

33   For an overview of Symmachus' time in Trier, see Sogno (2006) 1–30. On the religious policy of the Valentinian dynasty, see Lizzi Testa (2004).

34   For attendees of the Council of Aquileia, see Amb. *Acta*. The idea that it was the Bishop of Martigny who deposited the cup at the entrance to the mithraeum has been suggested by Wiblé (2004) 139. On Pegasius, see Julian, *Ep.* 19. Some letters may not have been written by Julian, however: see Elm (2016).

35   Bielmann (2013) 411.

36   On the fate of temples in Gaul, see Goodman (2011).

37   Goodman (2011) 179–80.

naked, was also found well-preserved. The preservation of the Sirona statue and the smaller Apollo makes Christian iconoclasts unlikely culprits, while there is no reason to assume the missing parts from the larger Apollo statue were removed to be destroyed; they may have been used as *spolia* or decoration elsewhere.[38] At Tawern, the coin series runs to the end of the 4th c., when the head of the Mercury statue was decapitated and thrown down a well, along with an inscription and two altars, while a broken statuette of Artemis was found in the temple enclosure.[39] Once again, this deposition of the Mercury head and the reliefs bears no clear evidence that Christians were responsible, while other examples of similar depositions, such as at Coventina's Well, have not been interpreted in such a fashion.[40]

Additionally, of the 15 instances where a church replaced, or was installed within, a temple in Gaul, there usually appears to have been a significant chronological gap between the abandonment of the temple and the appearance of the church. In fact, in most cases there was a period when the abandoned temples became necropolises, in a similar vein to contemporary secular buildings in the region. It was more likely because of the presence of these cemeteries that the churches were erected. This would also infer that Christians buried around abandoned temples did not fear being 'polluted' by them, from which, as Penelope Goodman observes "[W]e may postulate a more peaceable progression from polytheistic to Christian religious activity than the texts suggest".[41]

On the Danube frontier, by the late 4th c., Christian communities existed in the eastern and southern parts of the provinces, however the majority of the Mithraic evidence comes from the northern and western parts. A church is known to have existed at Lauriacum in the late 4th c.,[42] which would place a Christian community near to the mithraeum at Lentia. Yet in Lentia itself, the only evidence for a Christian presence is the tombstone of a Christian widow. Another female Christian tombstone was also uncovered at Ovilava, thus in close proximity to the Schachadorf Mithraeum, but in this case the wording on the tombstone suggests that her husband, who had it carved, was not a Christian, highlighting that Christian-'pagan' relationships could be harmonious.[43] Only at Poetovio is there substantial evidence for the cohabitation of Christian and Mithraic communities,

with the letters of Ambrose indicating that Poetovio was home to a bishop in the late 4th c. However, there is no mention of any conflict between the Christians and polytheists in the town, only a dispute between two rival claimants for the position of bishop: the Arian Julianus Valens and the orthodox Marcus.[44]

The use of 'negative evidence' to establish the presence of Christians along the Danube is not convincing. A number of temples that were found to have been destroyed and their images broken, including the Temple of Mars at Lendorf, near Teurnia, Mars Latobius at St Margarethen and the temple to Jupiter Dolichenus at Virunum, have been used to highlight Christian iconoclasm in this region in the past.[45] Yet none of these temples produced finds from secure contexts that postdate the end of the 3rd c.: the Dolichenum is likely to have been destroyed in the early decades of the 3rd c.; the usage of the Temple of Mars Lendorf can only be securely dated to the 2nd c.; and the temple to Mars Latobius was found to neighbour another temple that was systematically levelled in the final decades of the 3rd c.[46]

In Britain, much like the Danube frontier, it would not be until long after the Mithras cult had come to an end in this province that Christianity had a considerable impact. In terms of contemporary Christian and Mithraic evidence, there is little evidence to suggest any geographical correlation between the two, with the former found at southern sites such as Hinton St Mary and Lullingstone, while Mithraic sites bearing evidence of possible desecration lie on Hadrian's Wall in the north. Potential churches have been found on Hadrian's Wall at Borcovicium and Vindolanda, but these structures date to at least the turn of the 5th c., thus a considerable length of time after the mithraea went out of use.[47] In terms of 'negative evidence' for Christian presence in Britain, there is not a tremendous amount to go on. A curse tablet from Bath, which refers to "a holy place, wrecked by insolent hands and cleansed afresh", has been suggested as being evidence for Christian iconoclasts, particularly as another curse tablet references Christians from the same location, but this is highly speculative.[48] Other sites of possible iconoclasm have

---

38   Sauer (2003) 75–78.

39   Sauer (2003) 73.

40   Allason-Jones and McKay (1985).

41   Goodman (2011) 180–81.

42   Eckhart (1981).

43   Lentia: *CIL* 3.13532; Ovilava: Noll (1954) 47.

---

44   Amb. *Ep.* 10.9–10. The archaeological evidence for Christians in 4th c. Poetovio is not particularly forthcoming, thus far only consisting of two bronze candleholders bearing Chi-Rho symbols: see Korošec (1980).

45   Alfödy (1974) 210.

46   Walsh (2016) 232–33.

47   Rushworth (2009) 321–22.

48   Lewis (1966) 143–45; Thomas (1981) 133–36.

been identified at Silchester and Worth, although in neither case can a strong case be made.[49]

Turning to the interior provinces, early Christian evidence from Dalmatia is not in abundance either. Salona is known to have been a bishopric in the 4th c., while St Jerome's (b. 347) hometown of Stridon, on the border with Pannonia, is likely to have had a Christian community.[50] At the town of Narona (modern Vid), excavators have claimed to have found evidence of Christian iconoclasm in the archaeological record. An imperial cult building was found on the west side of the forum and contained a series of toppled statues and their bases, with pottery finds providing a *terminus post quem* for the temple's abandonment of the late 4th c. The statues depicted various emperors and members of their families from the 1st to early 2nd c. AD, most of which had had their heads removed, with some later found outside the temple. According to the inscriptions found in the temple there should also have been two silver statues of Venus, but these were absent. Three early Christian basilicas and a baptistery that date to the late 4th c. have been found in the town, so it is plausible that Christians may have been to blame.[51] However, it is also possible that, given the high quality of the statues, some of the heads were taken to be refashioned and reused, either as *spolia* or works of art. Furthermore, the absence of the silver Venuses is more likely due to their value than the desecration of the temple.[52] Of course, there is no guarantee that the removal of these items was contemporary to the destruction of the other images in this temple.

In the case of Rome and its hinterland in the 4th c., Christians were clearly present. It is only a question of whether there is any evidence of violence carried out by them against non-Christians in the city during the 4th c. The reference to the prefect Gracchus attacking a mithraeum has been discussed, but it is important to once again urge caution in using this as proof that Christians persecuted the Mithras cult in Rome during the latter half of the 4th c. Indeed, beyond this, there is little evidence indicating any sort of conflict between Christians and their neighbours in Rome during the 4th c. Inscriptions dedicated by both Christian and non-Christian aristocrats (including those who were part of Mithraic communities) uncovered on the Vatican Hill

do not present any evidence of any dispute between the two, and there is no indication of conflict in the literary texts.[53] In contrast, the textual evidence provides many examples of disputes within the Christian community, suggesting this was a much more frequent occurrence, such as during the papal election crisis of AD 366.[54] As Chenault observed, regarding the often-overstated importance of the debate surrounding the removal of the Altar of Victory from the Senate House, Christians were far more occupied with issues in their own ranks:

> ... the controversy over the altar of Victory was a sideshow in comparison to the far more contentious and consequential debates taking place within the Roman Church in the 380s. Neither Jerome or Ambrosiaster ever mentioned the altar, preoccupied as they were with questions about the proper interpretation and translation of Scripture ...[55]

In Syria there is evidence for a number of Christian communities in the province. Churches in this region dating from the 4th c. tend to be more extant than in other provinces, and can often be accurately dated from inscriptions recording their construction. For example, at Brad, a man named Julianus had a church constructed in AD 395–402, while Marcianus Cyris paid for a series of churches on the mountain road between Antioch and Aleppo at the turn of the 5th c. Similarly, a Bishop Flavian oversaw the construction of a martyr-church at Antioch in AD 380,[56] and Bishop Alexandros built the church at Hawarte over the mithraeum in AD 421.[57] At the same time, the textual record provides various examples of Christians involved in violent disputes with other communities, the most famous case of which was in AD 403 when the Bishop of Gaza, Porphyry, petitioned the hesitant emperor Arcadius to crackdown on the temples and idols present in the town, which subsequently led to an outbreak of violence. The named author of this account, Mark the Deacon, acknowledged that the Christians did not make up a considerable number of the population at the time of these events, only consisting of a few hundred people. Naturally, it is possible for even a relatively

---

49 Watts (1998) 43.

50 Wilkes (1969) 419, 430.

51 Christie (2011) 165.

52 Sauer (2004) 330 has argued that Christians would have been compelled to leave 'polluted' valuables in the temples they desecrated. If this were the case, then the evidence here is suggestive that Christians were not involved.

53 Gwynn (2011) 146.

54 Amm. Marc. 27.3.11–13. For the relationship between Christians and polytheists in 4th c. Rome, see Curran (2000); Cameron (2011); Mulryan (2011b); Ensoli and La Rocca (2000); Salzman, Sághy and Testa (2016).

55 Chenault (2016) 61.

56 Milburn (1988) 125–27.

57 Gawlikowski (2012) 490. See Trombley (1993–94) 2.339–74 for Christianity in rural Syria.

small group to cause trouble if they were backed by military force, but once again we should be cautious in overstating the backing of the imperial court for these activities, given the violent disruption they were likely to cause. Indeed, one may argue that Mark's assertion regarding the number of Christians actually downplayed their size in order to emphasis Porphyry's impact in the conversion of the population.[58]

Overall then, the evidence does not provide a strong basis for claiming Christianity played a decisive role in the end of the Mithras cult. Many of the mithraea that continued in use during the 4th c. were located in frontier regions that have produced only limited evidence for Christian communities, and such evidence, where it does exist, often lies some distance from the Mithraic material. For example, in Noricum and Pannonia, where the Mithras cult was still active on the frontier to the north-west, the evidence for a Christian presence is found only in the southern and eastern areas. By the time a notable Christian presence arises in the north-west, the mithraea had generally already been abandoned. The same pattern occurs for Britain. Equally, much of the so-called 'negative evidence' for the presence of Christians remains open to interpretation, with little in the way of firm evidence to prove their involvement in other anti-'pagan' iconoclasm. In Rome, various recent studies have also highlighted the lack of apparent conflict between Christians and the adherents of other cults in the 4th c., while in the imperial capital of Trier there is little indication of tension either.

However, this is not to say that Christian iconoclasts were blameless in the closure of certain mithraea. There is evidence for Christian communities existing close to active mithraea in the 4th c. in some locations in the inner provinces and in the East. At Hawarte, Christians do appear the most likely perpetrators of damage to the mithraeum there, given the evidence and the construction of a church on the site shortly after the abandonment of the mithraeum. At both Vulci and Les Bolards, the evidence also suggests Christian involvement, given the lack of attention paid to depictions of animals by those responsible for the breaking of the images (although the former cannot be dated). Additionally, Christians certainly lived in towns such as Martigny, Trier and Poetovio around the time the mithraea in these locations were desacralised, and thus cannot be excluded as possible culprits. Finally, the evidence also seems to indicate that Carnuntum I was the victim of

Christian iconoclasts, although this may have occurred long after it was abandoned, given the dearth of contemporary evidence for Christians in the surrounding area.

'Barbarian' Incursions

As we have seen, the movement of peoples across the Roman frontiers in order to raid and/or settle would have had considerable impact on these regions, regions which contained many active mithraea; such incursions may have resulted in their desecration or even destruction. By the latter half of the 4th c., the pressure that groups such as the Franks, Goths, Alammani and Sarmatians exerted on the Rhine and Danube frontiers had grown considerably. As a consequence of this, as highlighted in a previous chapter, the populations of many towns and *vici* in these areas fled to internal areas of the empire or sought refuge inside neighbouring forts.

The historical texts provide a number of instances where conflict flared along the northern frontiers throughout the 4th c. According to Ammianus, in the mid 4th c. the Quadi "got together and sent out parties to devastate our territory. They crossed the Danube and fell upon the country folk, who were busy with their harvest and had no thought of an enemy".[59] In the late 350s, Julian described in his *Letter to the Athenians* the destruction and desertion he was faced with on the Rhine, while Zosimus refers to around 40 towns being attacked by barbarians at this time.[60] Such problems were not only to be found on the frontiers, for the Alamanni were also attacking places as far south as Autun and around Auxerre.[61] In 365/66 the Alamanni crossed the frozen Rhine during winter, a move repeated by the Lentienses in 378. Around the same time in Dalmatia, Visigoths attacked cities along the Illyrian coast.[62] In the early 5th c. the situation did not improve, as the end of monetary circulation north of the Alps meant that those Roman forces that were left on the northern frontiers could no longer be paid. Also, "Vandal wanderings (401), Visigothic assaults (402) and plundering by the forces of the Goth Radagaisus (405/7) made the interiors of Pannonia and Noricum scarred battlegrounds".[63] Although uncommon, there are some accounts of assaults on religious sites during these incursions, such as at Clermont-Ferrand where Gregory of Tours describes the Alamanni completely destroying a temple.[64]

---

58 Trombley (1993–94) 1.191–204. Mark's hagiography was written in the 5th c., sometime after the events it describes, and he was not an eye-witness, thus to what degree it presents historical facts is debatable: see Lampadaridi (2016).

---

59 Amm. Marc. 29.6.
60 Zos. 3.1.
61 Amm. Marc. 16, 2; Lib. *Or.* 18. 43–45.
62 Jer. *Ep* 60.16.
63 Christie (2011) 86.
64 Gregory of Tours, *Hist.* 1.32.

FIGURE 46 *Headless Mithraic statuettes from the Dieburg Mithraea.*
PHOTOS BY CAROLE RADDATO.

As we have seen, attempting to identify barbarian presence in the archaeological record is problematic, but it is even more difficult to find clear evidence for any destruction or desecration of temples carried out by them. However, there is evidence from earlier periods regarding damage inflicted on mithraea by 'barbarians'. In the AD 260s the Roman empire abandoned its territories north of the Rhine, an area that contained various mithraea which then ceased to be used. At Dieburg, many of the fittings recovered from one of the mithraea were extensively damaged (fig. 46), with the large double-sided relief missing the heads of Mithras on one side and Phaeton on the other. Numerous statues were also beheaded, a statue of Mercury was smashed into at least 23 pieces, while elements of a tauroctony relief were discarded down a well outside the mithraeum.[65] Similarly, at Stockstadt, two mithraea were found to contain various statues and reliefs that were broken, with elements of the central relief from Mithraeum I found in the River Main, while Mithraeum II had been burnt down.[66]

The evidence from these earlier barbarian incursions also calls into question certain diagnostic traits of apparent Christian iconoclasm. A recurrent feature of the damage evident in many mithraea is the absence of heads from statues and reliefs, a feature commonly prescribed as a particularly 'Christian' act of iconoclasm.[67] However, a number of sites in Germany have produced evidence of destruction and damage dating to around the time of the Alamanni invasion, including the rural site of Harting in Germany where the remains of a family were recovered; they had been mutilated, scalped, their heads removed and their bodies

---

65 CIMRM 2. 1247–64.
66 CIMRM 2. 1158–215.

67 Heads Missing: Brocolitia: CIMRM 1. 850 (Cautes statue); Jajce: CIMRM 2. 1903 (Cautes statue); Konjic: CIMRM 2. 1896 (Mithras' head missing from main relief); Septeuil: Gaidon-Bunuel (1991) 55 (heads of Mithras and the bull missing from main relief); Timavo: Pross Gabrielli (1975) 18–33 (head of Mithras and bull missing from two reliefs); Vulci: Moretti (1979) 268–76 (heads of Mithras and the bull missing from two statues); Lentia: CIMRM 2. 1415 (Mithras' head missing from small relief); Carnuntum I: CIMRM 2. 1665, 1669 (Mithras' head missing from main relief and rock-birth statue); Poetovio II: CIMRM 2. 1511 (Mithras' head missing from relief); Poetovio III: CIMRM 2. 1600 (Mithras' head missing from relief). In instances where the heads of torchbearers are missing, one wonders if many could tell the difference between these and Mithras just by looking at their heads. Furthermore, the possible trinity of these three beings, as suggested in certain Mithraic reliefs (e.g. CIMRM 2. 1237), might mean that it was possible to worship Mithras through the torchbearers. On the destruction of heads being the work of Christian iconoclasts, see Sauer (2003) 79, 82.

thrown down a well.[68] The point of note here is that the bodies were mutilated and the heads were absent, mimicking the fate of the Mithraic statuary, while the deposition of the bodies down the well echoes the fate of the Mercury statue from Dieburg, and elements of the main relief from Stockstadt I. Indeed, it is perhaps no coincidence that the Biesheim mithraeum, which was partially burnt down and its statuary broken towards of the end of the 3rd c., lay in relatively close proximity to Harting. Arguably, the events at Harting suggest the aforementioned desecration of the temple at Tawern could also have been a victim of barbarian incursions, given that a statue of Mercury there was beheaded and thrown down a well.

Several small finds found beyond the Rhine frontier may also be an indication of valuable items being taken from mithraea by raiders. It has been suggested that a miniature of the bull-slaying scene in bronze found in the River Salle near Halle, was taken from a mithraeum as booty to Germania Superior sometime in the mid 3rd c.,[69] while bronze dagger-hands from the bull-slaying scene have been recovered beyond the Rhine frontier at Hamburg, Flechtorf and Berlin. The Hamburg hand was found in the River Alster, while the original provenance of the Flechtorf hand is unknown, and the Berlin example has been lost. However, given that the two finds with known provenances were recovered from rivers, ritual deposition cannot be excluded, although trade may also have resulted in them being found outside of the Roman sphere.[70]

In Britain, it is even harder to judge if 'barbarian' conflict occurred around Hadrian's Wall when the mithraea here went out of use. According to the literary evidence, there were problems with the Picts during Constantius Chlorus' reign, while Constantine's title *Britannicus* may refer to a campaign in the province.[71] Around 367 the so-called 'Barbarian Conspiracy' occurred, which began with the rebellion of garrisons on Hadrian's Wall that allowed Picts to cross into the province, and led to the deaths of the *dux Britanniarum* and the commander of the coastal defences. It is possible that the description of these events was overblown by Ammianus in order to glorify Count Theodosius (father of the emperor at the time of Ammianus' writing), who was responsible for putting down this uprising, but that it required the elder Theodosius' attention does indicate there was significant unrest.[72] The destruction of the Brocolitia Mithraeum may have been a product of this unrest if groups had been allowed to cross Hadrian's Wall unchecked, while the earlier campaigns of the Constantinian dynasty would fit chronologically with the destruction of the Borcovicium Mithraeum, although without clearer details regarding all these events this can only remain speculation.

If barbarians were to blame for the fragmentation of Mithraic statuary in frontier regions, what was it that drove them to do this? As highlighted in chapter one, the epigraphic evidence indicates that in the early 4th c. the cult of Mithras still enjoyed a significant level of popularity amongst the military along the Danube frontier, which led to the imperial government displaying an unprecedented level of support for mithraea. Subsequently, although support for mithraea looks to have waned in the latter half of the century, there was continuing activity in mithraea while most other buildings fell into ruin. This suggests that Mithras was still held in some esteem among those who had come a generation or two after the Tetrarchs' dedication; it is not difficult to imagine that the coins deposited in mithraea were for good luck in coming conflicts. For barbarian tribes, crossing the frontier to fight and plunder, defacing this 'unconquerable' deity, so strongly linked with Roman power in the region, must have had some attraction. Just as the Tetrarchs' could deliver a message of supremacy to the troops by supporting the cult, so too could later barbarians have demonstrated their might over the diminished Roman forces by ritually 'killing' their unconquerable god.

The targeting of 'Roman' deities by those in conflict with the empire was not unheard of. When the Roman garrison left the town of Gholaia in North Africa around AD 260, the local inhabitants tore down the statues of Victory and Fortuna located within the military camp to demonstrate the weakness of Rome's power. Their continued worship of Jupiter Hammon in a temple constructed by the Romans for over another hundred years, is perhaps an indication they targeted deities they saw as connected to the Roman military.[73] The prefix *Deo Invicto* may even have seemed a challenge to those crossing the Rhine or Danube. In the midst of this, it would be unsurprising if mithraea, which usually lacked any protection, were abandoned and became the

---

68 Carroll (2001) 138. Also stated on the same page: "Ritual defacement and smashing of statues and monuments to Roman gods at vici such as Bad Wimpfen and Walheim and at the villa at Brackenheim-Hausen an der Zaber also seem more likely to have been acts of Alamannic vengeance".

69 Gordon (2004) 267.

70 Marquart (2004).

71 Mattingly (2006) 233–34.

---

72 Amm. Marc. 27.8.

73 Caseau (1999) 21–22.

victims of what was inherently anti-Roman, rather than anti-'pagan', destruction.

Turning to the eastern frontier, it is possible that incursions by the Sassanids adversely affected the cult. During the 3rd c., the border between the two empires destabilised considerably, culminating in the first case of a Roman emperor, Valerian, being captured. Although peace was largely restored under the Tetrarchy, conflict between the Romans and Persians arose again in the mid to late 4th c., during which time the Persians made significant gains. During the course of the 4th c., these conflicts had taken on a religious element, beginning with Constantine warning the Persian ruler Shapur that he should refrain from persecuting Christians, lest the Roman empire be forced into action to protect them, a persecution which was subsequently carried out in the AD 340s. The resumption of the conflict in the early AD 420s has been seen as being partially the result of the Persian persecution of Christians.[74]

In such circumstances, it is possible that the Persian aspects of the Mithras cult came under increasing scrutiny, especially in the eastern half of the empire where the cult was a rarity. As noted, Firmicus Maternus, in his criticism of the cult, talks more of its Persian origin than it being non-Christian.[75] For cults to be targeted because of their Persian origins (whether real or projected) was not unheard of in the Roman world. A law that was passed under the Tetrarchs against the Manicheans, a Persian sect that had arisen in the mid 3rd c., suggests that the 'Persian' origin of the cult was a point of contention:

> ... we have heard that they have but recently advanced or sprung forth, like strange and monstrous portents, from their native homes among the Persians—a nation hostile to us—and have settled in this part of the world, where they are perpetrating many evil deeds, disturbing the tranquillity of the peoples and causing the gravest injuries to the commonalties; and there is danger that, in process of time, they will endeavour, as is their usual practice, to infect the innocent, orderly and tranquil Roman people, as well as the whole of our Empire, with the damnable customs and perverse laws of the Persians as with the poison of a malignant serpent.[76]

It is perhaps no coincidence that of the four Mithraic sites which exhibit evidence of Christian desecration,

three (Doliche, Hawarte and Ša'āra) were located in close proximity to the eastern frontier, at places which were significantly exposed to Persian invasion. Indeed, Doliche was sacked by the Persians in the mid 3rd c. Is it possible that the carving of crosses on the walls and reliefs of these mithraea represented not only the victory of Christ over the cult of Mithras, but the triumph of the Christian empire of Rome over the Zoroastrian Persians, with whom they identified Mithraic imagery? Could a general anti-Persian sentiment in the region explain why the cult remained relatively rare within the eastern provinces? One may wonder to what extant the Persian deity Mithra was recognised by those living along the eastern frontier of the Roman empire as being similar, or even the same, as the Roman Mithras. Was knowledge of the image of Mithra accompanying Shapur II (309–79) and his successor Ardashir II (379–83) standing over the fallen emperor Julian, carved into the rock at Taq Bostan (in modern Iran), transmitted across this frontier?[77]

That political and religious interests might collide in one instance is demonstrated by the attack on the Alexandrian Serapeum and the death of Hypatia, arguably two of the most famous examples of 'anti-pagan' violence in Late Antiquity. In both cases, it has become clear to scholars that these acts were perpetrated within a larger model of social and political unrest that had long been a feature in Alexandrian society. While they undoubtedly involved a religious dimension, the motivations behind these incidents were more complex than the traditional narrative would have us believe. Given the context of the desecration of the mithraea at Doliche, Hawarte and Ša'āra, the possibility that more than simply religious differences were at play here cannot be dismissed.

Civil War

Periods of civil war in the Roman world often resulted in the destruction or desecration of religious sites, but there is little indication that this was due to religious conflict in most cases. Instead, temples could be raided for funds, to make a political statement, or simply as an act of violence designed to inspire fear in the local population. As was outlined in the introduction, it would appear the violent fate met by various *dolichena* during the rule of Maximinus Thrax was related to at least the first two of these. Such motivations no doubt existed in the 4th c. as well. One should not assume they had any qualms in destroying or desecrating a mithraeum they

---

74   Holum (1977).

75   Firm. Mat. *Err. prof. rel.* 4.1.

76   *Mosaicarum et Romanarum Legum Collatio* 15.3. (transl. Hyamson (1913) 131).

77   For discussion of Mithra in this relief, see Adrych *et al.* (2017) 81–105.

had no connection to, especially if it provided prospects of booty.[78]

Unfortunately, attempting to establish a connection between the fate of mithraea and periods of civil war is immensely difficult. In Britain, the end of the Mithraic temples also finds a correlation with the apparent mass destruction of temples on military sites around the turn of the 4th c. Lewis postulated that this was the result of reprisals by Constantius Chlorus after his defeat of the Carausian revolt, but it is difficult to ascertain whether this was the case without further archaeological evidence.[79]

One mithraeum whose *terminus post quem* for abandonment does closely align with the occurrence of such conflicts is that of Septeuil. This mithraeum was clearly the victim of a vicious attack sometime in the 380s, and it is perhaps no coincidence that in AD 383 the usurper Magnus Maximus is recorded as having defeated Gratian just outside Paris.[80] Magnus' force consisted of troops he brought from Britain, a province where there is no Mithraic evidence dating to later than the early 4th c., thus his army likely had little to no affiliation with the deity. Subsequently, they may have seen the mithraeum at Septeuil as a site to be pillaged during their successful advance or, much like the possible motivation behind barbarian desecration of mithraea, as a demonstration that a deity followed by their foes was not as 'unconquerable' as they claimed. This is very hypothetical, but given the frequency of civil war in the late Roman period it is quite possible a mithraeum, even if not Septeuil, fell victim to such a fate.

Imperial Legislation

Amongst the factors contributing to the final closure of mithraea, imperial legislation is unlikely to have played a major role. Certainly, there is little evidence of a desire amongst the Roman authorities to legally justify religious violence in communities, as throughout the 4th and 5th c. it was reiterated that the destruction of religious buildings was not encouraged.[81] Even when it came to the laws demanding the closure of temples, it is questionable to what degree any of them were implemented. Many who held governorships and military commands adhered to polytheism, while bribery and ineptitude would also have played a part in limiting how effectively such legislation was exercised. Additionally, one wonders to what extent such laws could be implemented in rural areas. The fact that the legislation had to be repeated suggests that it had little impact, for as Bayliss observed "the Theodosian Law Code presents almost a collection of legal posterity rather than an efficient and effective source of reference by which to rule", while, as David Hunt succinctly comments, "laws, of course, 'do not a Christian make'".[82]

Equally, the laws concerning classical temples and rituals do not constitute a large portion of the prescriptions found in Book 16.5; there are only 25 laws applying to *De Paganis, Sacrificiis, et Templis*, while 66 laws were enacted against heretics, and 29 are filed under Jews, Caelicolists, and Samaritans. Although the imperial government was naturally concerned that people should not be carrying out 'improper rituals', particularly related to oracles and soothsayers, the laws indicate that they were more concerned with suppressing unorthodox forms of Christianity. As observed above, clashes between different Christian groups were more common than those between Christians and non-Christians, and the legislation reflects this. Perhaps the only locations where the closure and dismantling of a mithraeum might relate to an imperial law are those in residential areas or on private estates in Gaul, where the aristocracy converted to Christianity more rapidly than their contemporaries elsewhere. Such elites might wish to have had traces of non-Christian activity removed from their land to demonstrate to any visitors that they were truly devout to the religion of the emperors. The levelling of the Bornheim-Sechtem Mithraeum in the early 5th c. might be one such case of this, situated as it was on a villa estate. The large mithraeum at Burdigala, situated next to a house, and apparently taken apart to be mined for *spolia*, might also have met its fate for this reason.

Relocation of Mithraic Initiates

In his study on the fragmentation of cult statues in Late Roman Britain, Ben Croxford observed:

> [A]t the end of Roman Britain, with the arrival of outsiders and the threat of barbarian invaders, these fragments may have been especially valuable to individuals suffering perhaps uncertain times; they may have been used as apotropaic amulets or as personal objects of veneration, a private piece of the divine ... to suppose that everyone abandoned

---

78   To what extent mithraea contained valuable objects is unclear, but some have been recovered in a few examples, such as the silver plaque from Mithraeum I at Stockstadt (*CIMRM* 2. 1206) and a bronze plaque of unknown provenance currently on display in the New York Metropolitan Museum of Art (Picón *et al.* (1997) 17). It is worth noting that, prior to the discovery of a large hoard of silver in a Dolichenum at Mauer an der Url, we did not know that dolichena could contain so much wealth: see Noll (1938), Hörig and Schwertheim (1987) 187–207.

79   Lewis (1966) 143.

80   Leeham (2010) 167–69.

81   *Cod. Theod.* 16.10.8, 15, 18.

82   Bayliss (2004) 117; Hunt (1993) 143.

or even deliberately destroyed their 'old faith's' idols and images is now unsupportable.[83]

Such a description of 'uncertain times' could also apply to the Rhine or Danube frontiers, with many mithraea located in perilous positions, and many of the local inhabitants having fled or withdrawn to defensive positions. Is it possible that those who attended the mithraea in these places might have sought, as Croxford suggests, to remove parts of the cult images, and used them as more portable forms of Mithraic worship? As was illustrated in the previous chapter, in at least some Mithraic communities the ritual fragmentation of objects certainly occurred, with certain elements retained and still seen as significant. With this in mind then, at least some of the fragmented Mithraic sculptures and reliefs that have been found were perhaps not broken by people from outside the cult community, but by those within it.

However, for those who wished to take important items from mithraea, carrying the reliefs or statues may have been impractical, either because these items were too large or because there were no longer enough worshippers to warrant transporting the whole relief to a new location. In such circumstances, the fragmentation of a relief or statue, and the subsequent removal of the head or hands—arguably the two most important features of Mithras as they bore his image and the dagger which slew the bull—may have provided a method of retaining the essence of the image in a more portable form, in much the same fashion as the relics of saints would later be viewed as being as powerful as the whole body.[84] Indeed, when one surveys the remains of the statues and reliefs from mithraea a pattern does emerge: the head of Mithras, occasionally along with that of the bull, is absent in many cases. Furthermore, it is notable that the mithraeum at Dieburg—abandoned in *ca.* AD 260 during the Roman cessation of land beyond the Rhine—has produced numerous sculptures and reliefs also missing their heads. Could this have been the work of initiates fleeing the oncoming Alamanni, rather than the Alamanni themselves?

Are there any other cases where we might detect the hand of Mithraic adherents in breaking the images in order to remove certain elements? One possible example is the mithraeum at Septeuil. Here, the heads were removed from one statue and the main relief, the latter of which was heavily fragmented, but another relief was left intact and exhibits blows to the face of Mithras. Given that this mithraeum lay in the path of Magnus

Maximus's army and looks to have been abandoned at this time, it is possible that the Mithraic adherents sought to remove the head of Mithras and the bull from the main relief, as well as from the statue of the rock-birth, before Magnus' army reached the site.

Such a scenario could also explain the state of the evidence in some of the Dalmatian mithraea. At Jajce, a headless statue of the torchbearer was found, yet the main relief was left intact except for Mithras' dagger hand, which had been removed. Such precise removal of certain features of the image, while other elements were left untouched, suggest this damage was not born out of animosity. At Konjic, on one side of the main, double-sided relief, all depictions of Mithras (three in total) have had their heads removed, while in the top corners of the same side the images of Sol and Luna had been removed. On the reverse, which depicts Mithraic adherents recreating the banquet of Sol and Mithras, all the figures remain intact (fig. 47).[85] Thus, the heads of the deities were removed with precision, which suggests some care was taken to do this. While one may argue that this could have been outsiders attempting to negate the power of enemy gods or demons, then why did they leave the reverse image alone? How would they know the figures on the other side were human and not divine?

Even if this careful treatment of the reliefs only took place in a few instances, this would mean that the worship of Mithras survived beyond its disappearance from the archaeological record in the early 5th c. Whether such worship was undertaken communally or individually is unclear, although if the latter then we can say it no longer constituted a 'cult' of Mithras.

Natural Disasters and Accidental Destruction

The damage to, and destruction of, temples caused by natural disasters is very difficult to establish. Earthquakes appear to have brought about the destruction of the *temenos* of the Temple of Apollo at Hyle in Cyprus, as well as the second phase of damage inflicted on the Temple of Zeus at Cyrene. In the case of the latter, this is indicated by the "even eastward collapse of the pronaos and opisthodomos", but as to how common a fate this was for temples is unclear.[86] Mithraea are no different in this regard, but Carnuntum provides a rare example of where such an event was highly likely to have impacted on the Mithraic temples in the town. When Ammianus visited Carnuntum with Valentinian I in AD 375, he described it as "deserted and in ruins".[87] As we have

---

83 Croxford (2003) 93–94.
84 Brown (1981) 78.

85 Jajce: *CIMRM* 2. 1902–1903; Konjic: *CIMRM* 2. 1896.
86 Hyle: Trombley (1993–94) 1.177; Cyrene: Bayliss (2004) 25.
87 Amm. Marc. 30.5.2.

FIGURE 47 *The two-sided Mithraic relief from Konjic. After CIMRM 2. 1896.*
DRAWN BY LLOYD BOSWORTH.

seen, urban decay was common in this region during the latter half of the 4th c., but excavation at Carnuntum has uncovered extensive destruction levels dating to the mid 4th c., which occur in both secular and religious buildings. The type of damage evident is consistent with the impact of a seismic event, and the fact that Carnuntum lays only 8 km north-west of the Lassee Fault Line[88] also makes an earthquake the most plausible explanation for the ruination of the town. The mithraea in Carnuntum were unlikely to have remained untouched by the effects of the earthquake, thus at least some of the damage to them must have resulted from this; there is also no evidence of activity in either structure that post-dates the earthquake. As suggested, some of the damage found in Mithraeum I could indicate Christian involvement, but given the evidence relating to the earthquake and the lack of evidence for contemporary Christian activity in the region, any Christian iconoclastic activity is likely to have post-dated the abandonment of the temple.

---

88   Decker *et al.* (2006); Kandler (1989).

Finally, it is worth mentioning the mithraeum at Schachadorf. It contained a burnt layer inside its *cella*, but the recovery of an intact rock-birth statue from this deposit infers that this burning was not part of a violent act. Mithraea certainly presented a high-risk of fire given the lamps used therein. Naturally, it is difficult to prove if the fire at the Schachadorf Mithraeum was accidental, but certainly such occurrences must have taken place at times, and this is by far the most likely example from the archaeological record for an accidental fire in a mithraeum.

Conclusion

The fate of most mithraea from the late 3rd to the early 5th c. was predominantly a violent one, with 26 destroyed or found with their images broken. Only 16 mithraea had their images removed or left intact, while five were used as sources of *spolia* or were utilised for a different function. Chronologically speaking, in the early 4th c., the fate of mithraea was at its most varied, with some mithraea abandoned, some reused and others desecrated. By the mid 4th c., this is less apparent with most mithraea simply being vacated and their images removed. In the final decades of the 4th c., there is a considerable increase in the number of mithraea whose images were broken, while the number of those destroyed also rose. In terms of geographical distribution, most of the mithraea that were destroyed or had their images broken were to be found on the frontiers throughout the 4th c., while in the interior provinces the form of closure of mithraea apparently remained relatively benign until the late 4th c., when there is an increase in desecration in these regions.

Who was to blame for these closures and destructive activity? Contrary to what the traditional narratives would have us believe, in total only four mithraea (Doliche, Hawarte, Ponza and Šaʻāra) can be archaeologically proven to have been desecrated by Christians, and even then, only at the Hawarte Mithraeum did this probably coincide with the closure of the temple. Furthermore, the context of the mithraea at Doliche, Hawarte, and Šaʻāra suggests that their desecration by Christians may have been motivated by more than just the desire to destroy the temple of a 'pagan' god. Lying close to the frontier with Persia, it is not difficult to imagine that mithraea might have attracted the anger of locals who saw them as places used to worship an enemy (Persian) deity. As the cult was not particularly common in the East, unlike the West, this may also have contributed to it being seen as an alien, rather than Roman, religious movement. Much like the destruction of the Serapeum and the death of Hypatia in Alexandria, the closure of the Hawarte Mithraeum may well have been due to political, as well as religious, factors.

If we use other possible diagnostic traits to identify Christian iconoclasts, an interesting case is the mithraea at Carnuntum (Mithraeum I), Vulci and Les Bolards, which contained images of animals that were left intact while other figures were destroyed, so these examples may have been victims of Christian iconoclasm. Extra credeence is given to this interpretation by the fact that such evidence was present in the mithraeum at Šaʻāra, which was certainly desecrated by Christians. However, questions remain regarding the interpretation of some of these sites. At Gimmeldingen, the lack of damage to the Mithraic images may indicate that, if this was the work of Christian iconoclasts, they had little issue with Mithras or his cult, so we cannot be sure if such damage marked the end of worship in the mithraeum. At Carnuntum I, the lack of any evidence for a Christian presence in the area makes it unlikely that it was this group who forced the closure of the mithraeum; rather, the earthquake of the 4th c. was probably being the biggest contributing factor here, although Christians may have desecrated the temple at a later stage.

In reality, there was little scope for Christians to actively persecute the Mithras cult given that the two groups operated in largely different areas in the 4th c. Christianity was gaining popularity in the East, around the Mediterranean, and had penetrated Gaul, but the cult of Mithras was mainly found along the northern frontiers and in Rome itself.

The evidence suggests that barbarian incursion may have been a more common factor behind the destruction and desecration of mithraea. During the course of the 4th c., mithraea in frontier regions, such as on Hadrian's Wall, Poetovio, Lentia, Mackwiller, Ad Enum and Pons Saravi, all found themselves beyond the defences of their respective settlements, thus leaving them open to assault by external threats. That mithraea would be desecrated during incursions by barbarians does appear to have a precedent. This was the damage inflicted on the fittings of mithraea in the Rhineland in the early 3rd c., following the end of Roman hegemony there. There is also evidence for the continued destruction of mithraea in the late 3rd and early 4th c. in the same area. The mithraea destroyed in earlier periods and in the 4th c. have all produced various statues and reliefs missing their heads, which, given that groups such as the Alamanni would decapitate their victims and dispose of their heads separately, perhaps represents a 'ritual'

THE FATE OF MITHRAEA

killing of Mithras. Along the Danube and Hadrian's Wall, Mithras had been strongly associated with the Roman army, and in the case of the former being named the 'Protector of the Empire' by the Tetrarchs. This may have also made his temples an attractive target to barbarians who wished to demonstrate that Roman power was no longer what it once was.

Of course, we must also bear in mind that accidents and natural disasters, such as the earthquake at Carnuntum, can result in the destruction of images and structures. The situation at Carnuntum serves to highlight the lack of commitment that the cult now garnered from its followers in some areas. The Tetrarchs had restored a mithraeum and erected a dedication to Mithras at Carnuntum, calling him the 'Protector of their *Imperium*', suggesting a highly committed Mithraic community in the town. Yet only a few decades after this, following the earthquake, there was no apparent attempt to repair either of the mithraea at Carnuntum, nor is there evidence of another being constructed. At Schachadorf, the discovery of an intact image of the rock-birth in the remains of a burnt mithraeum may indicate an accidental fire. Once again, there was no attempt to rebuild the structure.

Another viable alternative view, based on the evidence, is that it was Mithraic adherents themselves who broke their images, in order to take certain elements with them when abandoning a temple. The absence of heads from many mithraea has been assumed to indicate the involvement of Christians, but given that the head is the most expressive part of an image, and a whole relief or statue was very heavy, breaking it into these individual elements might have provided a way of keeping something of it. Modern excavations of mithraea have demonstrated that Mithraic communities did indeed retain fragmented items and believed them to still be sacred; such evidence has also been found in other cultic contexts in this period. If this practice took place in mithraea, then it raises important questions regarding whether the end of the mithraea and the organised cult of Mithras actually represented the demise of Mithraic worship, or whether this actually continued, with individuals now honouring individual pieces of reliefs or statuettes they had carried away from former temples. Naturally, without finding the missing heads or other fragments this can only remain conjecture, but even if such worship did take place, it is unlikely these artefacts retained their cult status beyond one or two generations; they would have eventually found themselves used for other purposes. However, the recent work that has highlighted the significance of fragmentary objects in Mithraic contexts leaves us with tantalising possibilities.

Conclusion

During the course of writing this monograph, I read Neil Gaiman's *American Gods* and John Julius Norwich's *The Popes: a History*. The former is a work of fiction and the latter popular history, but both in their own way are about how religion has changed over the course of the last few thousand years. What struck me was that both books referenced (very briefly) the cult of Mithras. In *American Gods*, Mithras is described as being down on his luck after he was replaced by Jesus, while in *The Popes* the cult of Mithras is mentioned as major rival of early Christianity. What was apparent to me is that two very different books highlighted the almost tragic dimension the cult of Mithras has taken on since it first became a subject of study: an almost-ran next to Christianity, whose fate was inextricably bound to the 'victory' of the Church. Here were two cults which arose around the same time, matured together and then, like Romulus and Remus, fought a violent struggle for ownership of Rome and her subjects. As this study has shown, this popular image is far from reality. Certainly, in some cases, Christians were to blame for the desecration of mithraea. Yet the claim that Christianity was the single or dominant factor behind the end of the Mithras cult does not stand up to scrutiny.

Before disentangling the fate of the cult of Mithras from the rise of Christianity, however, it was necessary to dispel any notions that in the 4th c. the cult of Mithras was a homogenous entity, with Mithraic communities uniform regardless of place or time. If we are to understand why the cult of Mithras failed in Late Antiquity, we must first understand what the cult of Mithras *was* at this time. To amend the famous phrase of Tertullian: what has Brocolitia to do with Hawarte?

I argued in the introduction that we should see deities as having cultural biographies; as they travel across wide areas via 'world empires' and are integrated into local communities they undergo a series of transformations. We can see this in the cult of Mithras during Late Antiquity. From the late 1st to early 3rd c., the cult spread across the Roman world and, while there were some regional differences, the evidence does remain largely uniform, with mithraea following a set layout, with the central tauroctony present everywhere. Mithraic rituals (initiations, sacrifices, and feasts) did vary to some degree, such as with the possible application of a bow and arrow in initiations performed in Mithraic communities near the Rhine, but in essence the way in which they were conducted and their intended aims do not appear to have differed significantly on a regional level in this period.

By the 4th c. the picture is far more variable. In the East, the isolated mithraeum at Hawarte was highly unique, with its own distinct iconography and a *cella* containing an L-shaped bench. In Dalmatia, some Mithraic communities called Mithras 'Meterae', met in mithraea with just a single bench running down one side of the *cella*, and a tauroctony carved into a rock-face. At Rome, there were Mithraic communities built around senators who took on Mithraic, alongside many other, titles as they sought to differentiate themselves from the 'new men' entering the Senate. Oddly, some of these men held the titles of *pater* and *corax* simultaneously, the highest and lowest Mithraic grades respectively, while at *Via Giovanni Lanza* 128 there was a mithraeum dating to this period that had no benches at all. In Gaul, it appears that some Mithraic communities worshipped Mithras as a healing deity, with mithraea situated alongside temples devoted to such practices, altars referring to Mithras as 'helper', and a doctor serving as the head of a congregation. Unlike Hawarte, Dalmatia and Rome all the mithraea in Gaul in use at this time contained two benches running in parallel to each other. In contrast, on the Danubian frontier Mithras retained a strong affiliation with the military and was arguably one of, if not the, most popular god in this region in the early 4th c. We can see this at Lentia, where a mithraeum took pride of place alongside a temple to *Dea Roma* and the *Genius Augusti*, while other mithraea in the surrounding area had received the benefaction of the imperial government, which was unheard of elsewhere in the empire. At Gimmeldingen in Germany, a mithraeum referred to as a *fanum* was erected in AD 325, while among this congregation they also spelt the words for Mithras and *corax* uniquely. Finally, across the north-eastern provinces a great number of coins were being deposited in mithraea as votives, in much the same way that neighbouring temples and sacred springs also received such offerings, but we do not see this at Hawarte or in Rome.

This is a broad sketch, but the evidence outlined indicates that the Mithraic cult, although initially relatively uniform, had seemingly come to mean different things to different people in different places by the 4th c. Indeed, one might go so far as to say that by the 4th c., there were now *cults* of Mithras in operation across the Roman world.

A degree of regionalisation is also evident as to when support for mithraea began to decline. While in areas such as the Upper Danubian provinces and Rome the cult appears to have maintained a strong following into mid 4th and late 4th c. respectively, along the

---

© KONINKLIJKE BRILL NV, LEIDEN, 2019 | DOI 10.1163/9789004383067_007

Rhine, in Gaul and in Italy (outside of Rome) support for mithraea was already on the wane going into the 4th c. In Britain, the cult was almost completely extinct in the early decades of the 4th c., while in Dalmatia, in spite of a notable rise in the number of mithraea in the late 3rd c., support seems to have rapidly cooled, with no subsequent alterations to pre-existing mithraea or the construction of new ones after the early 4th c.

Unfortunately, it is almost impossible in most cases to establish whether there was a commensurate decline in mithraea attendance, for the diminishing numbers of coins being deposited at the end of the 4th c. might be the product of declining circulation. Mithraea might even have played host to *more* people in the 4th c. than before, although if this were the case it did not result in any continuing investment in these spaces. A decline in attendance can be traced in Trier, however, where the numismatic data from the mithraea rapidly decrease in quantity from the mid 4th c., in contrast to the evidence elsewhere in the town.

Why did such a decline in support for mithraea occur? The major problem faced by Mithraic communities, particularly on the frontiers, was the changing social context from which they drew adherents. The declining urban fabric of many frontier towns and *vici*, driven by the migration of large numbers of their population to safer areas as Roman hegemony collapsed, had a significant impact on the quantity and commitment of followers that the cult could attract. The considerable decrease in the population of these areas alone would have meant many mithraea became redundant; why would places such as Aquincum, Carnuntum, or Poetovio need multiple mithraea when their populations were now so severely depleted?

The changing social make-up of potential worshippers may also have had a negative impact on the numbers joining the Mithras cult. As highlighted, sociological studies indicate that religious choices are largely determined by social networks, and the 4th c. brought massive changes to the networks of people living on the frontiers. Mithraic initiates in previous periods would have spent much of their time together outside of the mithraeum, either as soldiers on campaign or working as *portoria* slaves, which would have reinforced their commitment to the cult, as their social capital was well-served via their membership. However, soldiers in the 4th c. now found themselves increasingly living side-by-side with their families and other civilians inside the fortifications. This is not to say the barrier between the two had never been permeable, naturally the two spheres had often mixed and lived in close proximity, but now the social dynamics had significantly shifted. Furthermore, those recruited to the Roman army, as well

as those they were led by, were increasingly recruited from tribes wishing to relocate into Roman territory. These people came with their own gods and traditions; they did not adhere to those of the Roman army, which Mithras may have been seen as. As a result of these reorientations in social networks in the 4th c., those who traditionally would have stood to have enhanced their social capital by joining the cult may have found this was no longer the case, and they may have found that their religious choices were now better served in investing in other cults.

In Rome too, we find a similar problem with the senatorial Mithraic worshippers, whose vast array of priesthoods and expansive social networks meant that they were constantly exposed to other cults and rituals that may have come to provide a greater source of social capital. Of course, this was not so much due to the changing times, as on the frontier, but more the whim or fortunes of a wealthy patron. As we see in Londinium and the Mithraeum of Victorinus at Aquincum, the support for a mithraeum by such an individual and his family could not always be guaranteed at any time; a simple change in circumstances might bring the use of a mithraeum to an end.

It is also likely that the declining fortunes of mithraea were related to the transformation of Mithraic rituals during the 4th c. Almost no materials relating to initiations or sacrifices have been found in 4th c. Mithraic contexts, while at the same time we see a rise in coins being deposited as votives (fig. 48), a practice common across the Roman world at various temples, shrines, and sacred sites, including some that lay within a short distance from mithraea. The implication of this shift is that mithraea were now more accessible and perhaps no longer required any distinctly Mithraic rituals to be performed by members, expect perhaps for ritual meals. Without these initiation rituals to bind members to the community, the cult lost the glue that bound its worshippers together; it is also possible that whatever ritual the specific design of mithraea was designed to facilitate ceased to be practised. In short, it is difficult to see why, by the latter half of the 4th c., people would feel any great need to support a mithraeum when they could practise the same rituals elsewhere, including at natural locations such as springs and caves. Mithras was born of a rock and was known as the 'eternal spring', so why should natural features not provide a place to worship him?

I am aware that some will argue the lack of objects relating to initiations need not mean such rituals had ceased to be conducted in the mithraea of the north-west provinces in the 4th c. Yet, when this absence of evidence is coupled with these new forms of ritual

FIGURE 48 *Artist's impression of coins offered as votives in a mithraeum during the 4th c.*
ARTIST: CHRIS NEWMAN.

activity in mithraea, and the evident decline in support for these structures, there were clearly major changes occurring in the Mithras cult. It would also be foolish to dismiss the notion that it was beyond the ability or will of Mithraic communities to marginalise or completely abandon some of their central rituals. The first chapter of this study highlights how Mithraic communities grew and altered over time and that, particularly in the drastic circumstances of the 4th c., radical alterations to Mithraic practice could occur.

Of course, it was not the same situation everywhere, with the senatorial Mithraic groups in Rome operating in a very different context, and there is no evidence of any dramatic shift in rituals here that we see north of the Alps. However, the alterations to traditional grades, evident from the epigraphic record, and Ambrosiaster's account—suggesting that the initiations men (and boys) undertook were not as intensive as their predecessors—infers that these members were also not as tightly bound to the cult as previous initiates.

Whether or not it was to Christianity or another cult that many Mithraic worshippers turned to, is unclear, although along the frontiers this is unlikely to have been the case given the dearth of Christian material, although at Trier we may speculate that is was indeed Christianity that drew Mithraic adherents away. The context of this mithraeum, with the temples around it being torn down in the shadow of Constantine's basilica and the Christian imperial court, may have led Mithraic worshippers to accept that the cult's days were numbered, and that Christianity might serve as a better investment. Indeed, Salzman's quantitative study of aristocratic conversion to Christianity demonstrates that the presence of the imperial court in Gaul had a significant impact in speeding this process up in comparison to elsewhere. There is also reason to believe that, even if the worshippers who used the Trier Mithraeum were not from the highest echelons of society, they too would follow a similar pattern.

This gives us some ideas as to why the cult of Mithras declined, but what was it that dealt the final blow? Christian iconoclasts were certainly responsible for the desecration of some mithraea. In four examples, this is indicated by the carving of crosses into the walls of the temple. However, only at Hawarte was the desecration by Christians likely to have been contemporary to the abandonment of the mithraeum, given that the *terminus post quem* for its abandonment dates to only shortly before the erection of a church over the site. Yet the circumstances in which this mithraeum found itself suggest the violent expulsion of the Mithraic congregation was perhaps driven by more than just religious fervour. Hawarte is the only extant mithraeum located in the East that was certainly in use during the 4th c., and it appears that this community continued to conduct their rituals in private, unlike many of their western counterparts, with no evidence of mass coin deposition present. Furthermore, the iconography of this mithraeum indicates a Mithraic group that had perhaps been influenced by Zoroastrianism, which, together with the cult's various Persian aspects (such as Mithras' garb and the Persian grade), may have attracted the anger of outsiders, given the state of war between 'Zoroastrian' Persia and 'Christian' Rome at the time.

It is perhaps no coincidence then that of the three other examples of Christian graffiti appearing in mithraea, two (Doliche and Ša'āra) were located near the eastern frontier, with Doliche even having been sacked by the Persians. In his tirade against the cult, Firmicus Maternus was keen to point out the dangers of allowing a 'Persian' cult to poison Roman society.[1] Equally, the laws issued by the Tetrarchs against the Manicheans indicate that apprehension regarding 'Persian' influence was a real issue at this time. Naturally, it is difficult to prove these desecrations had a political dimension, but recent studies that have emphasised how the attack on the Alexandrian Serapeum by Christians should be viewed through the lens of political conflict in Alexandria, could also apply to the eastern frontier.

There are a couple of other cases where Christian iconoclasts appear the most likely culprits behind the desecration of mithraea, although the evidence in these instances is by no means conclusive. At Les Bolards and Vulci, statues were not only broken but display evidence of nicks and abrasions, and in both cases images of animals were left completely intact. Given this evidence suggests a particularly zealous attack on the sculptures, the decision of the perpetrators to leave the images of animals untouched must have been a conscious one. It need not definitely be Christians, but such specific targeting does make them the most plausible culprits. However, it is worth reiterating that the evidence from Vulci is undated and could have occurred long after the mithraeum was abandoned. It is also possible that the relief depicting a naked Mercury, found at Gimmeldingen, may have been targeted by Christians, but the Mithraic items were left largely untouched, so we can exclude this as a possible example of anti-Mithraic violence.

Nonetheless, even if we accept that all six of the aforementioned mithraea were attacked by Christian iconoclasts, it is important to highlight that they do not constitute the majority of mithraea active in the 4th c. In most cases, it is unlikely that such iconoclasts were responsible for the fate of mithraea, as many were situated on the northern frontiers (along Hadrian's Wall, the Rhine, and on the Danube), which were areas where Christianity had yet to make a substantial impact, as attested to by the limited material culture and literary references of Christians in these regions. Even in Rome, Christianity was still far from the dominant faith, with many of the city's inhabitants, including leading senators, continuing to practise polytheism. Additionally, while it might be that the prefect Gracchus did launch an attack on a mithraeum in Rome, Jerome's absence from the city at the time and the fact that this mithraeum

---

1 It is also worth noting how often the Roman cult of Mithras is referred to as being a 'Persian' cult in modern literature.

remains unverified in the archaeological record, leaves his account open to doubt.

Finally, the patterns of fragmentation we see on items found in mithraea are also very random, with some sculptures of Mithras left intact while others were broken, with some depictions of animals vandalised alongside untouched Mithraic images, and many nude images left unmolested. This does not mean Christians are absolved of all blame in these cases, but it does serve to highlight how we lack reliable methodologies to detect their involvement.

As a result, we must seek alternative explanations for the fate of mithraea in the West, with the most likely candidates being barbarians. That they were responsible for the abandonment of many mithraea located in frontier regions is plausible for a number of reasons. First, the majority of the mithraea situated in these regions lay beyond the defences of the Late Roman settlements, often lying in derelict areas of the civilian towns or among dilapidated *vici*. Also, various mithraea located in Germania Superior were destroyed and desecrated following the cessation of Roman control in the mid 3rd c., with statues and reliefs found in much the same state as those recovered from mithraea abandoned in the 4th c. At the same time, there is evidence of mithraea being destroyed on the Rhine frontier in the late 3rd c. Equally, groups such as the Alamanni appear to have beheaded people and deposited the heads separately from the bodies, thus the ritual 'killing' of statues in such a fashion should not be ruled out either. It is also possible that Mithras' connection with the Roman army and his status as 'unconquerable', made his temples an attractive target for enemies of Rome who wished to demonstrate that Roman military power was no longer what it once was. Once again, there can be no certainty surrounding this, but such motives appear the most viable for explaining the demise of mithraea along the northern frontier.

There were also occasional instances where mithraea appear to have been abandoned for reasons other than Christian iconoclasm or barbarian attacks. Some, such as at Septeuil, may have been the victims of civil war. At Septeuil, the location and *terminus post quem* of the abandonment of this site correlates with Magnus Maximus' defeat of Gratian in the AD 380s. Magnus' troops had come from Britain, a province that does not appear to have contained any active mithraeum for nearly half a century before this, so it is possible that the image of the rock-birth at Septeuil was the subject an unsympathetic Roman soldier. Of course, one should always be wary of applying the historical sources to the archaeological evidence, but it is worth acknowledging that such a scenario was probably not unheard of at temple sites in the Late Roman world.

Additionally, natural disasters and accidental destructions may account for the violent fate of some mithraea, such as those at Carnuntum (earthquake) and Schachadorf (fire).

Of course, various mithraea have been uncovered that have yielded no evidence for a violent end, suggesting their congregations had either lost interest or moved somewhere else for mundane reasons. This would appear to be the case for a number of mithraea in Rome, which were left with their images mostly untouched, while various others situated in the interior provinces were found simply with their images removed. Precisely what became of these images is unclear, but it might be that such mithraea were simply used for a different function for a time, a function that left no explicit mark on the archaeological record.

Thus, there is no one single explanation as to why numerous mithraea were abandoned during the 4th c. If we are to rate the possible factors that caused the abandonment of mithraea at this time in terms of their frequency, barbarian incursion appears to be the most common. This is followed by Mithraic worshippers abandoning the mithraeum for passive reasons, such as their patrons dying or losing interest or Mithraic worshippers focusing their religious activity elsewhere. Christian iconoclasm would follow next in terms of frequency, with occasional examples that may have been victims of civil war, natural disaster, or accidental destruction.

So ended the worship of Mithras in mithraea amongst highly organised Mithraic communities, but did this mean that the worship of Mithras completely ceased? Recent evidence would suggest perhaps not, for, as we have seen, the fragmentation of images in mithraea need not necessarily represent a violent end. The evidence from Bornheim-Sechtem indicates that at least some Mithraic congregations at this time still viewed such items as being sacred and sought to retain them. Indeed, the evidence from this site points to a Mithraic congregation who rescued broken and burnt statuary from another mithraeum that had been destroyed in the latter half of the 4th c. The prevalence of broken Mithraic reliefs and statues that are missing the heads of Mithras, and on occasion his dagger hand and the head of the bull, in frontier regions, is a common theme. It may be that some Mithraic adherents sought to remove the most expressive parts of the image to carry as personal objects, especially if they felt the mithraeum was under threat. At Septeuil, the contrasting fates of two reliefs may indicate that this occurred here, with the rock-birth still whole but the face having received several heavy blows, while the main relief was broken into many pieces with the heads of Mithras and the bull removed.

CONCLUSION

The fate of the images at Konjic and Jajce may also have resulted from the adherents abandoning the mithraea, but not the worship of Mithras, given the precision used to remove certain parts of the images, and the lack of defacement on the others that remained. As a result, while the cult of Mithras may cease to be evident in the archaeological record from the early 5th c., the worship of Mithras, in at least some locations, may have continued. What form this took is impossible to discern. However, it is not difficult to imagine that as one generation moved to the next, these sculptural fragments, now far removed from their original context, would enter a new stage of their cultural biography. Just as sculptures can be refashioned or misidentified, so too may these last remnants of the Mithras cult have taken on new names and meanings, before being completely forgotten.

It is worth ending this study by identifying a number of lines of enquiry for future work that have emerged from it. Firstly, the evidence suggests that a significant review of many of the so-called archaeologically attested examples of Christian iconoclasm is required. Mithraea were supposedly frequently targeted by such groups, yet this study has shown that the evidence for this is not conclusive, and that much of the extant evidence has other, more viable interpretations. It is likely there are many other examples where Christian iconoclasm has long since been enshrined as the only, or at least most probable, reason for the demise of a mithraeum, yet a look at the original field report will show that this may not be the case. Indeed, during the writing of this thesis, I discovered a number of examples from Noricum and Pannonia of temples that were supposedly destroyed in the late 4th c., yet in the course of reviewing the excavation reports I could locate no secure dating

evidence for this. Often these dates were based on an unstratified coin, while the latest securely datable evidence originated from at least decades, sometimes centuries, earlier.[2] This also provides a cautionary tale for future archaeological investigations to avoid hastily interpreting the evidence to fit traditional narratives. Thankfully, with a high level of archaeological expertise now existing in many countries, future research may supply us with information that will help with the reinterpretation of older sites.

Another important point is that, as subsequent mithraea come to light and are excavated using modern techniques, one assumes a greater corpus of evidence will be amassed regarding the contexts of finds deposited in the late antique period. This will hopefully allow for future studies to assess the patterns of votive offerings and the retention of broken objects in these contexts; this will allow us to establish a more nuanced understanding of these ritual acts.

Finally, it is clear that there is much work still to be done concerning the religious life of the northern frontiers in this period, particularly concerning the accumulation of quantitative data. I know of no work that has collected any quantitative data on temples in Germany or the lower Danubian provinces, as Jouffroy has done for Italy and North Africa, or Fauduet for Gaul (this latter work only dealt with Gallo-Roman temples though). Once such datasets have been compiled, it will no doubt provide new and important insights into the transformation of the sacred landscape in these regions and the Roman world as a whole.

---

2 A discussion of this can be found in Walsh (2016).

Appendix A: Gazetteer of Mithraea Active in the 4th c. and Those That Exhibit Evidence of Christian Iconoclasm

A.   Britain

A.1   *Borcovicium (Housesteads)*
Selected Bibliography: *CIMRM* 1. 852–69; Bosanquet (1904); Clauss (1992) 82; Allason-Jones (2004) 184; Rushworth (2009) 242–43.

Excavated
1822 and 1898

Location
The mithraeum was built over a natural spring in an area known as 'Chapel Hill', which was situated outside of the main fort in the adjoining *vicus*. A temple to Mars Thincus existed nearby, as well as another cultic building that like the mithraeum was built over a natural spring. The latter contained numismatic evidence running to the reign of Constantine.

Structure
The temple lay on an east-west axis, measuring 4.80 m × 12.80 m. The entrance lay in the east wall, while the cult niche (2.13 m × 0.76 m) lay at the opposite western end. The north-west corner of the temple was uncovered in an excavation of 1822, but this was subsequently demolished. The outline of where this section of the building had stood could still be established in the later 1898 excavation. The central aisle (w. 1.65 m) was paved with flagstone that, at least in one area, had been covered with planks of oak and small birch logs. The central nave was flanked by two wooden benches (w. 1.52 m), the remains of which were still present *in situ*. Into the middle of the aisle was inserted a stone shaft made of flagstone and clay, from which the water from the natural spring rose. Two gutters, running east alongside the benches, were cut into the earlier floor to drain excess water.

Finds
During the 1822 excavation of the western end of the temple, an image of the rock-birth, surrounded by the signs of the zodiac, was uncovered *in situ* in the cult niche. Along with this were found various altars, a headless statue of one of the torchbearers, and fragments of the central limestone tauroctony image.

During the 1898 excavations, statues of the torchbearers and Aion were found lying face down in the centre of the nave, along with a further four small pieces from the central relief. All the statues were headless, although the head of one of the torchbearers was found elsewhere in the temple. Two altars were also uncovered: one dedicated to both a local deity, Cocidius, and Jupiter, while the other honoured Mars and Victory. It has been suggested that these, and another altar to Cocidius found in the 1882 excavation, originated elsewhere and were brought to the temple. The rest of the finds assemblage consisted of red and black-glazed pottery sherds; an iron knife; a Collingwood type T knobbed bow brooch; a two-strand twisted bronze bracelet; and a jet armlet bead of late 3rd/early 4th c. date.

Epigraphic Record
The altars found in 1822 consisted of: a dedication to Cocidius, a local deity, made by a soldier of the sixth legion; another to Sol by an individual named Herion; an altar to Mars and Victory; one erected by a centurion, on behalf of himself and his son, in AD 252, which appears to have suffered notable weathering; and a dedication by a *beneficarius consularis* for himself and his family. The altar found in 1898 dedicated to Cocidius and Jupiter was erected by soldiers of the *legio II Augusta*.

Chronology
A coin of Faustina II (d. AD 175) was found deposited in the floor layer of the temple, but the building is generally considered to date to the Severan period based on the style of the altar erected by the *beneficarius consularis*. It was evidently in use into the latter half of the 3rd c., given the altar of AD 252. The presence of a jet armlet bead, dating to the turn of the 4th c., provides a *terminus post quem* for the abandonment of the temple. A charcoal layer found in the 1898 excavations indicates that the wooden roof of the temple burnt down, following which, given the weathering evident on the altars, it would appear that the temple was then left open to the elements.

A.2   *Brocolitia (Carrawburgh)*
Selected Bibliography: *CIMRM* 1. 844–51; Richmond, *et al.* (1951); Clauss (1992) 79; Allason Jones (2004) 183–84.

Excavated
1950

Location
The mithraeum lay outside the fort, overlying a natural spring, on the east bank of a valley which also contained a temple to Coventina. Reliefs and altars from the Temple of Coventina were found deposited in a well nearby, although they had evidently been placed with care as they were still intact. On top of these items were found 16,000 coins (the latest dating to

AD 388) and items of jewellery. An open-air shrine dedicated to the Nymphs was also located next to the mithraeum, although this had been dismantled by the turn of the 4th c.

Structure

The mithraeum lay on a north-west by south-east axis. In its first phase, the temple consisted of a single room built from stone measuring 5.58 m × 7.92 m. The doorway (w. 1.28 m) was not located on the central alignment of the temple, but rather slightly off to the right. The first 1.28 m of the room was separated from the rest by a wooden screen, two stumps of which were found *in situ*, thus creating an antechamber. On the right-hand side of the anteroom was a drain from which water, emanating from a natural spring under the mithraeum, could be accessed. Another wooden stump, near the north-eastern wall, looks to have supported an item of furniture, possibly a cupboard. The nave consisted of a gravel strip (4.42 m × 1.27 m) and aligns with the door, rather than the central axis of the building. Nothing of the benches from this phase remained. At the far end of the temple, post-holes provided an indication of some form of frame, perhaps from which curtains hung to hide the altar platform. The remains of a small hearth (0.15m^2), which was bordered by slabs on its north-east and south-east sides, were also found in this area of the mithraeum. It contained a sizable amount of charcoal and three chicken bones. To the south-east of this, closer to the aisle, fragments of another Mediterranean pinecone were found underneath two slabs, along with a small deposit of hazel charcoal. No trace of a roof structure was found, but the excavator suggested a simple gabled roof may have been in place.

In building phase II.1, an extension terminating in an angular apse (1.74 m × 1.71 m) was added to the north-west end. The niche contained a platform which would have held the main cult image. The central aisle (now 1.88 m × 8.84 m) was moved to align with the central axis of the mithraeum. The anteroom was also expanded (now 2.23 m in length) by moving the line of posts further into the temple. The drain was completely sealed and a stone bench was installed on its south-west side; evidence of a hearth was found next to it. The remains of the stone foundations for the benches that ran either side of the nave, along with the steps that provided access to them on their south-east ends, were also recovered from this phase. As one entered the main chamber from the anteroom, one would have found oneself flanked by a base on either side, upon which probably stood images of the torchbearers.

Phases II.2 and II.3 did not include any structural changes, but consisted of a refurbishing of the inside of the mithraeum. There is, however, evidence that the roof required reinforcing, as nine post-holes appear in phase II.2 at irregular intervals in front of the benches, with three on the north-east side of the nave and six on the south-west. The floor of the sanctuary was raised up, paved and covered in a layer of heather. This also meant stepped access to the benches was no longer required. In the anteroom, the floor now reached the level of the small bench on its south-west side, and a pit was dug into the floor and cut through the bench. The pit was 0.48 m wide, 2.13 m long and 0.46 m deep, large enough for a person to fit into, but was only found to contain a few sheep bones.

In phase II.3 the pit was covered over when the floor of the mithraeum was raised again, this time using clay and covered with oak boards. New post-holes for roof supports were installed, two on the north-east edge of the nave and three on the south-east, this time at regular intervals. To the right of the cult niche was a group of posts that appear to have supported storage tables or stands, close to which fragments of amphorae were found. A new bench was also installed in the antechamber.

The third phase of the mithraeum began with the building being completely reconstructed at a higher level (only the capitals of the pedestals of the torchbearers from previous phases could be seen rising from the floor), but it retained roughly the same dimensions as its predecessor. It was predominantly a clay-brick building, although some masonry from the older phases was reused. The doorway (w. 1.07 m) was still offset from the main axis. The anteroom was expanded once again, now measuring 2.45 m across, and still contained a hearth on a raised platform. The floor was made of reused stone and clay. In the north corner of the room stood a pedestal, at whose base was found a broken statue of the mother goddess and a large jar, perhaps for offerings to her. There were fewer post-holes designating the partition between the anteroom and main chamber, but their size (0.13 m^2) indicates the poles were larger than in previous phases.

The length of the benches was reduced to 4.87 m, and they were once again fronted with wattle. In front of the benches ran a line of oak roof-posts at 1.5 m intervals. Four small altars were placed along the sides of the nave with two on each side; evidence for a plaster coating was found over the wattle and around these altars. The cult niche was reduced in size and was fronted by three larger altars.

Finds

Various items used in the operation of the mithraeum were found across the different occupational phases, including 19 drinking vessels, platters, an iron fire-shovel, a thatch-hook, and a candlestick. A great deal of animal bone was also found in all levels of occupation, including a significant number of bird and pig remains, along with some lamb bones. The three large altars which sat in front of the cult niche are very different in style: one depicts an image of Sol, garbed in a tunic and radiate crown, and holding a whip; the other two bear no images and are simply inscribed. Under these altars was a pit containing intentionally packed rubble in its top layer, below which was deposited a small, upright Castor-ware beaker, bordered on three sides by stones. Inside the vessel were

APPENDIX A

two lumps of pinecone fuel, along with the head and two vertebrae of a domestic fowl. Alongside the beaker was a small tin cup, which also contained a small amount of pinecone fuel, while to the left of the altars a Mediterranean pinecone was found. Four smaller altars were also found, one of which (erected originally to the 'Mothers' by Albinus Quartus) shows evidence of weathering, suggesting it was brought from elsewhere. Additionally, this altar was also turned to face the bench, so the face bearing the inscription to the Mothers could not be seen, suggesting it might have been reused as a Mithraic altar with a new inscription (now lost) painted on the plain side. Whether this altar bore any relation to the mother goddess image found in the anteroom, is unknown.

Epigraphic Record

All three of the large altars were erected by prefects: both Lucius Antonius Proculus and Aulus Cluentius Habitus were recorded as coming from the first cohort *Batavians Antoniniana*, while Marcus Simplicius does not provide the name of his cohort. It is reasonable to assume, however, that Simplicius was also a prefect of the *Batavians Antoniniana*, and that the role of prefect in this cohort was linked to the upkeep of the temple; it may be that by this point, with the two altars already in place, he had no need to record his title. The four small altars do not provide any epigraphic information, aside from one which was erected to the 'Mothers' by Albinus Quartus.

Chronology

The precise date of construction is unknown, but its use by the *Batavians Antoniniana* indicates it probably lies in the Severan period. Layers from Phases I–II.3 all contain 3rd c. pottery, indicating that the temple was refurbished throughout this period, probably due to structural problems caused by drainage. The end of phase II.3 is marked with evidence for the burning of the screen dividing the anteroom and main chamber, and the burning of the wattle edge of the benches, as well as the breaking of a fine stone laver. The disturbance of the floor levels has been suggested as being the result of people looking for hidden valuables, although one cannot rule out accidental destruction either.

The final phase (III) occurred at the turn of the 4th c., with the final occupational layer containing 4th c. pottery and five coins, the latest of which dated to the reign of Maximian (AD 296–308). This phase does not appear to have lasted long, as a rubbish deposit lay across the ruins of the temple, among which was found a coin of Magnentius (AD 350). The fate of the temple fittings was varied: one of the torchbearer statues had its head removed (although dowel-holes present in the neck line suggest that, rather than beheading, the head was simply removed), while the other was cut down at the shins. The image of the mother goddess, which stood in the anteroom, was left untouched, and the main cult relief was removed, although it may have been broken, as a fragment of one of the bull's horns was left behind.

A.3   *Londinium (London)*

Selected Bibliography: *CIMRM* 1. 810–26; Grimes (1968); Shepherd (1998); Clauss (1992) 80–81; Bryan *et al.* (2017).

Excavated
1954

Location
The mithraeum was situated on the east bank of the Walbrook River. Recent excavations suggest it was bordered to the north and south by housing.

Structure
The temple (19.27 m × 7.84 m) was constructed over rubbish dumps laid down in the first half of the 3rd c. Its foundations consisted of mortared rag-stone rubble, while its walls were built from coursed rag-stone. It follows the standard layout of a mithraeum, although its apse was rounded (as opposed the more common square format) and required three external buttresses. The mithraeum lay on an east-west axis, with the entrance located in the east wall. Recent excavations have uncovered evidence of at least two anterooms, one of which contained a well. The stone threshold at the entrance to the building had sockets for two doors. Two steps led down from the entrance to the sunken floor of the temple, which was re-laid nine times during the course of occupation. The remains of sleeper-walls indicated where the side benches had been, the tops of which were lined with column bases, seven on each wall. Evidence of timber fittings for the benches was found on top of the walls. A timber lined channel was cut into the nave floor alongside the north sleeper wall when floor phase 3 was in use. In the period of floor phases 3 and 4, a timber frame, which could have supported a great weight, was added to the south bench. The laying of the fourth-floor phase brought the level of the nave to the same as the sleeper walls, necessitating the raising of the benches via the addition of squat walls between the columns. In the south-west corner of the mithraeum, to the left of the apse, was a well. Directly in front of the apse was at least another two steps; given the height between the second step and the dais, a third may have been either removed or destroyed. Inside the apse was a plinth on which the tauroctony was displayed; both this and the inside of the apse showed evidence of contemporary plastering. Also present along the curve of the apse were four holes, all the same size and roughly equidistant to each other, which may have held posts to support more furnishings. During the time of the fourth-floor level, a recess was created just below the plinth, which probably resulted from the removal of the tauroctony image paid for by Ulpius Silvanus.

Finds

The group of sculptures buried in pit A, when floor level five was in use, included marble heads of Mithras, Sarapis and Minerva, a large hand of Mithras, a forearm from the main cult image (the only piece of it found), a marble Mercury statuette, and a stone laver. The head of Mithras had been separated from the neck via a blow from a blunt instrument, although both head and neck were buried together otherwise undamaged, while the heads of Sarapis and Minerva do not show any sign of such damage and had probably been attached to bodies fashioned separately. The hand of Mithras holds the remnants of a knife pointing downwards, but whether the hand was part of a larger scene or stood alone could not be ascertained. The limestone left hand and forearm of Mithras, his arm wrapped in a sleeve, is smaller than a life-size equivalent; the hand grasps the upper lip of the bull. The statue of Mercury depicts the naked god reclined on his cloak, accompanied by a ram and tortoise. Barring the break on Mithras' neckline, none of these objects show any sign of intentional damage and are incredibly well-preserved.

Several other marble items found during construction work in 1889 are believed to have also originated from pit A, as they were recorded as having been found next to it. These include the upper body of a water-deity, a statuette of a *genius* with its head missing, and a round relief of the tauroctony that is bordered by the signs of the zodiac. This relief was dedicated by Ulpius Silvanus, a veteran of the *legio II Augusta*.

Found *in situ* in floor level 6 is part of an inscription which might be Mithraic. What remains uses the term *invictus* and mentions the Tetrarchy; it is dated to AD 307–308. Given the excellent state of preservation provided by the waterlogged environment in which the mithraeum was discovered, a great many other finds were also uncovered, including pottery, items made of wood, iron, copper alloy, leather and bone. A Mediterranean pinecone was found partly burnt in the layers dating to the second half of the 3rd c.

Epigraphic Record

The only person we know from the mithraeum is the aforementioned *emeritus legionis* Ulpius Silvanus.

Chronology

The layers immediately preceding the construction of the mithraeum contained pottery that was dated, at the latest, to the mid 3rd c. Given that floor level two also contained pottery dating to the mid 3rd c., the construction of the mithraeum evidently lay sometime around AD 240–50. In total, there are nine distinct floor levels known to have been laid in the building, the first four of which belong to its time as a mithraeum. The rapid addition of new floors was probably due to the unstable ground on which the temple was constructed; as areas subsided, the floor required patchwork additions to keep it relatively level. Floor level three contained a coin

of the usurper Marius (AD 269). Floor four, the last definite Mithraic floor level, cannot be dated, but the inscription referring to the second Tetrarchy (AD 307–308), found in floor level six appears to be Mithraic, which, along with coins from floor five, indicates that the building ceased to be a mithraeum in the first decades of the 4th c. Into floor level five, near the entrance of the central sanctuary, a pit was cut, into which sculptures from the mithraeum were deposited, although the feature contained no dating evidence. The mithraeum appears to have been subsequently transformed into a building to worship another deity, possibly Bacchus. The colonnades in front of the benches were removed, the floor level of the nave rose to that of the benches, and the well was covered over, thus a flat and open surface—very different to a standard mithraeum—was created. We do not know whether the anteroom existed when the building was used as a mithraeum—it can only be definitely linked to the later phases—although the presence of such a space is typical among mithraea.

B.   Germany

B.1   *Biesheim*

Selected Bibliography: Pétry and Kern (1978); Kern (1991); Plouin (2004).

Excavated

1976–79

Location

The mithraeum lay on the edge of the *vicus* in an area that does not appear to have been densely populated.

Structure

The mithraeum was orientated north to south and was constructed out of basalt masonry blocks. It measured 11.50 m × 7.25 m and consisted of the main cult room and two anterooms. One of the anterooms, which was 7.00 m in length, was attached to the building at a later stage. The entrance was 1.40 m wide and one had to descend two steps, following which one would then pass through the second anteroom with a small storage space on both the left and right. Inside the *cella*, the benches (l. 5.80 m × w. 1.80 m) ran either side of the nave, the surface of which consisted of silty clay and gravel, and at the terminus of the nave stood the cult niche. In the south-east corner of the room there was also a small well.

Finds

Remains of the main cult image, which was made of limestone, were found scattered across the floor of the *cella*. In the second anteroom, various pot-sherds were also found, upon which were depictions of a lion, snakes, a female head, a torchbearer, and Mithras as the bull-killer. Coins deposited

APPENDIX A

during the second phase of occupation were found scattered across the floor, but a list of these has not been published. A pit was cut into the floor sometime in the late 4th c., into which the skull of an ox was placed.

Chronology

The mithraeum was constructed over occupational layers dated to the 1st c. AD, giving the temple an approximate construction date of the early 2nd c. This is complemented by ceramic finds of the 2nd and 3rd c. found in the mithraeum and surrounding pits. At some point in the late 3rd c., the mithraeum suffered fire damage, and the reliefs and statues were broken into pieces. Following this, the temple appears to have continued in use; the fragments from the earlier phase, as well as some traces of wall-plaster, were covered over. This meant the floor level of the nave rose, but the benches were not raised to compensate. Given the burial of the sculpture fragments and the raising of the nave floor, it seems unlikely the building continued to be used as a mithraeum. There is no ceramic evidence from this final period, but around 200 coins were recovered, the latest dating to AD 395 after which date the building was burnt down.

B.2   *Bornheim-Sechtem*

Selected Bibliography: Ulbert (2004); Wulfmeier (2004); Ulbert, Wulfmeier and Huld-Zetsche (2004).

Excavated

1998–99

Location

The mithraeum was situated several metres from what appears to have been a villa. The villa has not been dated precisely, but finds indicate it was occupied between the 2nd and 3rd c., while nearby burials run to the first half of the 4th c. Early medieval burials were also found in the same area, suggesting perhaps a period of abandonment before occupation resumed. Unfortunately, the rest of the settlement has not been subject to excavation.

Structure

The mithraeum appears to have had three phases of occupation. In all phases it lay on a north-east to south-west orientation. All that can be discerned about the first two phases is that it the building covered *ca.* 13.5 × 6.8 m, contained a shaft in the centre of its nave, and there was a channel that flowed out of the temple just in front of the south-west wall.

In its third and final phase, the mithraeum was reduced in size to *ca.* 7.2 × 5.0 m. The floor of the *cella* was probably around 1 m below the ground level. Two benches ran either side of the central aisle at a width of 1.70 m. In the centre of the nave was a shaft *ca.* 0.50 m deep and lined with tufa blocks, which was dug next to the shaft from the first phase. Situated

in line with this shaft was a niche in the north-west wall. At the western end of the mithraeum were two sandstone blocks, one in the corner and the other in the central aisle. There was no remaining evidence of the cult niche or platform that held the tauroctony here.

Finds

In the central shaft of the final phase mithraeum the left leg of a statuette was found, as well as a yellow-glazed ceramic relief depicting Cautes, a coin of Valentinian damaged by fire, a cup, a boar's tooth, and slag. In the niche, various sculpture fragments damaged by fire were discovered, along with a yellow-glazed ceramic fragment depicting a lion, and a small silver leaf inscribed with "*D(eo) I(nvicto Mithrae) BENAGIVS V(otum) S(olvit) L(ibens) M(erito)*". Buried under the niche was another cup. In front of the south-east wall, presumably where the cult image had stood, 25 coins had been deposited, which ranged from the reigns of Postumus and Laelianus (both AD 260) to Valentinian III (d. AD 402). A shaft from the first phase was found in the middle of the nave, which contained another piece of yellow-glazed ceramic depicting a snake. The three sherds of yellow-glazed ceramic appear to all be from the same vessel, despite being buried in different contexts. Evidently, the vessel was broken in the first phase, with one sherd being placed in the shaft and the others being kept by the adherents, suggesting that some particular importance was attached to them. From the sculpture fragments, statuettes of Cautes and Cautopates have been discerned, with the former dated to the 2nd c. by the style of his tunic, although many parts of the statuettes were also absent, including their heads. These sculptural elements also exhibited fire damage, but no traces of destruction by fire were discerned from the later *cella*; this suggests they may have come from another mithraeum, and are perhaps related to the burnt coin of Valentinian I. Fragments of what may have been the central relief were found on the *cella* floor, but no traces of Mithras or the bull were evident among these.

In the vicinity of the mithraeum were various pits, one of which had been cut straight through the entrance to the shrine. Two large pits just beyond the limit of the surrounding structure, which look to predate the later mithraeum stratigraphically, were found to contain nothing but sherds of pottery, although there may have been material that has since decomposed. Another pit, even further to the north-east, contained architectural remains from the temple, as did another pit situated 3.5 m west of the mithraeum.

Chronology

The mithraeum appears to have undergone three building phases. The earliest two are evident from the earlier masonry found under the north-western corner of the later mithraeum, and from surrounding patches of gravel which are also stratigraphically below the later *cella*, but these cannot be dated.

The construction of the final phase may date to the mid 4th c., given the presence of the Valentinan coin in the later shaft, and the fact that the majority of the coins found on the mithraeum floor dated to the mid to late 4th c. At the turn of the 5th c. it appears that the mithraeum was levelled, with various architectural elements buried in surrounding pits.

B.3 *Gimmeldingen*
Selected Bibliography: *CIMRM* 2. 1313–22; Schwertheim (1974) 140; Clauss (1992) 110.

Excavated
1926

Location
The mithraeum was located in a rural setting near to the Mußach stream.

Structure
No record.

Finds
All the altars and reliefs were made of sandstone. The main cult relief was found intact, but a statue of Cautes was missing its upper half, and a relief of Mercury displayed evidence of damage to the god's face and the caduceus in his left hand. The upper part of a relief depicting a bearded man alongside Minerva was also found, but there is no indication of specific damage to their faces. Three altars were uncovered, one of which was fragmented.

Epigraphic Record
Materninius Faustinus held the supposed lowest grade of *corax*, yet he was evidently a wealthy individual as he paid for the mithraeum and several altars. A man named Potentianus also served as a *pater*. No additional information is known about either man. The terms used in the inscriptions here differ from what one usually finds, such as 'Midre' instead of Mithras and '*carax*' instead of *corax*.

Chronology
The temple was badly recorded, and little information survives with which to build a chronology. An inscription on the main cult relief, however, does provide us with a precise date (22nd January AD 325) for the consecration of the mithraeum. It appears to have been destroyed by fire, but no dating evidence for when this occurred was retrieved.

B.4 *Reichweiler*
Selected Bibliography: Bernhard (1990).

The mithraeum, which was located in rural marshland, was first acknowledged in 1588 and its remains sketched in 1824.

The temple no longer exists today, aside from the natural rock-face onto which it was attached, but a general illustration of it has survived; it was a 5.15 m long wooden structure, with a side room and gabled roof. The main cult image was carved into the rock-face. Ceramics and a small number of coins (running from the reign of Claudius Gothicus to that of Constans) found nearby indicate activity in the 3rd and 4th c. here, although given the context of their discovery they cannot be considered entirely reliable.

B.5 *Rockenhausen*
Selected Bibliography: *CIMRM* 2. 1272–74; Schwertheim (1974) 135.

Excavated
1898

Information regarding the supposed mithraeum at Rockenhausen is scant, with the excavator's notes the only record, and these are often conflicting. It was situated in the grounds of a rural estate, and the structure was recorded as having been evidently destroyed by fire. Around 50 coins were found at the site and date to between AD 330 and AD 395. Two fragments from a relief appearing to depict the head and body of a torchbearer were found in the sanctuary, and the presence of these is the main reason for its identification as a mithraeum. Along with these was found the head from a statue of a bearded man, and a dedication to Mercury.

C. Noricum

C.1 *Ad Enum (Pons Aeni)*
Selected Bibliography: Garbsch (1985); Steidl (2008).

Excavated
1978–80

Location
Ad Enum lay across the river from Pons Aeni, which marked an important road junction and acted as a customs station, trading hub, and pottery manufacturing centre. The mithraeum itself was situated on a hillside 70 m from the bank of the river.

Structure
The sanctuary was *ca.* 8.75 m × 12.10 m and was built on a north-south axis. Two podia (w. 1.90 m × h. 0.5 m) were located on either side of the central nave (w. 3.57 m). Both the floor and the podia had mortar surfaces which were probably covered with planks of wood. A tiled roof was supported by beams, the existence of which were denoted by brick panels. The entrance to the mithraeum (w. 1.50 m) was located in the south wall and was covered by a wooden porch

APPENDIX A

(w. 2.00 m). A layer of burning was found at the threshold of the mithraeum, probably the remains of a series of wooden steps that descended into the sanctuary.

In the central nave three pits were discovered. Pit 1 (semicircular: 1.80 m × 1.40 m × d. 0.50 m), located just in front of where the cult image stood, contained two layers: a top layer of gravelly-humus and a lower layer of loamy humus containing charcoal, mortar and tuff rubble and numerous altar fragments, shards, broken glass, nails and coins. Pit 2 was approximately trapezoidal (3 m × 1.8 m × d. 0.4m). It had a single fill of black humus with many numerous broken altar remains, bricks, broken glass, nails and coins contained within it. Pit 3 was rectangular (2.00 m × 1.10 m × d. 0.20 m) with a single dark black fill containing a lot of charcoal.

Finds

570 coins were found in and around the mithraeum, of which 553 could be identified. Which coins were from the sanctuary and which came from outside of it is unclear, as they were all assumed to have initially been deposited within the mithraeum and subsequently washed down the hill. The majority of the coins were minted in the 4th c., including the largest known collection of coins from the reign of Magnus Maximus (AD 383–88) discovered in the region. In Garbsch's opinion, this vast number of coins does not come from a single hoard, but rather was possibly deposited in the sanctuary as votive offerings.

Chronology

A recent reappraisal of the site by Steidl has placed the construction of the mithraeum in the mid to late 2nd c. It appears to have been abandoned *ca.* AD 395 when the last coin was deposited.

C.2   *Lentia (Linz)*

Selected Bibliography: *CIMRM* 2. 1414–21; Karnitsch (1956) and (1962).

Excavated

1953–54

Location

The mithraeum was situated in what may have been the temple district of the town. Alongside the mithraeum two other temples were found, one of which was identified (somewhat tenuously) as being dedicated to the Capitoline Triad, due to the division of one side of the building into three *cella*. The other structure was identified as a temple to *Dea Roma* and the *Genius Augusti*, although in this case statue bases survive to confirm this. Both neighbouring temples were destroyed in the latter half of the 3rd c., although the temple to *Dea Roma* was rebuilt at the same time as the mithraeum was constructed.

Structure

The mithraeum was not a completely new construction, but rather made use of the remains of a pre-existing building. It was aligned south-east to north-west and consisted of several rooms and two anterooms. The room furthest south appears to have been a kitchen (l. 6.90 m × w. 4.50 m) and was subdivided by a low wall. The middle room (l. 5.40 m × w. 2.70 m) housed a well (radius 1.24 m). To the north of this room lay the main sanctuary (l. 5.10 m × w. 2.70 m), which, unusually, contained no benches, but it is likely these were made of wood and destroyed by the fire that occurred in the *cella* when the mithraeum was abandoned. A small balustrade, upon which monuments could be placed, was found at the end of the nave. The floor of this room was made of mortar and retained traces of red paint, while its roof was probably vaulted and used wicker-work and loam.

Finds

The mithraeum did not yield much in the way of finds. A small circular medallion relief depicts the tauroctony, and has the rare addition of a lion being featured along with the other animals. It also depicts three additional scenes, one of which remains indistinct, while the others show interactions between Mithras and Sol. Two fragments of a border which encircled this relief were also found. Originally the relief displayed numerous scenes, but now only those with images of the rock birth and a goat (or possibly an ibex) with another animal's feet resting on it, are all that remain. Fragments of an altar were found, along with the remains of numerous ceramic vessels, including sherds, which appear to have been part of vases decorated with snakes encircling their handles. A terracotta plate, with graffiti etched on the centre of one of its faces, has seven holes through its edge. Alongside 122 coins, a silver votive plaque, with either horns or a crescent moon inscribed onto it, was also found. Finally, traces of fruit (4210 g) were also uncovered in the kitchen, including vines, prunes, berries, apple-pips, walnuts and millets. Although assumed to be votives by the excavators, the presence of a kitchen may indicate these were to have been used for the sacred meal.

Epigraphic Record

Two fragments of a stone altar bore the name of the veteran Tiberius Ursalus.

Chronology

Six coins were found underneath the nave, all of which pre-date AD 275, while of the 122 coins found within the mithraeum, nearly 60% date to AD 363–78, 10% were from AD 330–63 and less than 8% were from beyond AD 378, with the final coin dating to the reign of Honorius (AD 394). One hundred and eight of these coins were found in a layer of burning which covered the floor of the *cella*, suggesting that a fire signalled the end of the sanctuary's use.

C.3 *Schachadorf*

Selected Bibliography: *CIMRM* 2.1409–12.

Excavated
1935–36

Location
The mithraeum lay close to the town of Ovilava, one of the main imperial administrative centres in Late Roman Noricum.

Structure
It consisted of two rooms, a vestibule and the main sanctuary (l. 8.00 m). The vestibule had two bases, presumably for the torchbearers; located beside each of these were two lamps.

Finds
The mithraeum contained 23 coins dating from Claudius II to Valentinian II, giving a *terminus post quem* for the end of structure's use of AD 392. Additional finds included an iron dagger, a knife, and chicken, sheep and pig bones. A depiction of the rock-birth was discovered at the far end of the second room, with a base on the far wall designed to hold it. In this image, Mithras holds two objects which cannot be discerned, while a snake can be seen winding its way up the rock and over Mithras.

Chronology
Judging from the coin finds, the mithraeum was probably constructed in the late 3rd c. and survived until the late 4th. The image of the rock-birth was found in a layer that provided evidence of burning, but given that this image remained intact, the fire may have been accidental.

C.4 *St. Urban*

Selected Bibliography: *CIMRM* 2.1442–43; Leber (1955) 187–91.

Excavated
1838

Location
The shrine was located in a small natural grotto, situated on the south side of Lake St. Urban in the central Carinthian Lakes region.

Structure
It was a mithraeum of modest size (8.50 m × 5.50 m). Its floor had been partially paved and the remains of a water-pipe were discovered. An even smaller grotto (w. 5.00m) is connected to this and also appears to have also been used as part of the mithraeum.

Finds
Little is known about its excavation, but finds, such as animal bones, pottery fragments, and pieces of charcoal, give some indication of the ritual meal possibly being performed here. Oddly, children's teeth were also apparently among the assemblage. The smaller grotto yielded a limestone slab bearing an inscription stylistically dating to the 3rd c. Coin finds from the larger grotto include those of Constantius II, Crispus, Valentinian I, Valens and Gallus, which suggests a short period of occupation in the mid 4th c.

Chronology
The mithraeum appears to have been in use in the mid to late 4th c.

D. Pannonia

D.1 *Aquincum IV ('of Symphorus')*

Selected Bibliography: *CIMRM* 2.1767–72; Tóth (1988) 46–51.

Excavated
1942

Location
This mithraeum was discovered in a residential area close to the southern town wall. It lay *ca.* 150 m south of the Mithraeum of Victorinus, which was constructed in the early 3rd c.

Structure
The mithraeum (l. 17.00 m × w. 9.00 m) was orientated east to west and appears to have had two construction phases. Initially, when one entered the mithraeum one found oneself in an anteroom, from which one could proceed forward into the *cella* or turn left into another anteroom. The *cella* consisted of the standard tripartite plan. On the back western wall was a platform (w. 2.00 m × d. 0.40 m) with a niche for the central relief. In the second phase, the *cella* was enlarged, with benches no longer reaching the back wall; they were now 2 m away from it. The niche was refashioned and decorated with stucco and had a cult statue placed in it, while the room to the south was also repaired. The anteroom located to the side was also enlarged and divided into two.

Finds
Small fragments of a statue depicting Mithras slaying the bull were found in front of the niche, along with the remains of statues of the torchbearers either side. A terracotta relief of a goddess, who may be Venus, was also discovered in the *cella*. A limestone altar was found to the right side of the podium wall and a fragment of another was found near the entrance, alongside which the remnants of a marble water basin were situated. Other finds included: sherds of a *terra-sigillata* bowl, with its handle moulded like a dog's head; a vase depicting a serpent; four pine-apples made of sandstone; 23 balls of stone; and seven altars made of sandstone (bearing no inscriptions).

APPENDIX A

Chronology

The mithraeum underwent two construction phases. Its precise construction date is unknown, but judging from the coin evidence it was probably built in the mid 2nd c. The expansion of the building is thought to have occurred under the Severans, when widespread construction work was undertaken in Aquincum. A total of 32 coins have been recovered from the mithraeum, dating from Domitian to Constantine (the latest coin appears to be from *ca*. AD 319). There were only two Constantinian coins uncovered, with no Tetrarchic coins. The majority of the coins come from the 2nd and 3rd c., with Probus (AD 276–82) the latest pre-Constantinian emperor.[1]

D.2   *Carnuntum I*

Selected Bibliography: *CIMRM* 2. 1664–80; Clauss (1992) 158–59.

Excavated

1852

Location

The shrine was located on the side of a hill outside of the town, not too far from the large cult complex at Pfaffenberg.

Structure

The report does not provide much detail in terms of the dimensions of the mithraeum. The apse, which is described as being built from a mix of the natural rock and masonry, was the only part of the temple to be found extant to a substantial degree at the time of excavation. The remains of a wall with an entrance were also uncovered.

Finds

The sanctuary produced the remains of four statues, two of which had their heads removed (both are likely to have been Mithras). Seven altars (one in marble the others in sandstone), several of which bore inscriptions, were also recovered mostly intact. Evidence for coal and wood burning was found, with layers of ash (containing bones and teeth from oxen, sheep and goats) discovered, along with fragments of terracotta vessels.

Chronology

An inscription on one of the altars refers to the *legio XIIII gemina*, suggesting that the mithraeum came into existence in the first decades of the 2nd c. It was restored at some point by C. Atius Secundus, although the exact date of this remains unknown. Two coins were found, one of Gordianus III (AD 238–44) and another of Constans I (dating from his elevation to Caesar in AD 333). The latter provides a *terminus post quem* for the occupation of the mithraeum, but given the

---

1   I am grateful to those at the BTM Aquincum Museum for providing me with this information.

lack of adequate recording this dating cannot be considered definitive.

D.3   *Carnuntum III*

Selected Bibliography: *CIMRM* 2. 1682–1722; Bormann (1895); Clauss (1992) 159–60.

Excavated

1894

Location

This mithraeum was located on the eastern edge of the civilian town, although what buildings it neighboured is unclear.

Structure

This mithraeum is one of the largest ever discovered (l. 34.00 m × w. 10.00 m). It was constructed on an east-west axis, with its entrance at the eastern end. First, one passed through two anterooms (l. 8.50 m and l. 3.50 m) before finally entering the *cella* (l. 8.00m), which contained the usual nave (w. 4.00–4.50 m) and parallel benches (h. 0.60 m × w. 1.50–1.85 m × l. 15.00 m).

Finds

The central sandstone tauroctony was found at the western end of the nave in pieces, of which numerous fragments were missing. It has now been restored and is one of the largest bull-slaying scenes ever found (h. 2.75 m × w. 3.88 m). Judging from holes on the reverse of the relief, it was originally attached to the wall. Another sizable find was an altar carved from stone, which was supported by six figures and decorated with a further three. These nine figures, beginning from the front of the altar and circling it clockwise, have been interpreted as Caelus, Ver, Favonius, Autumnus, Eurus, Septentrio, Hiems, Auster and Aestas (i.e. the winds and the seasons). Smaller finds included lamps, pottery, vessels decorated with snakes, and a shell carved from sandstone which most likely served as a water basin. No additional Mithraic reliefs, other than the central taurocteny, were found in the mithraeum, although another bull-slaying relief was found nearby. Additionally, a statue depicting a lion with its front paws resting on the bull's head, another lion on a block of sandstone, and the head of a Medusa, were also found in the temple.

Chronology

A coin of Macrinus (AD 217–18), which was found near the entrance of the mithraeum, provides us with the earliest dating evidence. There is no subsequent information regarding dating, but the Tetrarchic dedication of AD 308, recording the restoration of a mithraeum, is believed to relate to this temple. The altar on which the dedication was inscribed was found sometime prior to 1795, but where is unclear. However, there are three reasons to believe this altar originated from this temple. Firstly, the altar depicting numerous deities is unlikely to have been originally erected in a Mithraic context and it may have been brought to the temple as part of the Tetrarchic renovation. Secondly, Bormann argued that ceramic fragments found under a wall of the anteroom indicated that this wall was of a later date than the original structure. Thirdly, as the identification of Mithraeum 'II' remains uncertain, that Mithraeum 'I' lay far outside the town, and Mithraeum 'III' was not only the largest of these three, but one of the largest provincial mithraea known to exist, it appears the likely candidate for the imperial restoration. If this is the mithraeum referred to in the inscription, then this provides a *terminus post quem* for when it was abandoned.

D.4 *Poetovio II (Ptuj)*

Selected Bibliography: *CIMRM* 2. 1509–77; Abramić (1925) 63–73; Selem (1980) 43–83; Beskow (1980); Horvat *et al.* (2003) 173–74.

Excavated
1901

Location
The mithraeum was located *ca.* 20 m from Mithraeum I in an area of the town that also contained warehouses, administrative buildings, and temples to the *Nutrices* and Jupiter.

Structure
The mithraeum measured 13.40 m × 7.30 m and the majority of its floor-plan was taken up by a central nave *ca.* 4.00 m wide. Worshippers entered from the eastern end via an anteroom. The benches (h. 0.70 m × w. 1.00 m) ran down both the north and south sides of the sanctuary. The surfaces of the benches were covered in loam. The sanctuary was constructed over a spring, which was channelled up into a marble-plated water-basin (h. 0.65 m × w. 0.85m–0.92 m), from which the water was drained away by a canal. The water-basin was later repaired using material from the nearby sanctuary of the *Nutrices*, which included an altar dedicated to the *Nutrices* by Fl. Iovinus. The same Fl. Iovinus appears on an inscription from the mithraeum as well, dating to AD 244, thus the repairs to the drain must have occurred sometime around this date. At the far western end of the interior nave is a niche (h. 0.80 m × w. 2.35 m × d. 0.90 m) which held the cult relief.

Finds
Twelve trapezophores (supports for low tables) were recorded, six lined against each bench. Abramić describes them as being adorned with the images of lion's heads, but the only trace of such decoration is a single complete example adorned with a paw. Another marble water-basin, with a rose design, was also found near the entrance. The remains of various altars, reliefs and statuettes were also present. Only a few of the altars survived relatively intact. The largest of these was erected by M. Antonius Celer, while another was paid for by Epictetus

and Viator, and the other is not inscribed. The main cult relief had been broken into numerous pieces. Several other reliefs were discovered, the largest of which depicts several scenes involving Mithras, Sol, and what could be Cautes and Cautopates emerging from cypresses alongside Mithras. Another smaller fragment depicts a person in oriental dress walking to the right. These fragments would have bordered the relief's right-side, while Abramić records a piece of the border, which ran along the top of the tauroctony, which was engraved with images of Aion, a serpent and Caelus, but the whereabouts of this piece is unknown. Along with numerous fragments of reliefs, various other elements of representations have been found, including a number of marble heads wearing Phyrgian caps, and other body parts. One damaged statue depicts a version of the rock-birth in which Mithras is being entwined by a snake. Aside from the usual characters depicted, Luna appears on one relief, Hercules is alongside Jupiter on another, while Jupiter also appears alone, possibly battling the giants, in another engraving. It is also worth mentioning that, similar to some of the imagery of several other mithraea in the region, a lion is depicted with a pig's head in its grasp.

Chronology
The earliest evidence we have is an inscription that refers to Geta as Caesar, which would provide a date of AD 198–209. The sanctuary was certainly still in use sometime during the 4th c., as the vast majority of coin finds date from the 330s–70s, with a *terminus post quem* for the end of the mithraeum of AD 388. Eighty of these coins were found in the water basin, most of which dated to the first half of the 4th c.

D.5 *Poetovio III*

Selected Bibliography: *CIMRM* 2. 1578–1612; Abramić (1925) 172–93; Selem (1980) 84–109.

Excavated
1913

Location
The mithraeum was built near the Drava River, some distance from Mithraea I and II, between two villas. A statue of Magna Mater was found in the remains of a building to the east of the mithraeum, perhaps denoting this was also a religious building.

Structure
The occupation of the mithraeum consisted of at least two phases, with the walls of the first building (l. 11.20 m × w. 6.85) constructed out of pebble and the later additions erected in brick. The original structure had an adjoining anteroom, which was incorporated into the *cella* in the second phase, while another anteroom was added in front of this to compensate. Extensions were also added to the eastern and western sides

APPENDIX A

of the mithraeum, with the former acting as a possible storage area for ritual artefacts. In both phases, the temple conforms to the typical mithraeum plan, with a central nave formed by two benches running parallel down the side walls, which in the second phase were lengthened to the end of the former anteroom. At the north end of the nave a base constructed out of brick was used as a podium, upon which the central cult image sat. This was later enlarged to be the same breadth as the nave. Evidence of red paint and stucco could be found to the right side of this platform, and the side walls were painted white with red edges. The roof may have been made of wood, given that traces of loam were found on the floor of the mithraeum.

Finds

The fragments of the main relief were found at the terminus of the nave, where it originally would have stood. Only the sheath of Mithras' dagger and the part of the bull being stabbed by Mithras survive from the two central actors, along with the images of the serpent, the dog and the upper part of one of the torchbearers. Based on the surviving pieces, Vermaseren (in *CIMRM*) observed that the scene was occurring within a cave. Bordering this relief were smaller depictions, including various interactions between Sol and Mithras, who wear the usual eastern attire. A large marble altar, found just in front of the remains of the relief, depicts the water miracle, along with a scene described by Vermaseren as showing Mithras appearing to offer Sol a dagger, with pieces of meat speared onto it across a burning altar. The altar is inscribed with reference to Augustus Flavius Aper, who commanded the *legio V Macedonia* and the *legio XIII Gemina*. Another well-preserved marble altar was found halfway down the nave on the right-hand side, while opposite it was a marble stone into which a unique depiction of the rock birth was carved. It shows Mithras emerging from the rock, being helped on either side by torchbearers, while above him Saturnus is crowned by Victory. Along the bottom of the carving is an inscription that refers to the *legio V Macedonia* and the *legio XIII Gemina*. Only a few remains of statuettes were found in this temple, which contrasts with Poetovio II, although Vermaseren suggests that the bases located on the corners of the benches held statues of the torchbearers. From Abramić's work, we know there were remnants of trapezophores, two of which stood in front of the left bench. In contrast to Poetovio II, this mithraeum did produce ceramic evidence, including lamps, dishes, vases, and brown-glazed scale pottery. On one sherd of pottery the name 'Valerius M ...' was inscribed. Additional figures depicted in the sanctuary were Luna and Silvanus.

Chronology

Despite inhabiting a different area of the town to Mithraea I and II, Mithraeum III appears to have been contemporary to both of them. The Flavius Hermadion referred to in an inscription from the mithraeum, is almost certainly the same L. Flavius Hermadion who appears in a Mithraic inscription from Rome in the latter half of the 2nd c. The activity in the mithraeum appears to have reached its apex in the mid 3rd c., however, as most of the inscriptions were dedicated by soldiers of the *legio V Macedonia* and the *legio XIII Gemina*, who were garrisoned in Poetovio during the reign of Gallienus (AD 258–68). The mithraeum also contained 317 coins dating from Augustus to Theodosius (the latest coin is dated to AD 392), with particular concentrations from the time of Gallenius (AD 260–268), Claudius Gothicus (AD 268–70) and the Constantinian dynasty. However, given that the coins were recorded without provenance, how they relate to the use of the mithraeum is difficult to discern, and a late 4th c. date for its abandonment can only be tentative.

D.6 *Poetovio v*

Selected Bibliography: Tušek (1990); Ertel (2001).

Excavated
1987

Location

The context in which the mithraeum existed is unknown.

Structure

The excavations uncovered the poorly preserved foundation walls of the temple (h. 0.80 m × w. 0.55–0.60 m), along with some reliefs and altars. The walls do not appear to have been very sturdy, but the remains of marble pillars indicate that the structure was reinforced. It has been suggested that the architectural design of this mithraeum was quite similar to other religious and civic buildings in the town, as the columns that were used in the temple were stylistically similar to those found elsewhere.

Finds

A large marble altar, which was inscribed during the consulships of Severus and Quintianus (AD 285), was disturbed by machine digging, which led to the discovery of the temple. The other finds were found deposited in a pit that had been dug within the mithraeum. Another sizeable altar made of yellow sandstone was also discovered, as were the heavily weathered fragments of an altar relief. A fragment of a large enamel jug is the only significant pottery find, which bore a depiction of a snake winding its way around the vessel and then up the handle, before resting its head on the top. Of the eleven coins found, one was minted in the reign of Caracalla, another under Gallienus; the rest date from the reign of Constantine up to AD 379.

Chronology

Judging from the finds, the mithraeum is likely to have come into being in the 3rd c., perhaps during the Severan period, and remained active until the end of the 4th c. It appears that the altar relief was broken and the fragments were left in the open for some time, and then perhaps buried when the mithraeum was either levelled or had collapsed, given that the foundations were not particularly sturdy.

E. Dalmatia

E.1 *Arupium (Prozor) I and II*
Selected Bibliography: *CIMRM* 2. 1851–52; Beck (1984).

Excavated
1896 and 1900

Two mithraea were discovered in the late 19th c. in the countryside of Arupium. The first consisted of a space enclosed by rocks. At the eastern end of this space, a badly weathered representation of the tauroctony had been carved in a natural niche. In a case of modern damage to a cult image, the central relief had been used for target practice by Soviet troops in the 20th c. A small number of coins had been deposited in front of the niche, the dates for which ran from AD 260 to 360.

A second mithraeum, found near to the first, was also built into an enclosed, rocky space, and once again utilised a natural niche that contained a heavily weathered image of the tauroctony. As with the first mithraeum, a small group of coins were found in this space that dated to the mid 4th c. The numismatic data thus indicate that the two temples were active at the same time and, given the similarity between their styles, Beck has suggested that the carving of the two reliefs may have even been carried out by the same artisan.

E.2 *Epidaurum (Cavtat)*
Selected Bibliography: *CIMRM* 2. 1882–84; Evans (1884) 20–23.

Excavated
1884

Like those in Arupium, the mithraeum at Epidaurum was located in the countryside in a natural grotto. A well was located at its entrance, where an image of the tauroctony was carved into a rock face. At the far end of the grotto, again carved into the wall, was another relief showing the mithraeum on the hill overlooking the settlement of Epidaurum, and featured Mithras as the bull-killer. In a natural groove in the rock-face under this relief were found three coins, dating from the reign of Aurelian to AD 324. Unfortunately, the mithraeum produced little else in the way of finds.

E.3 *Jajce*
Selected Bibliography: *CIMRM* 2. 1901–1905; Sergejevskij (1937).

Excavated
1937

Location
The shrine was situated on the bank of the river Pliva.

Structure
The mithraeum lay on an east-west axis; only a cult room survives, dug 2.80 m below ground level. It was made of marlstone blocks on three sides that abutted a natural rock-face, forming an irregular quadrangle shape. The central relief was carved into the rock-face. Two steps lay in front of the relief, while another two were located in the south-west corner, most likely where the entrance was situated. As opposed to the standard plan of two benches flanking a nave, only one bench is present here, against the south wall.

Finds
A statue of Cautopates was found headless, while that of Cautes is completely absent. In two small, triangular hollows either side of the main relief broken pottery sherds were found, while in front of the relief more fragments of pottery, a fibula, and various coins were found amongst rubble deposited in front of the relief. Six altars were found, but only one bears an inscription (simply '*invicto*').

Chronology
It is not possible to reconstruct any clear chronology for the site. The coin finds range in date from the reign of Trajan to Constantine, although the majority date from the latter period. This suggests occupation of the temple was limited to the first half of the 4th c. The pottery and fibula found with the coins were also identified as Late Roman in date. It was the belief of the excavator that the temple, which was not built in a particularly sturdy fashion, collapsed due to the exceedingly damp condition of the area.

E.4 *Konjic*
Selected Bibliography: *CIMRM* 2. 1895–99.

Excavated
1897

Location
The mithraeum was situated on a slope of a hill, close to the right bank of the Trstenic River.

Structure
The cult room alone (9.00 m × 5.00 m) was well-preserved. The mithraeum lay on an east-west axis and had a floor of stamped clay and pebbles, with a bench (l. 4.30 m) running along the left side of the nave. The remains of wedge-shaped blocks suggest the mithraeum had an arched roof.

APPENDIX A

Finds

The main cult relief, which apparently revolved, as it had images carved on both sides, was found in fragments. On one side of the relief was an image of the tauroctony, flanked by images of Mithras-*taurophorus*. On the other side, a Mithraic meal seems to be depicted, with the *pater* and *heliodromos* being attended by figures wearing lion and raven masks, as well as an unmasked man. In the case of the tauroctony, all the three images of Mithras have had their heads removed. For unspecified reasons, Vermaseren (in *CIMRM*) suggested that the relief was made in the 4th c., but the dating is likely correct given that, of the 91 coins found across the floor of the shrine, 67% are 4th c. in date, the latest of which was minted in AD 383.

Chronology

Given that there is a relatively even chronological distribution of coins dating to between AD 260 and 383, it would seem that the temple was erected in the late 3rd c. and abandoned in the final decades of the 4th c.

F. Italy (Excluding Rome and Ostia)[2]

F.1 *Capua*

Selected Bibliography: *CIMRM* 1. 180–99; Vermaseren (1971); Clauss (1992) 51.

Excavated
1922

Location
The mithraeum was located not too far from the *capitolium*, although the actual context in which it existed is unknown.

Structure
The temple was located underground and consisted of an adapted 'L' shaped *cryptoporticus*. The first section ran north to south for a total of 13.32 m and was 4.41 m wide. When one reached the end of this passage, on the left-hand side would be the main *cella* (l. 12.27 m × w. 3.37 m), running on an east to west axis. This was stuccoed and painted all over, with scenes of Mithraic lore on the walls and stars on the vault. Remains of blue glass found on the floor of this room may have come from the holes visible in the centre of these stars, so that they would twinkle when reflecting the light from the lamps and candles below. The central aisle (w. 1.60 m) was inlaid with marble, and a threshold was placed in the floor just over 3 m out from the cult niche. The aisle was flanked by two benches, which were extended from 1.40 m to the door in a later phase (as indicated by the older paintings disappearing behind the

extensions). In both benches, water basins were included halfway along. Near to the basins, small niches were cut into the front of the benches, which, based on the evidence for burning within them, were probably used for lamps. The cult niche, which was painted with an image of the bull-slaying scene, was located in the western wall and contained a podium that ran across its entire width (2.83 m).

Finds

The remains of various lamps, amphorae, and animal bones were found amongst the rubbish dumped in the mithraeum, but no reliefs or statues remained.

Chronology

Vermaseren was able to distinguish different phases of painting, pointing out that the different style and colour scheme used in the painting of panel III differs from the others, and highlighted that there was a figure in this panel that had been later covered over. Based on the style of panel III, which is similar to the fourth Pompeian style, the mithraeum may have come into existence in the first half of the 2nd c. The rest of the paintings, evidently composed by a different artist, were dated by Vermaseren to the Antonine period.

The final period of alteration came with the enlargement of the benches that covered some of the earlier paintings. The benches were subsequently decorated with initiation scenes that Vermaseren dated stylistically to the early 3rd c. Precisely when ritual activity ceased cannot be ascertained, but this had certainly occurred by the first half of the 4th c., as amongst the rubbish dumped in the mithraeum was a coin of Constantine. Given the damage to the eyes and nose of Mithras in the central tauroctony painting, one might assume that—based on other examples such as Hawarte—that this was the work of Christians, but the damage actually occurred during the excavation process. The facts behind this are unclear, with Vermaseren remarking, "According to the custodian [the damage] had been inflicted by playing children".

F.2 *Ponza*

Selected Bibliography: Vermaseren (1974).

Excavated
1866

Location
The shrine was located just outside of one of the island's ports, although what lay in its immediate vicinity is unknown.

Structure
Ten steps were uncovered leading down to the sanctuary, with a platform situated between steps eight and nine. The mithraeum itself (l. 10.90 m × w. 6.45–6.90 m) is on an east-west axis and consisted of a central aisle of stamped earth and

---

2 For Rome, see Bjørnebye (2007); for Ostia, see White (2012).

two parallel benches, over which was a vaulted roof painted with signs of the zodiac. A low podium had been cut into the left-hand wall, its function unknown. At the western end, the cult apse, which was flanked by pilasters, contained a ridge about 1 m high, which may have been the remains of a podium that held the image of the tauroctony. To the right of the main apse was a smaller niche.

Finds
This mithraeum appears to have had its contents removed upon abandonment.

Chronology
Given its irregular construction, the temple was almost certainly not a mithraeum at first, but later converted. There were no inscriptions or datable finds, but Vermaseren placed the construction of the mithraeum in the 3rd c., based on the style of the zodiac painting that decorated its roof. A cross found hewn into the wall opposite the entrance may suggest that desecration by Christians occurred following its abandonment, but when this took place cannot be established. Without any remains of reliefs or sculptures, we cannot say how extensive any desecration of the sanctuary was.

F.3 *Spoletium*
Selected Bibliography: *CIMRM* 1. 673–82; Gori (1879) 55–62, 252–56.

Excavated
1878

Location
Just outside the city gate.

Structure
The mithraeum was connected to a series of other rooms, which Vermaseren suggests may have acted as a living space. The sanctuary (l. 21.10 m × w. 3.90 m) was set on a north-west to south-east axis. Accessed was provided via a door placed in the middle of the south-west bench; the parallel bench had a gap, without a door, to match this. Four niches were made in the faces of the benches, situated opposite each other in pairs. Into the benches, above one of the pairs of niches, water basins had been installed. At the far end of the shrine were three recesses a central niche (in front of which stood the base of a pillar), to hold the bullslaying-scene, that was flanked by two smaller ones, most likely for representations of the torchbearers. Another smaller bench (or shelf?) was situated between the left-hand niche and the north-east bench. The aisle and walls were paved with marble, while the benches were covered in plaster, and bore traces of red colouring.

Finds
A votive altar was found near point B on the plan, while an earthen lamp and a bone statuette depicting a young man wearing a tunic, cloak and laurel wreath, were also found in the *cella*. In the adjoining rooms, a sacrificial knife and a piece of marble inscribed with signs of the zodiac were present.

Chronology
The only dating evidence from the mithraeum came in the form of coins from the reigns of Constantine and Gratian. Thus, the construction is likely to have been in the early 4th c., with its abandonment in the late 4th c. It was burnt down, although given that all the cultic objects had been removed (apart from the odd small fragment) the fire may have occurred post-abandonment.

F.4 *Timavo*
Selected Bibliography: Pross Gabrielli (1975); Clauss (1992) 68.

Excavated
1965

Location
The mithraeum was situated in a grotto on the side of a hill overlooking the coast.

Structure
The mithraeum (*ca.* 48 m^2) was located in a natural cave and contained a central nave (w. 2.6 m) flanked by parallel benches (h. 0.45 m × w. 0.70 m); in front of each bench stood three pillars. The cave also had a well dug into it, and the remains of tiles and a wooden truss suggest the ceiling may have been covered over.

Finds
The contents of the mithraeum were found deposited across its floor. They included fragments of two broken reliefs, both depicting the tauroctony; in both cases, the majority of the images are missing, including the heads of Mithras and the bull. Also found was an iron knife, a piece of a spear, ceramic fragments from amphorae, cups, saucers and (around 70) lamps. Dating can be established by the *ca.* 300 coins found, which run from the reign of Antoninus Pius to that of Theodosius, the last dating to AD 379. Unfortunately, the chronological distribution of these coins has not been recorded. A square block of limestone, which appears to have been used as an altar, was found in the middle of the nave.

Epigraphic Record
On the two reliefs, five names were recorded. On one were the names of three brothers from the Tulli family, while the other

bears the name of Aelius. On the altar are the names Aurelius Hermes and Aurelius Protemus. Unfortunately, nothing else is known about any of these men.

Chronology
Dating the mithraeum is somewhat difficult given the lack of information provided regarding the coins. It would seem they all came from the same layer as the reliefs and ceramic fragments, indicating that this damage occurred at the end of the 4th c., while a construction date cannot be established any more securely than the latter half of the 2nd c.

F.5 *Vulci*
Selected Bibliography: Moretti (1979); Clauss (1992) 50.

Excavated
1975

Location
The mithraeum was built between what appears to have been the slave-quarters of a large *domus* and the so-called the 'House of the *Cryptoporticus*'. The area to the north-east of the sanctuary remains unexplored.

Structure
The mithraeum (l. 13.20 m × w. 5.10 m) lay on an east to west axis, cut into a natural slope. The two benches (h. 1.20 m × w. 1.20 m) border an earthenware central aisle and contain six niches in their front faces that run deep under them. At the end of the aisle, in front of the niche, two shallow pits had been dug into the floor (l. 0.38 m × w. 0.25 m × d. 0.32 m and l. 0.62 m × w. 1.14 m × d. 0.78 m), the larger of which contained a hole at the bottom that fed into an underlying channel.

Finds
Several statues were found in the mithraeum. Two of these depicted the tauroctony, the larger of which was found in a fragmentary condition to the left of the main altar; various pieces were missing, including Mithras' head and most of his arms, and nicks and abrasions were evident across the statue. The smaller tauroctony statue was also found on the floor in a fragmentary state, next to the altar abutting the south wall of the mithraeum. Once again, various parts are missing, such as Mithras' head, segments of his arms and horns of the bull, while blows are also evident across the statue. Both sets of statues have been dated to the mid 3rd c. due to the style of the carving. Sculptures of a raven and Cautes were also found; the former at the entrance to the mithraeum relatively intact, the latter in the central aisle, broken in two, missing one of its arms and, like the tauroctony statues, it displays evidence of chips and abrasions.

Chronology
Moretti's stylistic dating of the sculptures is the only evidence with which the mithraeum can be dated, placing its occupation sometime in the mid 3rd c. When the mithraeum went out of use, and when the statues were desecrated, cannot be established. Given that this is one of the few examples where all the statues were fragmented, apart from the representation of an animal, it is one of the likeliest candidates for Christian iconoclasm directed at a mithraeum.

G. Gaul

G.1 *Augusta Treverorum (Trier)*
Selected Bibliography: Gose (1972) 110–17; Walters (1974) 23–29; Ghetta (2008) 115–18.

Excavated
1928

Location
The mithraeum was located within a house at the north end of one of the two sanctuary areas in the valley of Altbach, which was populated by at least 30 other temples.

Structure
Rather than being a standalone structure, the mithraeum was a room (*ca.* 82 m^2) within a large building. The central nave (l. 8.70 m × w. 4.00 m) was flanked by benches, the eastern one of which was much wider (h. 0.40m × w. 1.20m/3.40m). At the far end of the nave lay a podium-wall, on which stood a large limestone block that supported an image of the rock-birth. This block was flanked by two small altars, with steps leading up to it, abutting the benches on both sides.

Finds
Some small fragments of the main relief were recovered from the temple. A sculpture of Mercury was found decapitated, but the head was left in the mithraeum, while a relief depicting Mithras emerging from the rock was uncovered completely intact. Several altars were also found, bearing inscriptions, as did several ceramic vessels that were painted with the phrase '*Deo Invictus*'. At the entrance to the *cella* was a rectangular pit (l. 1.84 m × w. 0.80 m × d. 0.45m) that contained a thick layer of ash. Deposited in the pit were bird bones and coins from the 4th c., the latest of which dates to the time of Honorius.

Epigraphic Record
The two altars were dedicated by the *pater* Martius Martialis. It was suggested by Walters that the name Martialis might be indicative that the man's origins were local. Another name,

'Nicasius', also appears on a votive *aedicula* from the sanctuary, but nothing else is known about this man.

Chronology

The house to which the mithraeum belonged appears to have been built in the 3rd c., but judging from the numismatic evidence the mithraeum was a later addition, probably in the final decades of the 3rd c. The mithraeum looks to have been abandoned in the late 4th c., with the deposit in the pit perhaps representing the ritual closure of the temple. The nearby temple area went out of use in the latter part of the 4th c., with some temples torn down and paved over to make way for a road, while others were converted into living spaces. A later wall was cut through the mithraeum, while a pan used for lime-burning was found in strata of this period. It is worth noting that many of the sculptures and reliefs in the mithraeum were made of limestone.

G.2   *Burdigala (Bordeaux)*

Selected Bibliography: Gaidon-Bunuel (1991); Barraud and Caillabet-Duloum (2007) 256–58.

Excavated
1986

Location

The mithraeum was situated on the southern edge of the Roman town. From what excavations have discerned, the surrounding area appears to have been predominantly housing.

Structure

The mithraeum was a subterranean structure, cut 2.6 m into the limestone natural. It was a particularly large mithraeum (18.4 m × 10.3 m) and was partially submerged, with access provided by ten steps at 90 degrees to the main axis. The nave (w. 4.00 m) is flanked by two benches (w. 2.50–2.77 m × h. 0.77 m), which look to have had columns placed on top of them to support the roof. The centre of the eastern bench was removed to accommodate another feature which is now lost. A small podium was placed in the south-west corner. At the northern end of the sanctuary was a raised niche of substantial size (4.70 m × 3.30 m), where the cult image looks to have been held. Just in front of this, two post-holes have been found on either side of the nave, suggesting that some form of screen or railing was erected in front of the image.

Finds

Fragments from the border of the main cult image were uncovered, but the majority of the relief was never found. Small statuettes of the torchbearers and one of the rock-birth were found headless, but a relief of Aion was found intact. An altar was also found broken in two.

Chronology

The style of the statues suggests that the mithraeum was constructed in the early 3rd c., while coins dating to the latter half of the same century were found in the annex. According to what has been published, the mithraeum was destroyed at the beginning of the 4th c. but was then subsequently rebuilt before being destroyed again. No dating material was provided for the interpretation of these latter stages.

G.3   *Forum Claudii Vallensium Octodurensium (Martigny)*

Selected Bibliography: Wiblé (1995), (2004), and (2008) 146–66.

Excavated
1993

Location

The mithraeum was located in the south-west part of the Roman town, close to other cultic buildings and a large bathhouse, in what may have been a temple precinct.

Structure

The mithraeum (l. 23.40 m × w. 9.00 m) was built on a southeast to north-west axis and was surrounded by a fence. The southern façade largely survived intact and indicated that the walls were at least 3.75 m high and that the structure was covered with a gabled roof. As one crossed the threshold of this enclosure, one would walk over a pit (l. 1.70 m × w. 1.10 m × d. 1.35 m) which contained a beaker incised with Greek graffiti honouring Mithras. The entrance to the anteroom lay in the south-west corner, so one would not be able to see straight into the mithraeum; the outline of what appears to have been a storage space (2.30 m × 3.00 m) was found in the northern corner of this room. A dry-stone surface, perhaps for food preparation, appears to have existed next to the south-east wall of this room. The *cella* (8.00 m × 14.40 m) is divided into three: the two benches and a central nave (w. 3.70 m); the left-hand bench was not built as a single whole, but originally had a gap about halfway along that was later bricked up in order to make a single unified bench. At the end of the nave was a niche that was covered in yellow stucco, to which a podium was later added.

Finds

Pieces of bronze statuettes, an unusual find in mithraea, depicting the tauroctony were found broken with various bits missing. From this, the image of Cautopates was found largely intact, save for his right leg, but Mithras and the bull are largely absent save for a few small parts. Three altars were found, one of which was erected to honour the restoration of a temple to Jupiter, another was in honour of all the gods, and the third was erected to Mithras. The altar from the temple

APPENDIX A

of Jupiter was placed in a pit, while the other two were found broken. There were 2091 coins found, the deposition of which became increasingly concentrated around the terminus of the nave; nearly all the coins deposited after AD 378 (28.2%) were found in this area, indicating perhaps changing practices over the course of the 4th c. Some 29,361 animal bones, consisting of a high proportion of fowl, were also found in and around the temple.

Epigraphic Record

On a cup, deposited at the threshold of the palisade surrounding the mithraeum, there was written, in Greek, an offering to Helios by a man named Theodore. On one of the altars, the governor of the province Publius Ancilius Theodore is referred to, but this altar was erected to all the gods, and so may have been brought to the mithraeum from a different context. The same can be said of one of the other altars, which had originally been set up in the temple of Jupiter, to commemorate its reconstruction by the governor at the end of the 3rd c., but it was moved to the mithraeum and the inscription painted over. This would suggest that the temple of Jupiter had gone out of use in the 4th c., while the mithraeum still attracted devotees. The altar dedicated to Mithras bears the name Condius Paternus, a former *duumvir* and priest of the imperial cult.

Chronology

The first floor of the *cella* was made of clay and was covered in the remains of bone, tile, pottery and coins, which date the construction of the mithraeum to the latter half of the 2nd c. Later alterations were made, such as the podium and the filling in of the south-west bench, although a precise date for these is not given. A stratum of mortar was laid over the original earthen floor in the AD 360s, as two coins predating this period were found sealed under the new floor. The latest coin to be found in the mithraeum dated to AD 394, after which the building was abandoned. One of its altars was subsequently buried in a pit, although wear and frost damage on it suggests that it was left out in the open for some time prior to this burial.

G.4 *Les Bolards*

Selected Bibliography: *CIMRM* 1. 917–28; Walters (1974) 11–17.

Excavated

1948

Location

A hypocaust and many *ex votos*, which appear to have been in connection to eye illnesses, were found near the mithraeum. Two kilometres from the mithraeum is the natural spring of La Courtavaux.

Structure

The mithraeum was partially submerged, requiring access via three steps. The size and general structure of the building were not recorded.

Finds

The statue of Cautes was found largely intact, but with a slightly damaged face, while the statue of Cautopates was found in pieces (the current whereabouts of both statues today are unknown). A statue of a lion was found near the entrance, untouched. Various fragments of other statues and reliefs were recovered: the head of an unknown beast; heads of two youths in Phrygian caps, probably from the tauroctony image; the foot and hoof of a bull, along with the jaw of a dog, also from the central relief; a woman (possibly Luna); and an image of Sol's head. Unusually for a mithraeum, there were a number of offerings found that look to have been *ex votos* connected to ailments, including a marble hand and two marble legs. Around 627 coins were found in the mithraeum, of which only 127 could be identified.

Chronology

Judging from the coin finds found in the mithraeum, it was active from sometime in the mid to late 3rd c. until around AD 393.

G.5 *Mackwiller*

Selected Bibliography: *CIMRM* 2. 1329–34; Hatt (1955) and (1957).

Excavated

1955–56

Location

The mithraeum was located in a rural setting, possibly near to a villa, alongside a small timber shrine.

Structure

The excavator was uncertain as to whether the remains of the structure, that had been transformed into a spring sanctuary, had originally served as the *cella* or the anteroom of the mithraeum (*ca.* l. 10.00 m × w. 8.19 m). It was assumed that this was an anteroom due to its square shape, but given the presence of the finds here, and the fact that other square-shaped mithraea are known (such as at Pons Saravi), it does appear that this was indeed the *cella*.

Finds

404 coins (over 80% dating between and AD 330 and 350) were found in an area of just *ca.* 0.50 m², along with sherds of a broken, fire-damaged pot. One might speculate that the coins were kept in this container, which had perhaps stood on

a wooden shelf that was incinerated when the building was burnt down. Strewn across the mithraeum floor were various fragments of Mithraic sculptures and reliefs, including elements of: the central tauroctony relief (half-life size); a statue of a man in a toga; fragments of a rock-birth statue; and a second, smaller tauroctony relief.

Epigraphic Record
Just one fragment of an inscription bearing a couple of letters is all that survives to provide any information, in this; which appears to refer to an equestrian.

Chronology
The foundation of the mithraeum is dated to the mid 2nd c., according to the style of the sculptures. Based on the numismatic evidence, the neighbouring shrine was destroyed sometime in the late 3rd c., at which point the mithraeum also suffered fire damage. The numismatic evidence for the mithraeum ends in AD 351, when it was completely burnt down and its sculptures broken. A wooden and dry-stone spring sanctuary appears to have arisen in its place (the coin series for which runs to around AD 388); this sanctuary was also eventually burnt down.

G.6   *Pons Saravi (Sarrebourg)*
Selected Bibliography: *CIMRM* 1. 965–84; Walters (1974) 17–23.

Excavated
1895

Location
The mithraeum was located on a hill outside of the town around 50 m from the Sarre River and near a natural spring.

Structure
The mithraeum (6.20 m × 5.48 m) lay on a north-south axis and was built against the side of a hill. Based on two angled blocks found near the entrance, the original excavation report suggested the mithraeum had been housed under a gabled roof, and from the angle of these blocks, Walters calculated the side walls had stood at least 2.9 m high. The building may have had an anteroom, given the paving slabs found at the entrance, while water from a nearby spring was brought into the temple via a conduit. The mithraeum was partially submerged, *ca.* 2 m below surface level, it being entered via a doorway (w. 1.25 m) which led to an anteroom via several steps. The inner sanctuary follows the standard ground plan: two benches (w. 1.35–1.38 m × h. 0.90 m × l. 4.80m), elevated by limestone fragments and clay, and supported by two parapet walls. The cult niche stood at the far end of the nave.

Finds
The main cult relief had been smashed into 300 identifiable pieces. Reliefs of the torchbearers were found broken, and

additional smaller statues were found of headless men (possibly Mercury and Mithras), while two heads of two female statues were recovered without their bodies. Of the pottery found, there was: a trachyte bowl which showed evidence of burning; a *mortarium* that had a lip in the form of a lion's head; a dark grey pot which contained ash and bird bone; a *terra sigillata* bowl depicted a hunting scene; and a lamp had an inscription that read *Soli*. Given this description of the pottery evidence, it seems unlikely it was rubbish dumped from elsewhere, as Walters postulated, as it actually consists of items used in Mithraic rituals.

Epigraphic Record
From two inscriptions, including the cult relief, we have the name Marceleius Marianus, but no other information about him.

Chronology
There were 274 coins found in the mithraeum, running from the 1st c. AD (one coin) to the reign of Theodosius (AD 394); the vast majority (250 coins) originated from the 4th c. The pottery suggests the mithraeum may have been built in the 2nd c., while the cult relief has been stylistically dated to the Severan period, but with no stratigraphy provided it is not possibly to give an accurate chronology. It would seem that the sanctuary met a violent end, with the statues exhibiting evidence of blunt trauma and the main cult relief smashed to pieces. Furthermore, where the cult relief would have originally stood the remains of a man bound in chains was found, although whether he had any connection to the mithraeum is unclear.

G.7   *Septeuil*
Selected Bibliography: Cholet (1989); Gaidon-Bunuel (1991).

Excavated
1984, 1985 and 1988

Location
Septeuil was located where the Flexanville River met the ancient road between Paris and Evreux. The precise location of the mithraeum in relation to the small settlement is unknown, but a large building, possibly a temple or bathhouse, stood close by.

Structure
The mithraeum was orientated east to west and lay 2.60 m below ground level. In order to create the mithraeum, a nymphaeum (*ca.* 42 m²) was divided in half, with the *cella* of the mithraeum to the south and an anteroom to the north. It was separated from the rest of the nymphaeum by a wooden partition inserted into a ditch, which ran the width of the building. The cult building consisted of a nave (w. 2.60m) panelled with oak, flanked by two benches (w. 1.50m)

APPENDIX A

that were propped up using architectural fragments. The entrance lay in the north wall, meaning that the right-hand bench had to be shorter than that on the opposite wall. The bases of two columns were also used to prop up the main cult image at the western end. Reused tiles were placed in the north-west corner of the room to create what might have been some form of platform, while a large hearth was also found in this room at the western end of the bench on the south wall.

Finds

The cult image was found broken, the heads of both Mithras and the bull absent. A relief with Mithras and a statue depicting the rock-birth were also retrieved. In the case of the former, the face of Mithras had been damaged using a blunt tool, while the statue was headless. Of the 1000+ coins distributed throughout the structure, there appears to have been a particular concentration in the nymphaeum basin, which post-dated the destruction of the mithraeum around AD 378 (see below): the last was dated to AD 388. Two fibulae, apparently military in design, were found which dated to the mid 4th c. and latter half of the 4th c. A large amount of animal bones and cooking ceramics were uncovered, indicating that the hearth in the northern room was frequently used.

Chronology

The mithraeum was constructed in a room of an earlier nymphaeum. The first stratigraphic layer associated with the mithraeum is dated by coin finds and a fibula to the mid-4th c., with coins post-dating 378 found in the destruction layer, giving a final abandonment date in the AD 380s.

G.8   *Tienen*

Selected Bibliography: Martens (2004); Lentacker, Ervynck and van Neer (2004).

Excavated

1998

Location

The mithraeum lay in the south-western edge of the *vicus*, close to a cemetery, in an area containing predominantly craft workshops. The mithraeum was surrounded on at least three sides by a palisade, and stood across the road from a plot of land containing various refuse pits and a sunken hut. A large number of pits, dated by their contents to the 2nd and 3rd c. AD, and believed to have been ritual in nature, have been uncovered in this area.

Structure

This mithraeum (l. 12.00 m × w. 7.50 m) stood on a south-west to north-east axis and was partially submerged, with the central aisle (l. 12.00 m × w. 2.00 m) laying 1.20 m below the Roman ground level. Given the large quantity of nails found in the

excavation, it has been suggested that the central aisle was covered with boards. It was flanked by benches that do not survive, but post-holes attest to their presence. In the centre of the aisle, a pit had been dug and lined with tiles, in which a container bearing burnt material was found. At the north-west end, a 2.00 m × 2.00 m square of hypocaust and roof tiles sealed a pit containing a sword, animal bone, and ceramics. Two channels were cut into the floor, one alongside the right-hand bench, the other perpendicular to this.

Finds

Pits located next to the south-west wall of the mithraeum were found to contain a variety of finds, including at least 89 lids; 85 dishes; 103 incense burners; 79 drinking vessels; 12 oil lamps; 14,000 animal bones and a host of other items. By far the most common animal remains found in these pits were chicken (*ca.* 90%), while sheep and pig remains (the latter of which were mainly adolescents) were also present. Analysis of the piglet and lamb remains indicated that they were killed around the end of June or beginning of July, most likely for a celebration of the summer solstice, while the fill of the pits indicates they were all filled in rapid succession. This has led to the conclusion that this may have been the remains of a large ritual feast, catering for at least 100 people.

Epigraphic Record

A votive offered by Tullio found just outside the Mithraeum bears the inscription *DIM* (*Deo Invicto Mithrae*). The name Spurius is also mentioned, but it is unclear whether Tullio was his slave or his son.

Chronology

The mithraeum itself contained four coins, one from the 1st–2nd c. A.D., the others from AD 310 to 350, while the pits contained coins from the 1st to mid 4th c. Beakers found in the pits date to the latter half of the 3rd c. Overall, the most likely date of construction for the temple is around the mid 3rd c. It would appear that the mithraeum was abandoned in the mid 4th c., but no reliefs, sculptures or altars remain.

G.9   *Venetonimagus (Vieu-en-Val-Romney)*

Selected Bibliography: *CIMRM* 1. 909–14; Walters (1974) 5–11.

Excavated

1840 and 1868–69

Location

Information regarding the Roman *vicus* and its topography is sparse, although the prefix '-magus' may indicate a market town. It has been suggested that this may have been sanctuary area, as parts of a colossal statue have been found nearby, as well as a large number of *ex votos* relating to eye diseases. To the south of the mithraeum lay the remains of what appear to be bathhouses, and Walters suggested that this complex might have been similar to the sanctuary of Apollo-Moritagus in Alise-Sainte-Reine. This interpretation is made even more likely by the close proximity of a natural spring.

Structure
Little was recorded regarding the structure. The mithraeum (l. 10.60 m × w. 3.40 m) appears to have been on a north-south axis and was accessed by a door to the south, which was sheltered on the outside by a portico. Inside, a channel ran along the west wall; the only remnant of the benches seems to have been a parapet wall.

Finds
Only an altar was recovered, with no trace of statues or reliefs.

Epigraphic Record
C. Rufius Virilis erected a Mithraic altar to his father, C. Rufius Eutactus, the *pater* of the Mithraic community, who we know from another inscription was a doctor.[3]

Chronology
The only dating evidence originating from the mithraeum consisted of coins dating to the reign of Claudius Gothicus (AD 269–70) and a small bronze coin from the reign of Magnus Maximus (d. AD 388).

H.   Spain

H.1   *Lucus Augusti (Lugo)*
Selected Bibliography: Alvar, Gordon and Rodriguez (2006).

Excavated
2003

Location
The mithraeum was installed across five rooms in a large house.

Structure
The mithraeum, which was orientated north-south, consisted of a rectangular *cella* (l. 15.70 m × w. 7.00 m), and four anterooms. The foundations of much of the building were dug into the natural substrate, although the eastern end of the mithraeum was constructed on a pre-existing cement platform, which had been enclosed by a wall. The north wall, where the cult niche would have been, had been completely destroyed, while there was also no trace of the entrance way from the anteroom to the *cella* in the southern wall. Along the central axis of the *cella* was a nave bordered by five equidistant pillars on both sides. No remains of benches have been found, but the existence of low walls between the pillars and outer

walls shows they were probably intended to support wooden examples. A system of drains ran under the mithraeum, and a well was discovered in the one of the adjoining rooms.

Finds
A fragment of a granite votive altar was found bearing the remains of the word *sacerdos*, although this looks as though it was used as *spolia* to support the north-west corner of the mithraeum. Another granite altar was also found the middle of the nave.

Epigraphic Record
The altar found in the middle of the aisle bears the name of C. Victorinus Victorinus (a centurion of the *legio VII Gemina Antoniniana*) and his two freedmen, Victorinus Secundus and Victorinus Victor. The presence of the *Legio VII Gemina* suggests that the inscription dates from AD 212–18. Albeit not a Mithraic adherent himself, Victorinus dedicated the altar in honour of his own freedmen, whom the mithraeum may have been installed for.

Chronology
The mithraeum seems to have been built in the early 3rd c., judging by the inscription of Victorinus. Part of the house was destroyed in AD 262 to make way for the city wall when the city was refortified, following a Frankish raid. However, the mithraeum was left intact and the numismatic data run until AD 350.

I.   North Africa

I.1   *Lambaesis*
Selected Bibliography: *CIMRM* 2.138A–F; Le Glay (1954); Clauss (1992) 248–49; Groslambert (2011) 94–96.

Excavated
1951

Location
The mithraeum was located outside the military camp, close to the temple precinct of the Asklepieion.

Structure
The mithraeum (l. 16.40 m × w. 8.40 m) is situated on an east-west axis. It was built using irregular stones and its interior was painted with plaster. Partially submerged 1.00 m below the Roman street level, it was entered via a door from the west that lay at the bottom of two large steps. Traces of the benches (h. 0.80 m × w. 2.00 m) were found *in situ*, which ran for the length of the main room, and were filled with stones and packed earth. The apse (l. 2.00 m × w. 1.80 m) was situated about a metre above the floor level and was accessed by four steps. Another room (l. 4.55 m × w. 3.65 m), accessed via a door

---

3   *CIL* 13. 2509.

APPENDIX A

to the south-west, was attached to the mithraeum. This room was constructed with different building material (cut bricks) from the mithraeum, thus it appears to be a later addition. A pipe ran along the front of the north wall of this room, which was intersected by another pipe coming from the north-west; these are likely to have fed a water basin.

Finds

A number of altars were found in and around the mithraeum, but all other portable fittings look to have been removed.

Chronology

The only datable evidence from the mithraeum comes from two of the three altars found here. The earliest was erected by M. Valerius Maximianus between AD 183 and 185. Notably, Maximianus was from Poetovio, which was one of the major centres of Mithraic activity in the Roman world. The second altar has been dated to the early 3rd c., and was erected by an *actuarius*, while the final altar was paid for by the governor of Numidia in AD 303, Valerius Florus. It is possible that the addition of the small adjacent room was contemporary to one of these altars, but this cannot be verified.

J.   The Eastern Mediterranean

J.1   *Caesarea Maritima*
Selected Bibliography: Bull (1978); Blakely and Horton (1987); Holum (1988) 148–53; Clauss (1992) 243; Patrich (2011) 103.

Excavated
1973–74

Location
The mithraeum was located in a vault under the audience hall of the *praetorium* of the Roman financial procurator.

Structure
The vault (*ca.* 101 m²) was divided into two along its north-south axis. The *cella* (l. 13.50 m) contained 0.40 m high benches running in parallel along the north and south walls. The eastern bench was divided into two by a low wall (l. 1.05 m × w. 0.32 m × h. 0.32 m). In front of this bench stood an altar (l. 0.60 m × w. 0.60 m × h. 0.22 m); a drain was found to the north-east corner of this. Traces of painted plaster were found on the north and south walls, as well as the ceiling. Nineteen small holes were cut in a line along the walls and ceiling 4.50 m from the end of the eastern end of the chamber. At the edge of one of these holes the impression of a wooden beam was found in the plaster, indicating a wooden structure was fitted here in order to divide this part of the mithraeum from the rest, although no vertical supports were found. Just behind this, to the east, was a small opening (0.2 m²) that allowed light to shine into the mithraeum, which would

align with the altar on the summer solstice. Another aperture (0.2 m²) was located at the western end and allowed light into the antechamber. At the western end of the room, a stone foundation (w. 3.25 m) was found that is believed to mark the entrance, although no traces of a door survive.

Finds
A small circular marble medallion (d. 0.075 m) was found bearing an image of the tauroctony. A white circular area (d. 0.08 m) was found on the small wall dividing the two end benches, suggesting it had been fixed here, so that one would view it just above the altar. There was no trace of the main relief or any other fittings.

Iconography
On the southern wall three painted scenes survived, albeit in poor condition. In the first scene (0.65 m × 0.50 m) the vague image of two figures could be discerned, one standing and one kneeling. The standing figure, on the left, appeared to be wearing trousers and a purple garment with a red border, with both hands extended to the kneeling figure. The other, kneeling figure was painted in red and wore a cloak, with his hands extended in the direction of the standing figure. He appeared to offer him a yellow sphere separated into two horizontally. To the right, a second panel (0.80 m × 0.50 m) depicted two figures in similar positions; although this time they were slightly further apart. The standing figure was again in trousers, though his cloak was blue with a red edge. The kneeling figure was completely red again, though he wore a green and blue cape. A faint red line that could be seen next to the standing figure indicated he was depicted holding something, perhaps a sword, which was resting on the kneeling figure's shoulder. Above and behind each figure were vague yellowish areas, the right one appearing to be a vase or bust. In the final panel, two figures are shown, both 0.43 m tall, between which stood a rectangular object, with a yellow disk positioned above it. The figure on the left once again held a sword(?), although this time it was upright. The two figures' right hands appeared to have been clasped over the yellow disk. The right-hand figure, who was naked apart from what may be a crown, appeared to have a yellow line coming out of his head. Who these scenes depicted is difficult to ascertain. Bull has suggested Mithras and Sol rather than scenes from a Mithraic initiation, but given what we know of such ceremonies from elsewhere, and a lack of parallels from iconographic representations of the Mithraic narrative, it is more plausible that these were indeed depictions of an initiation.

Chronology
The earliest strata of the floor revealed coins dating to the reign of Nero, and fragments of amphora used for wine and garum. Judging from the ceramic evidence, the vault was converted into a mithraeum in either the late 1st or early 2nd c. Towards the end of the 3rd c. the mithraeum ceased

to function and the vault was used for a different purpose; the floor was covered with a new plaster surface and traces of amphora, along with coins dating from the late 3rd to early 4th c., were found. This suggests the vault was now being used as a storehouse, its original purpose. Another layer above this contained Byzantine amphorae, which suggests the vault continued to be used for storage after the Roman period.

J.2   *Doliche*

Selected Bibliography: Winter (2000); Schütte and Winter (2004); Gordon (2007).

Excavated
1997–98

Location
Two mithraea were located within a natural cave on a hillside outside of the town.

Structure
The entrance (h. 1.4 m, although probably larger when the mithraea were in use) to the cave lays on the west side of Keber Tepe, the hill upon which Doliche is situated. Mithraeum I was about 40 m long and consisted of a long entrance corridor, which, after the first 15 m, had a rather steep gradient. At the end of this is an open area of about l. 10 m × w. 7 m, with various basins cut into the walls (these may be remnants of the extraction phase) and an image of the tauroctony carved into the far wall, offset from the axis of the entrance way. Mithraeum II was accessed via an entranceway on the south-east side of the corridor leading to Mithraeum I. The area within this cave is covered roughly l. 32 m × w. 18 m, but the actual space that could be used for the mithraeum was, like Mithraeum I, only *ca.* 10 m × 7 m.

Finds
A *tabula ansata* was found near the entrance of the cave system, but its 18 line inscription is unreadable. Some Greek graffiti are present on the south-eastern wall of Mithraeum II, but these are crudely drawn and are just the first letters of the alphabet.

Chronology
The phases of occupation in the two mithraea have been disputed, with Gordon providing a new assessment of the material, which led him to argue for a different sequence to that provided by the excavators. This discrepancy is unsurprising, as the strata of the mithraea have been disturbed, and toxic air inside the mithraea meant only limited excavations were undertaken around the main cult reliefs. It was the opinion of the excavators that the mithraea, or at least one of them, might be one of the earliest to be discovered in the Roman world, dating to the Late Hellenistic/Early Roman period, with its destruction occurring when Shapur sacked the city in AD 253. There are, however, numerous problems with this interpretation, which are discussed by Gordon in his review of the final report. I am inclined to agree with Gordon's chronology, which is what is outlined here.

Both caves were originally used as extraction sites for building blocks, with the walls of both producing evidence of step-wise extraction and niches for oil lamps, while the ceilings of both are almost completely level. In Mithraeum I, three blocks have been marked out on the wall and work had already begun on extracting them. It would appear that this activity ceased rather suddenly. Around the central relief in Mithraeum I, the first stratum above the natural limestone contains impacted limestone with no finds. This stratum is followed by a thin burnt layer which produced a coin of the Seleucid king Antiochus IX (114–95 BC). The next layer had been greatly disturbed, with no clear difference between the strata detectable. It contained various items, including broken roof tiles, eight pieces of *terra sigillata* A from the Late Hellenistic/Early Roman period, some glass, and two coins dating to the reign of Elagabalus. A burial, which had been disturbed, was found in the north-west corner of the mithraeum, dug into the top layer, which Gordon believes may either predate the use of the cave as a mithraeum, or may even be that of a Mithraic adherent. In Mithraeum II, again around the central relief, the bedrock and first two layers are the same as in Mithraeum I, although the burnt layer only existed around the relief. The next stratum consisted of brown earth, which had been set down as a floor, containing more *terra sigillata* A, and some local coarse-ware. Above this was a layer containing a volute lamp of the 1st c. AD. Finally, the top stratum consisted of dark brown earth with debris from the city (pottery and roof tiles), with two Warzen-lampen dated to the 3rd/4th and 6th c. Gordon believes that the *terminus post quem* for the mithraea's abandonment should be dated by the coins of Elagabalus. At some point, Christians entered the abandoned mithraea and vandalised the two central reliefs, replacing Mithras' face with a cross in Mithraeum I and etching crosses into various recesses around the cave. The top stratum of both mithraea suggests the site may have been used as a rubbish dump in the Late Roman period.

J.3   *Hawarte*

Selected Bibliography: Gawlikowski (2000), (2001), (2007).

Excavated
1998–2003

Location
The mithraeum was installed in a series of natural caves lying close to a village.

Structure

Five steps led from the entrance of the mithraeum (w. 1.50m) into the vestibule. The remains of a wooden frame for the door were found, along with two columns either side of it. The right-hand wall of the vestibule was covered in soot and bore two sets of horizontal holes running in parallel, indicating that a grille had been here. Directly opposite the foot of the stairs was a small bench. At the north end of the room a pit was dug into the ground that was 1.5 m deep and 1.70 m in diameter. It was partially covered by the wall, with its upper fill containing stones to support the wall. The lower fill was found to contain mostly chicken and sheep bones, along with some cattle and pig, but there was no dating evidence. The two fills were separated by a stone slab, indicating the pit had two distinct phases. At some point, the ceiling of this space developed a crack, stretching from one side to the other. Two pillars consisting of mismatched blocks, one of which cut through the corner of an earlier stone shelf, was erected to support the roof. Between the two pillars and over the shelf, a fill was found containing ash, animal bone, and culinary pottery dating to the late 4th c.

Proceeding from the vestibule, one would find a larger rectangular room (l. 6.0–6.6 m), identified by the excavators as the 'Outer Chamber'. The first thing encountered in this room was a square pillar (h. 0.65 m) of which only two blocks remained, while another pillar was found on the western side of the room. Gawlikowski suggested a third may have existed between them, and that they acted as roof supports. Against the north wall was a large recess (w. 3.5 m) containing a stone platform (h. 0.40 m). On the west side of the room was a passageway, bordered by two pillars and accessed by some small steps, which led to space D. The wall to the right of this passage bore the remains of painted plaster. The north wall was painted five times (as was the walls of the cella, suggesting all the painting is contemporary) and was erected to cut off the northern area of the cave.

The cella (l. 6.45–7.20 m × w. 4.80 m) was separated from the outer chamber by an ashlar wall that ran north to south. In the middle of the wall was an entranceway (h. 2.25 m × w. 1.70 m) which contained two steps. At the far end of the cella was a niche (h. 1.40 m × w. 1.40m) cut into the rock. The niche was bordered by two pilasters and a lintel that was slightly vaulted. It was initially painted red, then plastered and whitewashed. A series of steps, which were later covered partially by the podium, led up to the niche. On either side of the niche were two vertical grooves (h. 1.40 m × w. 0.04 m) that indicate where wooden shelving had existed. However, unlike the standard mithraea layout, there was only a single bench (h. 0.60–0.80 m × w. 2.00 m) which ran against the eastern wall, which turned at the corner and continued along the south wall, although it stopped short of reaching the western wall. The bench was plastered and reinforced with stone slabs. There was a narrow cut (h. 0.50 m × w. 0.25 m) through the western wall, located on one side of the door, which has been suggested to have been a light source for the room. The remains of a light shaft also appeared in the north-east corner of the ceiling, but the construction of successive churches over the mithraeum (see below) meant that it no longer reached the surface.

Finds

Six square altars were found broken in the rubble deposited in the cella, along with the cylindrical inscribed altar referred to above and a small statue base. Aside from the other small finds found in pits, the mithraeum was void of finds.

Iconography

The iconography of the Hawarte Mithraeum has been well-publicised for its uniqueness. Scenes were painted on the walls throughout the mithraeum, including across both the walls and ceiling of the cella. Of the five stages of painting, only the last two (four and five) can be distinctively analysed, although the images of period five are the same as of period four, just redrawn slightly. Depicted are various scenes from the life of Mithras and the battle between good and evil, the latter of which is presented in the form of black demons. The good versus evil images include: a depiction of lions devouring these demons; another image from the outer room consisting of a man in Persian garb (Mithras?) holding the chains of a short, black two-headed being, while standing in front of a large white horse; and a city wall topped by various black heads, with rays of light descending on (or attacking) them. The eyes of the demons in these depictions have been scratched out, possibly by Christians. Such images are unparalleled in other mithraea, and Gordon has suggested that this was the product of a distinctly local tradition that has been influenced by Zoroastrianism. The depictions of Mithras' life include: the rock birth; the tauroctony; Mithras in a tree; and Mithras holding an arrow. The scenes from Mithras' life were found in the cella, while the demons adorned the walls of the other rooms, indicating there was a particular spatial arrangement. Other images, within the cella, include: images of items representing the seven Mithraic grades (located underneath the tauroctony painting); hunters on horseback dressed in Phrygian hats chasing animals; Helios; Transitus; and Zeus. Little of the ceiling painting in the cella survives, but from the phase four painting, an inscription could be discerned which read: "The fortune of the [invincible] Mithras [wins!]", which may be an adaption of a hippodrome chant.

Chronology

The earliest activity from the site has been detected in space 'D', where a pit was found to contain ceramic material from the 1st c. BC that was later covered over by a bench. In the same area, another pit, possibly contemporary to the bench, was found to contain ceramics from the 1st c. AD. Another pit, located in the *cella* of the mithraeum, also contained ceramic material, along with glass vessels, animal bones and ash, from the latter half of the 1st c. AD. This was also later covered by a bench. Who it was that deposited these remains is unknown, but the deposits predate the Mithraic structure by centuries. An altar dumped amongst the rumble of the cave bears a short Greek inscription referring to M. Longinus. This has been matched to another inscription on an altar that dated to AD 142/43, which was found in a previous excavation in a modern building nearby. Neither altar bears any indications of being Mithraic.

The mithraeum itself appears to date to the turn of the 4th c., as stratum just above the bedrock produced a coin of Diocletian and two others dating to the 2nd c. In the mid 4th c., alterations were made, with the addition of the podium in front of the niche in *cella*, under which coins of Constans and Constantius II were found. Around the same time, the first images were painted onto the walls and the podium. Another stratum covers the floor level, which produced lamps and coins dating to the 4th c. The walls and podium were repainted five times, until a pedestal was added to the right-hand wall of the niche. Between the wall and the pedestal was a fill containing lamps and coins, the latter of which dated to the reigns of Theodosius and Arcadius (d. 408). In space 'D' two coins of Arcadius were also found. The temple must have been abandoned shortly after these coins were deposited, as an inscription from the church erected above it attests to a construction date of AD 421. Probably around the time the church was constructed, the mithraeum was the victim of Christian vandals: the altars were broken, the eyes of the figures on one of the wall paintings were etched out, and a cross was engraved on the wall opposite the entrance. The mithraeum was subsequently filled in, after which the foundation trenches for the church were cut through it. Parts of the mithraeum were used in the substructure of the church, such as the doorjambs of the *cella*, which were utilised in the foundation of the narthex.

J.4 *Šaʿāra*
Selected Bibliography: Kalos (2001).

Excavated
2000

Location
Two mithraea were situated in a cave system outside the village. It was located in close proximity to several other buildings, two of which appear to have been military in nature.

Structure
The mithraea were located in two separate caves, the entrances of which were surrounded by wall that created a courtyard area. The side of the hill was covered with a 43 m long façade, which currently stands at 3–4 m tall. The remains of porticoes have been found in front of these caves, as have the slots for doorposts at the entrances to the caves.

Little survived in one of the caves, although amongst the rubble found therein were the remains of a rock-birth image. At the entrance to this cave, a lintel was found with two crosses carved into it.

The mithraeum located in the other cave provided much more information. This cave had been artificially divided into two rooms, the first being a hall, roughly square in shape (h. 7 m × w. 7 m). The section of the roof closest to the door consisted of flat basalt slabs, while at the far end is a lowered barrel vault supported by corbels. The walls of the hall were made of basalt blocks, which have produced traces of lime mortar and were most likely painted. Along the south and side walls were niches, about 1–1.3 m off the ground and 0.6–0.8 m deep. The remnants of basalt slabs used to pave the floor survived, but did not stretch to the walls, with a band of 0.4–0.6 m running around the outside. Kalos believed that this space was occupied by benches, taken out at a later stage. In the north-eastern corner of the room there was another doorway which led to another courtyard.

Accessed via an entrance in the northern side of the hall (w. 2.6 m), the apse, which was a natural crevice, was raised to 1 m higher than the floor of the hall. Around the border of the lower half of the apse were depictions from Mithras' life, while around the upper half, and arching over its roof, were images of the Zodiac. The majority of these images had been chiselled away, except for the depictions of foliage. The apse is offset to the west of the axis of the main entrance, so it could not be seen directly. Evidence for doors, in the form of jambs, have been uncovered. To the west of the apse were three small niches, which were possibly used to store sacred objects.

Chronology
Although medieval occupation had severely disturbed the site, a coin dating to the reign of Trajan was found in the mithraeum. Kalos has compared some of the architectural features of this mithraeum to that of Dura-Europos, such as the raised podium and the intention to make the inner sanctuary as cave-like as possible. This, along with the similar zodiac reliefs found at both sites, led him to suggest that the second mithraeum at Šaʿāra was built around the same time as that at Dura, so in the late 2nd c.

When the Šaʿāra mithraea went out of use cannot be dated. The vandalism of the images on the arch, chiselled away systematically apart from the foliage, and the two crosses etched above the doorway to the mithraeum, indicate that the mithraic complex was the victim of Christian iconoclasts. Yet the lack of finds from the mithraea suggests the Mithraic adherents had abandoned the structure prior to this attack. Kalos postulates that the vandalism occurred in the Byzantine period (when several churches were constructed near the site) rather than in the Late Roman era.

Appendix B: Mithraea Constructed and Repaired *ca.* AD 201–400

TABLE B.1 *Construction of Mithraea*

Province	Location	Constructed	Median Date	Reference
Ostia	Ostia ('Planta Pedis')	204–11	207	White (2012) 442
Ostia	Ostia ('Del Palazzo Imperiale')	193–225	210	White (2012) 442
Italy	Aveia	213	213	Jouffroy (1986) 144
Britain	Vindobala (Rudchester)	Early 3rd c.	215	Gillam and MacIvor (1954) 186
Pannonia	Carnuntum III	Early 3rd c.	215	*CIMRM* 2. 1696
Pannonia	Fertőrákos	Early 3rd c.	215	*CIMRM* 2. 1646
Pannonia	Aquincum II	Early 3rd c.	215	Póczy and Zsidi (1995) 36
Spain	Lucus Augusti (Lugo)	Early 3rd c.	215	Alvar, Gordon and Rodriguez (2006) 267
Pannonia	Poetovio II	Early 3rd c.	215	Beskow (1980) 5
Syria	Doliche	Early 3rd c.	215	Gordon (2007)
Italy	Ostia ('Menandro')	Early 3rd c.	215	White (2012) 442
Rome	Crypta Balbi	Early 3rd c.	215	Saguì (2004) 167
Rome	Baths of Caracalla	Early 3rd c.	215	*LTUR* 3 (1996) 267
Gaul	Bordeaux	Early 3rd c.	215	Gaidon-Bunuel (1991) 56
Britain	Borcovicium (Housesteads)	Severan	215	*CIMRM* 1. 862
Britain	Brocolitia (Carrawburgh)	Severan	215	*CIMRM* 1. 845
Italy	Castrimoenium	Severan	215	Jouffroy (1986) 143
Rome	San Clemente	Severan (?)	215	Bjørnebye (2007) 42
Germany	Aquae Matticae	218	218	*CIMRM* 2. 1235
Italy	Sentium	219	219	Jouffroy (1986) 144
Noricum	Rüse	235–40	237	*CIMRM* 2. 1448
Britain	Londinium	250	250	Shepherd (1998) 61
Dalmatia	Arupium (Prozor) I	Mid 3rd c.	250	*CIMRM* 2. 1851
Dalmatia	Arupium (Prozor) II	Mid 3rd c.	250	Beck (1984) 367
Gaul	Tienen	Mid 3rd c.	250	Martens (2004) 26
Gaul	Venetonimagus	Mid 3rd c.	250	Walters (1974) 9–10
Germany	Reichweiler	Mid 3rd c.	250	Bernhard (1990)
Pannonia	Heviz	Mid 3rd c.	250	Müller (2006) 92
Noricum	Zgornja Pohanca	Mid 3rd c. (?)	250	*CIMRM* 2. 1461
Italy	Ponza	3rd c.	250	Vermaseren (1974) 13
Italy	Vulci	3rd c.	250	Moretti (1979) 265
Italy	Ostia ('Lucrezio')	3rd c.	250	White (2012) 442
Italy	Ostia ('Baths of Mithras')	3rd c.	250	White (2012) 442
Moesia	Biljanovac	252	252	*CIMRM* 2. 2201
Noricum	Ad Enum	258	258	Steidl (2008)
Italy	Ostia ('Fructosus')	251–300	275	White (2012) 442
Italy	Ostia ('Porta Romana')	251–300	275	White (2012) 442
Noricum	Lentia	275	275	Karnitsch (1956) 197
Italy	Ostia ('House of Diana')	Late 3rd c.	280	White (2012) 443
Rome	Ospedale San Giovanni	Late 3rd c.	280	Santa Maria Scrinari (1979) 224
Rome	Foro Boario (Circus Max)	Late 3rd c.	280	Bjørnebye (2007) 34
Dalmatia	Epidaurum (Cavtat)	Late 3rd c.	280	*CIMRM* 2. 1882
Dalmatia	Konjic	Late 3rd c.	280	Sauer (2004) 346
Gaul	Trier	Late 3rd c.	280	Sauer (2004) 348
Noricum	Schachadorf	Late 3rd c.	280	*CIMRM* 2. 1411
Italy	Ostia ('Felicissimus')	Late 3rd c.	280	White (2012) 443

© KONINKLIJKE BRILL NV, LEIDEN, 2019 | DOI 10.1163/9789004383067_009

126 APPENDIX B

TABLE B.1 *Construction of Mithraea* (cont.)

Province	Location	Constructed	Median Date	Reference
Italy	Ostia ('Serpents')	Late 3rd c.	280	White (2012) 443
Pannonia	Poetovio V	285	285	Tušek (1990) 271
Syria	Hawarte	Tetrarchic (?)	290	Gawlikowski (2007) 350
Gaul	Les Boldards	Tetrarchic	290	Walters (1974) 14
Rome	Phrygianum	313	313	CIMRM 1. 523
Dalmatia	Jajce	Constantinian (?)	324	CIMRM 2. 1905
Rome	Via Giovanni Lanza 128	Constantinian	324	Bjørnebye (2007) 50–51
Italy	Spoletium	301–50	325	CIMRM 1. 682
Germany	Gimmeldigen	325	325	CIMRM 2. 1315
Germany	Rockenhausen	330	330	Schwertheim (1974)
Gaul	Septeuil	Mid 4th c.	350	Gaidon-Bunuel (1991) 57
Noricum	St Urban	Mid 4th c.	350	CIMRM 2. 1442
Rome	House of the Olympii I	Mid 4th c.	350	CIMRM 1. 400–405
Rome	House of the Olympii II	385	385	CIMRM 1. 406

TABLE B.2 *Repair of Mithraea*

Province	Location	Date	Median Date	Reference
Syria	Dura-Europos	210	210	CIMRM 1. 34
Italy	Capua	201–50	225	Vermaseren (1971) 51
Noricum	Virunum	239	239	Piccottini (1994)
Syria	Dura-Europos	240	240	CIMRM 1. 34
Gaul	Martigny	3rd c. (?)	250	Wiblé (2004) 138
Britain	Vindobala (Rudchester)	Mid 3rd c. (?)	250	Gillam and MacIvor (1954) 196
Britain	Brocolitia (Carrawburgh)	Mid 3rd c. (phases II.1–3)	250	Richmond, Gillam and Birley (1951) 9–28
Italy	Ostia ('Planta Pedis')	253–59	256	White (2012) 489–91
Pannonia	Poetovio III	260s	265	CIMRM 2. 197
Rome	Castra Peregrinorum (Santo Stefano Rotondo)	Late 3rd c.	280	Bjørnebye (2007) 30
Britain	Londinium	Late 3rd c.	280	Shepherd (1998) 78
Gaul	Burdigala (Bordeaux)	Late 3rd c. (?)	280	Gaidon-Bunuel (1991) 56
Rome	Crypta Balbi	Late 3rd/ Early 4th c.	301	Ricci (2004) 162
Britain	Londinium	Tetrarchic (?)	301	Shepherd (1998) 89
Britain	Brocolitia	Late 3rd/Early 4th c.	301	Richmond, Gillam and Birley (1951) 34
Pannonia	Poetovio IV	Late 3rd/Early 4th c.	301	CIMRM 2. 1614
Pannonia	Carnuntum III (?)	308	308	CIMRM 2. 1698[a]
Noricum	Virunum	311	311	CIMRM 2. 1431
Rome	Foro Boario	301–50	325	Bjørnebye (2007) 34
Syria	Hawarte	Mid 4th c.	350	Gawlikowski (2007) 348

APPENDIX B

Province	Location	Date	Median Date	Reference
Numidia	Cirta	364–67	365	*CIMRM* 1. 129
Gaul	Martigny	360s	365	Wiblé (2004) 137
Germany	Bornheim-Sechtem	360s	365	Ulbert (2004) 87
Syria	Hawarte	Late 4th/Early 5th c.	401	Gawlikowski (2007) 350

a Vermaseren gives the date of the Tetrarchic conference as 307, but this conference probably took place the following year in 308: see Leadbetter (2009) 200–205.

Bibliography

Ancient Textual Editions

I have sought to use translations based on respectable editions wherever possible. For the convenience of the reader, references to the ancient text are provided. In the case of Loeb translations, Greek and Latin text is provided alongside the English.

Amb. *Ep.* = J. H. W. G. Liebeschuetz transl., *Ambrose of Milan: Political Letters and Speeches* (Translated Texts for Historians 43) (Liverpool 2005). M. Zelzer ed., *Sancti Ambrosi Opera, Pars X, Epistulae et Acta* (CSEL 82) (Vienna 1982).

Amb. *Acta* = M. Zelzer ed., *Sancti Ambrosi Opera. Pars X, Epistulae et Acta* (CSEL 82) (Vienna 1982) 312–68.

Ambrosiaster, *Quaestiones veteris et novi testamenti* = A. Souter ed., *Pseudo-Augustini. Quaestiones Veteris et Novi Testamenti CXXVII* (CSEL 50) (Vienna 1908).

Amm. Marc = J. C. Rolfe transl., *Ammianus Marcellinus*, 3 vols. (Loeb Classical Library) (London-Cambridge, Mass. 1935–39). C. D. Yonge transl., Ammianus Marcellinus, *Roman History* (Bohn's Classical Library) (London 1862).

Apul. *Met.* = J. A. Hanson ed. and transl., *Metamorphoses*, 2 vols. (Loeb Classical Library) (Cambridge, Mass. 1989). R. Helm ed., *Apuleius I: Metamorphoseon Libri XI* (Leipzig, 3rd edn. 1968).

Caesarius, *Serm.* = M.-J. Delage ed. and transl., *Césaire d'Arles: sermons au peuple*, 3 vols. (Sources Chrétiennes 175, 243, 333) (Paris 1971–96). M. M. Mueller transl., *Sermons* (Fathers of the Church 3) (Milwaukee 1972).

Cod. Theod. = T. Mommsen and P. Meyer *et al.* edd., *Theodosiani Libri XVI cum Constitutionibus Sirmondianis*, 2 vols. (Berlin 1905).

Euseb. *Vit. Const.* = A. Cameron and S. G. Hall transl., *Life of Constantine* (Oxford 1999). F. Winkelmann ed., *Die Textbezeugung der Vita Constantini des Eusebius von Caesarea* (Berlin 1962).

Exodus = *The Bible, The New English Bible, Book of Exodus* (King James transl.) (Oxford 1970).

Firm. Mat. *Err. prof. rel.* = R. Turcan ed. and transl., *L'erreur des religions païennes* (Paris 1982) (French and Latin).

Greg. Naz. *Or.* = J. Bernardi ed. and transl., *Grégoire de Nazianze Discours 4–5 contre Julien* (Sources Chrétiennes 309) (Paris 1983). J-P. Migne ed., *Tou en hagiois patros hēmōn Grēgoriou tou Theologou, Archiepiskopou Kōnstantinoupoleōs ta euriskomena panta* (PG 35–36) (Paris 1885–86).

Gregory of Tours, *Hist.* = E. Brehaut transl., *Gregory of Tours, History of the Franks* (New York 1916). B. Krusch and W. Levison edd., *Gregorii episcopi Turonensis. Libri Historiarum X* (MGH SRM 1.1) (Hanover, revised edn. 1951).

Jer. *Ep.* = F. A. Wright transl., *Jerome, Selected Letters* (London 1933). I. Hilberg ed., *Hieronymus, Epistulae 71–120*, 4 vols. (CSEL 55) (Vienna, revised edn. 1996).

Julian, *Ep.* = F. C. Hertlein ed. *Iuliani Imperatoris quae supersunt praeter reliquias apud Cyrillum omnia* (Leipzig 1875–76).

Julian, *Mis.* = W. C. Wright transl., *The Works of the Emperor Julian*, vol. 2 (Loeb Classical Library) (London 1913) 421–512. F. C. Hertlein ed., *Iuliani Imperatoris quae supersunt praeter reliquias apud Cyrillum omnia* (Leipzig 1875–76). H.-G. Nesselrath ed., *Iulianus Augustus opera* (Berlin 2015).

Julian, *Or.* = W. C. Wright transl., *The Works of the Emperor Julian*, vol. 1 (Loeb Classical Library) (London 1913). F. C. Hertlein ed., *Iuliani Imperatoris quae supersunt praeter reliquias apud Cyrillum omnia* (Leipzig 1875–76). H.-G. Nesselrath ed., *Iulianus Augustus opera* (Berlin 2015).

Julian, *The Caesars* = W. C. Wright transl., *The Works of the Emperor Julian*, vol. 2 (Loeb Classical Library) (London 1913) 343–415. F. C. Hertlein ed., *Iuliani Imperatoris quae supersunt praeter reliquias apud Cyrillum omnia* (Leipzig 1875–76). H.-G. Nesselrath ed., *Iulianus Augustus opera* (Berlin 2015).

Just. *apol* = D. Minns and P. Parvis edd., *Justin, Philosopher and Martyr: Apologies* (Oxford 2009). E. J. Goodspeed ed., *Index apologeticus: sive, Clavis Iustini Martyris operum Aliorumque apologetarum pristinorum* (Leipzig 1912).

Just. *dial.* = P. Bobichon ed. *Dialogue avec Tryphon*, 2 vols. (Paradosis 47) (Fribourg 2003). E. J. Goodspeed ed., *Index apologeticus: sive, Clavis Iustini Martyris operum Aliorumque apologetarum pristinorum* (Leipzig 1912).

Lactant. *Div. inst.* = A. Bowen and P. Garnsey transl., *Lactantius: Divine Institutes* (Translated Texts for Historians 40) (Liverpool 2003). E. Heck and A. Wlosok edd., *Lactantius. Divinarum institutionum libri septem* (Munich-Leipzig 2005).

Lib. *Or.* = R. Foerster edd., *Libanii Opera*, 12 vols. (Leipzig 1903–27).

Mosaicarum et Romanarum Legum Collatio = M. Hyamson transl., *Mosaicarum et Romanarum Legum Collatio* (London 1913) (English and Latin).

Paul. *Carm.* = W. von Hartel ed., *Sancti Pontii Meropii Paulini Nolani Carmina* (CSEL 30) (Vienna 1894).

Paul. *Ep.* = P. G. Walsh transl., *Letters of St Paulinus of Nola* (Ancient Christian Writers 35) (London 1966). W. von Hartel ed., *Sancti Pontii Meropii Paulini Nolani Epistulae* (CSEL 29) (Vienna 1894).

Plut. *Vit. Pomp.* = B. Perrin transl., *Plutarch's Lives*, vol. 5 (Loeb Classical Library) (London 1955) 116–325.

BIBLIOGRAPHY

Plut. *Mor.* = F. H. Sandbach transl., *Plutarch's Moralia. Fragments from Other Named Works*, vol. 15 (Loeb Classical Library) (London 1969) 317–25.

Ruf. *HE* = P. R. Amidon transl., *The Church History of Rufinus of Aquileia Books 10 and 11* (Oxford 1997). J-P. Migne ed., *Tyranni Rufini Aquileiensis presbyteri opera omnia* (PL 21) (Paris 1878) 467–540.

Serv. *In Vergilii Carmina Commentarii* = G. Thilo and H. Hagen edd., *In Vergilii Carmina Commentarii* (Leipzig 1884).

Socrates, *Hist. eccl.* = G. C. Hansen ed., *Kirchengeschichte. Socrates Scholasticus: Historia Ecclesiastica* (GCS new series 1) (Berlin 1995).

Sozom. *Hist. eccl.* = J. Bidez and G. C. Hansen edd., *Sozomenus: Kirchengeschichte* (GCS 50) (Berlin 1960).

Stat. *Theb.* = C. S. Ross transl., *The Thebaid: Seven against Thebes* (Baltimore 2004). A. Klotz and T. C. Klinnert edd., *Thebais. Statius, P. Papinius* (Publius Papinius) (Leipzig 1973).

Suet. *Aug.* = J. C. Rolfe transl., *Lives of the Caesars*, vol. 1 (Loeb Classical Library) (London 1913).

Sulp. Sev. *Dial.* = J. Fontaine and N. Dupré edd. and transl., *Gallus. Dialogues sur les 'vertus' de Saint Martin* 2 vols. (Sources Chrétiennes 510) (Paris 2006). C. Halm ed., *Sulpicii Severi libri qui supersunt* (CSEL 1) (Vienna 1866).

Symm. *Ep.* = O. Seeck ed., *Q. Aurelii Symmachi quae supersunt* (Berlin 1883).

Tert. *De corona* = F. Ruggiero transl., *De Corona* (Classici greci e latini 30) (Milan 1992). J.-P. Migne ed., *Quinti Septimi Florentis Tertulliani presbyteri Carthaginensis opera omnia*, 2 vols. (PL 1–2) (Paris 1844–79).

Tert. *De Prae. Hae.* = T. H. Bindley transl., *Tertullian: On the Testimony of the Soul and on the "Prescription" of Heretics* (London 1914). J.-P. Migne ed., *Quinti Septimi Florentis Tertulliani presbyteri Carthaginensis opera omnia*, 2 vols. (PL 1–2) (Paris 1844–79).

Thdt. *affect.* = P. Canivet transl., *Thérapeutique des maladies helléniques*, vol. 1 (Sources Chrétiennes 57) (Paris 1958) (French and Greek).

V. *Porph.* = H. Gregoire and M.-A. Kugener edd., *Marc le Diacre: Vie de Porphyre* (Paris 1930) (French and Greek).

Zos. = F. Paschoud edd. and transl., (French) *Zosime Histoire Nouvelle* vols. 1–3.2 (Paris 1971–89). R. T. Ridley transl., (English) *Zosimus, New History* (Byzantina Australiensia 2) (Canberra 1982). L. Mendelssohn ed., *Zosimi comitis et exadvocati fisci Historia nova* (Leipzig 1887).

Modern Sources

Abramič M. (1925) *Poetovio. Führer durch die Denkmäler der römischen Stadt* (Vienna 1925).

Adrych A., Bracey R., Dalglish D., Lenk S. and Wood R. (2017) *Images of Mithra* (Oxford 2017).

Alföldi A. (1937) *A Festival of Isis in Rome under the Christian Emperors of the IVth Century* (Budapest 1937).

Alföldy G. (1974) *Noricum* (London 1974).

Allason-Jones L. (2004) "Mithras on Hadrian's Wall", in *Roman Mithraism: the Evidence of the Small Finds*, edd. M. Martens and G. De Boe (Brussels 2004) 183–89.

Allason-Jones L. and McKay B. (1985) *Coventina's Well: a Shrine on Hadrian's Wall* (Hexham 1985).

Alvar J. (2008) *Romanising Oriental Gods: Myth, Salvation and Ethics in the Cults of Cybele, Isis and Mithras* (Leiden 2008).

Alvar J., Gordon R. and Rodriguez C. (2006) "The mithraeum at Lugo (Lucus Augusti) and its connection with Legio VII Gemina", *JRA* 19 (2006) 266–77.

Athanassiadi P. (1981) *Julian and Hellenism* (Oxford 1981).

Bakker J. T. (1994) *Living and Working with the Gods: Studies of Evidence for Private Religion and its Material Environment in the City of Ostia (100–500 AD)* (Amsterdam 1994).

Barraud D. and Caillabet-Duloum G. (2007) *Burdigala: bilan de deux siecles de recherches*: http://www.cervantes virtual.com/bib/portal/simulacraromae/libro/c13.pdf (last accessed 4.2.16).

Bayliss R. (2004) *Provincial Cilicia and the Archaeology of Temple Conversion* (BAR-IS 1281) (Oxford 2004).

Beck R. (2006) *The Religion of the Mithras Cult in the Roman Empire* (Oxford 2006).

Beck R. (2000) "Ritual, myth, doctrine, and initiation in the mysteries of Mithras: new evidence from a cult vessel", *JRS* 90 (2000) 145–80.

Beck R. (1984) "The rock-cut mithraea of Arupium (Dalmatia)", *Phoenix* 38 (1984) 356–71.

Bedon R., Chevallier R. and Pinon P. (1988) *Architecture et urbanisme en Gaule romaine* (Paris 1988).

Bernhard H. (1990) "Reichweiler", in *Die Römer in Rheinland-Pfalz*, edd. H. Cüppers (Stuttgart 1990) 527–28.

Beskow P. (1980) "The portorium and the mysteries of Mithras", *JMithSt* 3 (1980) 1–18.

Bidez J. (1930) *La vie de l'empereur Julien* (Paris 1930).

Bielmann C. (2013) *A Christianisation of Switzerland? Urban and Rural Transformations in a Time of Transition—AD 300–800* (Ph.D. diss., Univ. of Leicester 2013).

Bird J. (2007) "Incense in Mithraic ritual", in *Food for the Gods: New Light on the Ancient Incense Trade*, edd. D. Peacock and D. Williams (Oxford 2007) 122–34.

Birley A. and Birley A. R. (2012) "A New dolichenum, inside the third-century fort at Vindolanda", in *Iuppiter Dolichenus: vom Lokalkult zur Reichsreligion*, edd. M. Blömer and E. Winter (Mohr Siebeck 2012) 231–58.

Bjørnebye J. (2016) "Reinterpreting the cult of Mithras", in *Pagans and Christians in Late Antique Rome: Conflict, Competition and Coexistence in the Fourth Century*, edd. M. R. Salzman, M. Sághy and R. Lizzi Testa (New York 2016) 197–212.

Bjørnebye J. (2007) *The Cult of Mithras in Fourth Century Rome* (Ph.D. diss., Univ. of Bergen 2007).

Blakely J. and Horton F. (1987) *Caesarea Maritima: the Pottery and Dating of Vault 1: Horreum, Mithraeum, and Later Uses* (Lewiston, New York 1987).

Bloch H. (1963) "The pagan revival in the West at the end of the fourth century", in *The Conflict Between Paganism and Christianity in the Fourth Century*, edd. A. Momigliano (Oxford 1963) 193–218.

Boin D. (2013) *Ostia in Late Antiquity* (Cambridge 2013).

Boon G. (1960) "A temple of Mithras at Caernarvon-Segontium", *Archaeologia Cambrensis* 109 (1960) 136–78.

Bormann E. (1895) "Das dritte Mithraeum", *AEM* 18 (1895) 169–201.

Bosanquet R. (1904) "Excavations on the line of the Roman wall in Northumberland", *Archaeologia Aeliania* 4 (1904) 193–305.

Bowden H. (2010) *Mystery Cults in the Ancient World* (London 2010).

Bradbury S. (1995) "Julian's pagan revival and the end of blood sacrifice", *Phoenix* 49 (1995) 331–56.

Brashear W. M. (1992) *A Mithraic Catechism from Egypt* (Vienna 1992).

Bremmer J. (2014) *Initiation into the Mysteries of the Ancient World* (Berlin 2014).

Brenot C. (1990) "La numismatique", in *Le site de Notre-Dame d'Avinionet à Mandelieu*, edd. M. Fixot (Paris 1990) 202–28.

Brewer R. J. (1993) "Venta Silurum: a civitas-capital", in *Roman Towns: the Wheeler Inheritance: a Review of 50 Years' Research*, edd. S. J. Streep (Council for British Archaeology Research Report 93) (York 1993).

Brewer R. J. (1990) "Caerwent—Venta Silurum", *Trivium* 25 (1990) 75–85.

Brown, P. (1981) *The Cult of the Saints, its Rise and Function in Latin Christianity* (London 1981).

Brown, P. (1970) "Sorcery, demons, and the rise of Christianity from Late Antiquity to the Middle Ages", in *Witchcraft Confessions and Accusations*, edd. M. Douglas (London 1970) 17–45.

Bryan J., Cubitt R. S., Hill J., Holder N., Jackson S. and Watson S. (2017) *Archaeology at Bloomberg* (London 2017).

Bull R. (1978) "The mithraeum at Caesarea Maritima," in *Etudes mithriaques: actes du 2e congrès international, Téhéran, du 1er au 8 septembre 1975*, edd. J. Duchesne-Guillemin (Leiden 1978) 75–90.

Cameron A. (2011) *The Last Pagans of Rome* (Oxford 2011).

Cammerer B. (1976) "Riegel Mithraeum", in *Die Römer in Baden-Württemberg*, edd. P. Filtzinger, D. Planck and B. Cammerer (Stuttgart 1976) 506–508.

Carroll M. (2001) *Romans, Celts and Germans* (Stroud 2001).

Caseau B. (1999) "Sacred landscapes", in *Late Antiquity: a Guide to the Postclassical World*, edd. G. B. Bowerstock, P. Brown and O. Grabar (London 1999) 21–59.

Chapula A. (2005) "Hyenas or lionesses? Mithraism and omen in the religious world of the Late Antiquity", *Religio: Revue pro religionistiku* 13 (2005) 198–230.

Chastagnol A. (1986) "La législation sur les biens des villes au IVe siècle à la lumière d'une inscription d'Ephèse", in *Atti dell'Accademia Romanistica Costantiniana. VI Convegno internazionale* (Naples 1986) 143–70.

Chenault R. (2016) "Beyond pagans and Christians: politics and intra-Christian conflict in the controversy over the Altar of Victory", in *Pagans and Christians in Late Antique Rome: Conflict, Competition, and Coexistence in the Fourth Century*, edd. M. Salzman, M. Sághy and R. Lizzi Testa (New York 2016) 46–63.

Chioffi L. (1996) "Iuppiter Dolichenus, Aedes", in *LTUR*, vol. 3, ed. E. M. Steinby (1996) 132.

Cholet L. (1989) "Le sanctuaire des eaux de Sepeteuil (Yvelines): recherches sur la persistance de la fonction cultuelle d'un site", *Connaître les Yvelines* 2 (1989) 19–21.

Christie N. (2011) *The Fall of the Western Roman Empire: an Archaeological and Historical Perspective* (London 2011).

Clauss M. (2012) *Mithras: Kult und Mysterium* (Darmstadt 2012).

Clauss M. (1992) *Cultores Mithrae* (Stuttgart 1992).

Collins R. (2012) *Hadrian's Wall and the End of Empire* (New York 2012).

Cristilli A. (2015) "Macellum and imperium. The relationship between the Roman state and the market-building construction", *Analysis Archaeologica* 1 (2015) 69–86.

Croxford B. (2003) "Iconoclasm in Late Roman Britain?", *Britannia* 34 (2003) 81–95.

Cumont F. (1896–99) *Textes et monuments figurés relatifs aux mystères de Mithra*, 2 vols. (Brussels 1896–99).

Curran (2000) *Pagan City and Christian capital: Rome in the Fourth Century* (Oxford 2000).

David J. (2000) "The exclusion of women in the Mithraic mysteries: ancient or modern?", *Numen* 47 (2000) 121–41.

David M. (2016) "Osservazioni sul banchetto rituale mitraico a partire dal 'Mitreo dei marmi colorati' di Ostia antica", in *L'alimentazione nell'antichità. Atti della XLVI settimana di studi aquileiesi*, edd. M. M. Roberti and G. Cuscito (Antichità altoadriatiche 84) (Trieste 2016) 173–84.

Decker K., Gangl G. and Kandler M. (2006) "The earthquake of Carnuntum in the fourth century AD—archaeological results, seismologic scenario and seismotectonic implications for the Vienna Basin Fault, Austria", *Journal of Seismology* 10 (2006) 479–95.

Deichmann F. (1939) "Frühchristliche Kirchen in antiken Heiligtümern", *JdI* 54 (1939) 105–36 (repr. with additions, in idem, *Rom, Ravenna, Konstantinopel, Naher Osten. Gesammelte Studien zur spätantiken Architektur, Kunst und Geschichte* (Wiesbaden 1982) 56–94.

Delmaire R. (1989) *Largesses sacrées et res privata: l'aerarium impérial et son administration du IVe au VIe siècle* (Rome 1989).

BIBLIOGRAPHY

Demarsin K. (2011) "'Paganism' in Late Antiquity: thematic studies", in *The Archaeology of Late Antique 'Paganism'*, edd. L. Lavan and M. Mulryan (Late Antique Archaeology 7) (Leiden 2011) 3–40.

Derks T. (1998) *Gods, Temples and Ritual Practices: the Transformation of Religious Ideas and Values in Roman Gaul* (Amsterdam 1998).

Dijkstra J. H. F. (2011) "The fate of the temples in late antique Egypt", in *The Archaeology of Late Antique 'Paganism'*, edd. L. Lavan and M. Mulryan (Late Antique Archaeology 7) (Leiden 2011) 389–436.

Eckhart L. (1981) *Forschungen in Lauriacum 11. 1–3, 1960–1966. Die Stadtpfarrkirche und Friedhofskirche St. Laurentius von Enns-Lorch-Lauriacum in Oberösterreich* (Linz 1981).

Elm S. (2016) "The letter collection of the emperor Julian", in *Late Antique Letter Collections: a Critical Introduction and Reference Guide*, edd. C. Sogno, B. K. Storin and E. J. Watts (Oakland 2016).

Ensoli S. and La Rocca E. (2000) edd. *Aurea Roma: dalla città pagana alla città cristiana* (Rome 2000).

Ertel C. (2001) "Zur Architektur der Mithräen von Poetovio", in *Archaeologia Poetovionensis Ptuj in Römischen Reich Mithraskult und Seine Zeit*, edd. M. J. Gojkovič (Ptuj 2001) 167–78.

Esmonde Cleary S. (2013) *The Roman West, AD 200–500* (Cambridge 2013).

Evans A. J. (1884) "Antiquarian researches in Illyricum", *Archaeologia* 48 (1884) 1–105.

Faber A. (1973) "Grada za topografiju antičkog Siska/ Zusammenfassung: materialien zur topographie der antiken stadt Siscia", *Vjesnik Arheološkog Muzeja u Zagrebu* 7 (1973) 133–62.

Fauduet I. (1993) *Les temples de la tradition celtique en Gaule romaine* (Paris 1993).

Fitz J. (1980) "The way of life", in *The Archaeology of Roman Pannonia*, edd. A. Lengyel and G. T. B. Radan (Budapest 1980) 161–75.

Forrer R. (1915) *Das Mithra-Heiligtum von Königshofen bei Strassburg* (Stuttgart 1915).

Fowden G. (1978) "Bishops and temples in the eastern Roman empire 320–435", *JThS* 29 (1978) 53–78.

Frankfurter D. (1998) *Religion in Roman Egypt: Assimilation and Resistance* (Princeton 1998).

Gaidon-Bunuel M. A. (1991) "Les mithraea de Septeuil et de Bordeaux", *Revue Du Nord-Archeologie* 73 (1991) 49–58.

Gaidon-Bunuel M. A. and Caillat P. (2008) "Honorer Mithra en mangeant: la cuisine du mithraeum de Septeuil (La Férie)", in *Archéologie du sacrifice animal en Gaule romaine: rituels et pratiques alimentaires* edd. S. Lepetz and W. van Andringa (Montagnac 2008) 255–66.

Gallo D. (1979) "Il mitreo di Via Giovanni Lanza", in *Mysteria Mithrae*, edd. U. Bianchi (Leiden 1979) 249–58.

Garbsch J. (1985) "Das Mithraeum von Pons Aeni", *Bayerische Vorgeschichtsblatter* 50 (1985) 355–462.

Gawlikowski M. (2012) "Excavations in Hawarte 2008–2009", *Polish Archaeology in the Mediterranean* 21 (2012) 481–95.

Gawlikowski M. (2007) "The mithraeum at Hawarte and its paintings", *JRA* 20 (2007) 337–61.

Gawlikowski M. (2001) "Hawarte: excavation and restoration work in 2001", *Polish Archaeology in the Mediterranean* 13 (2001) 271–78.

Gawlikowski M. (2000) "Hawarte: third interim report on the work in the mithraeum", *Polish Archaeology in the Mediterranean* 12 (2000) 309–14.

Ghetta M. (2008) *Spätantikes Heidentum: Trier und das Trevererland* (Trier 2008).

Gibbon E. (1781) *The History of the Decline and Fall of the Roman Empire*, vol. 3 (London 1781).

Gillam J. P. and MacIvor I. (1954) "The temple of Mithras at Rudchester", *Archaeologia Aeliana* 32 (1954) 176–219.

Glaser F. (2002) "Teurnia", in *The Autonomous Towns of Noricum and Pannonia: Noricum*, edd. M. Šašel Kos and P. Scherrer (Ljubljana 2002) 135–47.

Goddard C. (2006) "The evolution of pagan sanctuaries in late antique Italy (fourth-sixth Centuries AD): a new administrative and legal framework: a paradox", in *Les cités de l'Italie tardo-antique, IVe–VIe siècle: institutions, économie, société, culture et religion*, edd. M. Ghilaridi, C. Goddard and P. Porena (Rome 2006) 281–308.

Goddard C. (2002) "Les formes festives de l'allégeance au prince en Italie centrale, sous le règne de Constantin: un suicide religieux?", *MÉFRA* 114 (2002) 1025–88.

Gömöri J. (2003) "Scarbantia", in *The Autonomous Towns of Noricum and Pannonia: Pannonia I*, edd. M. Šašel Kos and P. Scherrer (Ljubljana 2003) 81–92.

Goodman P. (2011) "Temples in late antique Gaul", in *The Archaeology of Late Antique 'Paganism'*, edd. L. Lavan and M. Mulryan (Late Antique Archaeology 7) (Leiden 2011) 165–94.

Gordon R. (2009) "The Mithraic body", in *Mystic Cults in Magna Graecia*, edd. G. Casadio and P. Johnston (Austin, Texas 2009) 290–313.

Gordon R. (2007) "Mithras in Doliche: issues of date and origin", *JRA* 20 (2007) 602–10.

Gordon R. (2004) "Small and miniature reproductions of the Mithraic icon: reliefs, pottery, ornaments and gems", in *Roman Mithraism: the Evidence of the Small Finds*, edd. M. Martens and G. De Boe (Brussels 2004) 259–83.

Gordon R. (2001) "Trajets de Mithra en Syrie romaine", *Topoi* 11 (2001) 77–136.

Gordon R. (1999) Review of Sauer, *Mithraism* in *JRA* 12 (1999) 682–88.

Gordon R. (1980) "Reality, evocation and boundary in the mysteries of Mithras", *JMithSt* 3 (1980) 19–99.

Gordon R. (1976) "The sacred geography of a mithraeum: the example of Sette Sfere", *JMithSt* 1 (1976) 119–65.

Gordon R. (1972) "Mithraism and Roman society: social factors in the explanation of religious change in the Roman empire", *Religion* 2 (1972) 92–121.

Gori F. (1879) *Storico artistico archeologico e letterario della città e provincia di Roma* (Rome 1879).

Gorski G. J. and Packer J. E. (2015) *The Roman Forum: a Reconstruction and Architectural Guide* (New York 2015).

Gose E. (1972) *Der gallo-römische Tempelbezirk im Altbachtal zu Trier* (Mainz am Rhein 1972).

Graf F. (2015) *Roman Festivals in the Greek East: From the Early Empire to the Middle Byzantine Era* (Cambridge 2015).

Griffith A. (2006) "Completing the picture: women and the female principle in the Mithraic cult", *Numen* 53 (2006) 48–77.

Griffith A. (2003) "Cult and the ancient urban landscape: a case study of Mithraism and Roman topography", in *Theoretical Frameworks for the Study of Graeco-Roman Religions: Adjuct Proceedings of the XVIIIth International Association for the History of Religions*, edd. L. H. Martin and P. Pachis (Thessalonikia 2003) 67–82.

Griffith A. (2000) "Mithraism in the private and public lives of 4th-c. senators in Rome", *Electronic Journal of Mithraic Studies*: http://www.mithraeum.eu/liber/mithraism_in_the_private_and_public_lives_of_4th_c_senators_in_rome (last accessed 23.1.16).

Griffith A. (1993) *The Archaeological Evidence for Mithraism in Imperial Rome* (Ph.D. diss., Univ. of Michigan 1993).

Grimes W. F. (1968) *Excavation of Roman and Mediaeval London* (London 1968).

Groh S. (2005) "Amphitheater in Noricum", *ÖJh* 74 (2005) 90–91.

Groslambert A. (2011) *Lambèse sous le haut-empire (1er–III siècles): du camp à la cité* (Paris 2011).

Gugl C. and Kremer G. (2011) "Soldaten, Bürger, Kaiser—Mithras at Carnuntum", in *Götterbilder—Menschenbilder: Religion und Kulte in Carnuntum*, edd. F. Humer and G. Kremer (Carnuntum 2011).

Gwynn D. M. (2011) "The 'end' of Roman senatorial paganism", in *The Archaeology of Late Antique 'Paganism'*, edd. L. Lavan and M Mulryan (Late Antique Archaeology 7) (Leiden 2011) 135–61.

Hahn J. (2004) *Gewalt und religiöser Konflikt: Studien zu den Auseinandersetzungen zwischen Christen, Heiden und Juden im Osten des Römischen Reiches (von Konstantin bis Theodosius II)* (Berlin 2004).

Hannestad N. (2001) "Castration in the baths", in *Macellum. Culinaria archaeologica. Robert Fleischer zum 60. Geburtstag von Kollegen, Freuden und Schülern* edd. N. Birkle, I. Domes and S. Fähndrich (Mainz 2011) 67–77.

Hanson R. P. C. (1978) "The transformation of pagan temples into churches in the Early Christian centuries", *JSS* 23 (1978) 257–67.

Hatt J.-J. (1957) "Découverte d'un sanctuaire de Mithra à Mackwiller (Bas-Rhin)", *Cahiers Alsaciens d'Archéologie et d'Histoire* 1 (1957) 51–81.

Hatt J.-J. (1955) "Découverte d'un sanctuaire de Mithra à Mackwiller (Bas-Rhin)", *CRAI* 99 (1955) 405–409.

Henig M. (1998) "Appendix 1: the temple as a bacchium or sacrarium in the fourth century", in *The Temple of Mithras London: Excavations by W. F. Grimes and A. Williams at the Walbrook*, edd. J. Shepherd (London 1998) 230–32.

Holum K. (1988) *King Herod's Dream: Caesarea on the Sea* (London 1988).

Holum K. (1977) "Pulcheria's crusade AD 421–22 and the ideology of imperial victory", *GRBS* 18 (1977) 153–72.

Hörig M. and Schwertheim E. (1987) *Corpus Cultus Iovis Dolicheni* (Études préliminaires aux religions orientales dans l'empire romain 106) (Leiden 1987).

Horvat J., Lovenjak M., Dolenc Vičič A., Lubšina-Tušek M., Tomanič-Jevremov M. and Šubic Z. (2003) "Poetovio: development and topography", in *The Autonomous Towns of Noricum and Pannonia: Pannonia I*, edd. M. Šašel Kos and P. Scherrer (Ljubljana 2003) 153–89.

Hudeczek E. (2002) "Flavia Solva", *The Autonomous Towns of Noricum and Pannonia: Noricum*, edd. M. Šašel Kos and P. Scherrer (Ljubljana 2002) 213–12.

Huld-Zetsche I. (1986) *Mithras in Nida-Heddernheim: Gesamtkatalog* (Frankfurt am Main 1986).

Hunt D. (1993) "Christianising the Roman empire: the evidence of the code", in *The Theodosian Code: Studies in the Imperial Law of Late Antiquity*, edd. J. Harries and I. Wood (London 2010) 143–58.

Hunter D. G. (2004) "Fourth-century Christian writers: Hilary, Victorinus, Ambrosiaster, Ambrose", in *The Cambridge History of Early Christian Literature*, edd. F. Young, L. Ayres and A. Louth (Cambridge 2004) 302–317.

Iannacone L. R. (1994) "Why strict churches are strong", *American Journal of Sociology* 99 (1994) 1180–211.

Iannacone L. R. (1990) "Religious practice: a human capital approach", *Journal for the Scientific Study of Religion* 29 (1990) 297–314.

Jackson R. (1988) *Doctors and Diseases in the Roman Empire* (London 1988).

Jeremić M. (1995) "Architectural stone decoration of Sirmium in the first half of the 4th century—the age of tetrarchs", *Scientific Meeting* 75 (1995) 138–55.

Jones C. P. (2012) "The fuzziness of 'paganism'", *Common Knowledge* 18 (2012) 249–54.

Jouffroy H. (1986) *La construction publique en Italie et dans l'Afrique romaine* (Strasbourg 1986).

Kalos M. (2001) "Un sanctuaire de Mithra inédit en Syrie du sud", *Topoi* 11 (2011) 229–77.

Kandler M. (1989) "Eine erdbebenkatastrophe in Carnuntum?", *ActaArchHung* 41 (1989) 313–36.

Kandler M. and Vetters H. (1986) *Der römische Limes in Österreich* (Vienna 1986).

Karnitsch P. (1962) *Die Linzer Altstadt in römischer und vorgeschichtlicher Zeit* (Linz 1962).

Karnitsch P. (1956) "Der Heilige Bezirk von Lentia", *Historisches Jahrbuch der Stadt Linz* 5 (1956) 189–287.

Kellner H.-J. (1995) "Pfaffenhofen am Inn", in *Die Römer in Bayern*, edd. W. Czysz, K. Dietz, T. Fischer and H.-J. Kellner (1995) 498.

Kempf T. K. (1979) "Das haus der heiligen Helena", *Neues Triererisches Jahrbuch 1978* (1979) 3–16.

Kent J. P. C. (1994) *The Roman Imperial Coinage X: the Divided Empire and the Fall of the Western Parts AD 395–491* (London 1994).

Kenyon K. M. (1935) "The Roman theatre at Verulamium, St Albans", *Archaeologia* 84 (1935) 213–61.

Kern E. (1991) "Le mithraeum de Biesheim-Kunheim (Haut-Rhin)", *Revue du Nord-Archeologie* 73 (1991) 59–65.

King A. C. (2008) "Coins and coin hoards from Romano-Celtic temples in Britain", *Continuity and Innovation in Religion in the Roman West*, vol. 2, edd. R. Haeussler and A. C. King (JRA Supplementary Series 67) (Portsmouth, Rhode Island 2008) 25–42.

Korošec P. (1980) "Starokrščanska svečnika iz rogoznice v Ptuju", *Arheološki Vestnik* 31 (1980) 55–61.

Knox W., Meeus W. and t'Hart M. (1991) "Religious conversions of adolescents: testing the Lofland and Stark Model of religious conversion", *Sociological Analysis* 52 (1991) 227–40.

Kortüm K. and Neth A. (2005) "Mithras im Zabergäu. Die Mithräen von Güglingen", in *Imperium Romanum: Roms Provinzen an Neckar, Rhein und Donau*, edd. H.-J. Trinker (Darmstadt 2005) 225–29.

Kortüm K. and Neth A. (2002) "Römer im Zabergäu: Ausgrabungen im vicus von Güglingen, Kreis Heilbronn", *Archäologische Ausgrabungen in Baden-Württemberg 2002*, edd. J. Beil (Stuttgart 2002) 116–21.

Kosorić M. (1965). "Spomenik Mitrinog Kulta Iz Okoline Zvornika", *Članci Grada za Kulturnu Istoriju Istočne Bosne* 6 (1965) 49–56.

Lampadaridi A. (2016). *La conversion de Gaza au christianisme: la Vie de S. Porphyre de Gaza par Marc le Diacre* (Brussels 2016).

Láng O. (2012) "New results in research on the southeastern part of the civil town in Aquincum—the so called 'Painter's House'", *Aquincumi Füzetek* 18 (2012) 17–36.

Laurence R., Esmonde Cleary S. and Sears G. (2011) *The City in the Roman West, c. 250 BC–c. AD 250* (Cambridge 2011).

Lavan L. (2011) "The end of temples: towards a new narrative?", in *The Archaeology of Late Antique 'Paganism'*, edd. L. Lavan and M. Mulryan (Late Antique Archaeology 7) (Leiden 2011) xv–lxv.

Lavan L. and Mulryan M. (2011) edd. *The Archaeology of Late Antique 'Paganism'* (Late Antique Archaeology 7) (Leiden 2011).

Lazar I. (2002) "Celeia", in *The Autonomous Towns of Noricum and Pannonia: Noricum*, edd. M. Šašel Kos and P. Scherrer (Ljubljana 2002) 71–101.

Le Glay M. (1954) "Le Mithraeum de Lambèse", *CRAI* 3 (1954) 269–78.

Leadbetter B. (2009) *Galerius and the Will of Diocletian* (London 2009).

Leber P. (1955) "Aus dem römischen Kärnten", *Carinthia I* 145 (1955) 183–212.

Lee A. D. (2000) *Pagans and Christians in Late Antiquity: a Sourcebook* (London 2000).

Leeham D. (2010) *Born for the Good of the State: Emperor Flavius Magnus Maximus, Wales, and the Later Roman Empire 367–411* (Chester 2010).

Lewis M. J. T. (1966) *Temples in Roman Britain* (Cambridge 1966).

Lentacker A. Ervynck A. and van Neer W. (2004) "The symbolic meaning of the cock: the animal remains from the Mithraeum at Tienen (Belgium)", in *Roman Mithraism: the Evidence of the Small Finds*, edd. M. Martens and G. De Boe (Brussels 2004) 57–80.

Liebeschuetz J. H. W. G. (1999) "The significance of the speech of Praetextatus", in *Pagan Monotheism in Late Antiquity*, edd. P. Athanassiadi and M. Frede (Oxford 1999) 185–205.

Liebeschuetz J. H. W. G. (1966) *Temples in Roman Britain* (Cambridge 1966).

Lissi-Caronna E. (1986) *Il mitreo dei Castra Peregrinorum (S. Stefano Rotondo)* (Leiden 1986).

Lizzi Testa R. (2004) *Senatori, popolo, papi. Il governo di Roma al tempo dei Valentiniani* (Bari 2012).

Lolić T. and Wiewegh Z. (2012) "Urbanism and architecture", in *The Archaeology of Roman Southern Pannonia*, edd. B. Migotti (BAR-IS 2393) (Oxford 2012) 191–224.

Lowther A. (1937) "Report on excavations at Verulamium in 1934: Insula XVI", *AntJ* 17 (1937) 28–51.

Luginbühl T., Monnier J. and Mühlemann Y. (2004) "Le mithraeum de la villa d'Orbe-Boscéaz (Suisse): du mobilier aux rites", in *Roman Mithraism: the Evidence of the Small Finds*, edd. M. Martens and G. De Boe (Brussels 2004) 109–33.

Lunn-Rockliffe S. (2007) *Ambrosiaster's Political Theology* (Oxford 2007).

MacMullen R. (1997) *Christianity and Paganism in the Fourth to Eighth Centuries* (London 1997).

MacMullen R. (1982) "The epigraphic habit of the Roman empire", *AJP* (1982) 233–46.

Macready S. and Sidell S. (1998) "The environmental evidence", in *The Temple of Mithras London: Excavations by W. F. Grimes and A. Williams at the Walbrook*, edd. J. Shepherd (London 1998) 208–15.

Mader I. (2004) "Vindobona", in *The Autonomous Towns of Noricum and Pannonia: Pannonia II*, edd. M. Šašel Kos and P. Scherrer (Ljubljana 2004) 67–74.

Márity E. (1992) "Chronological problems and special features in the structure of the civilian town of Aquincum", *Communicationes Archaeologicae Hungariae* 10 (1992) 65–73.

Marquart M. (2004) "Mithras aus bronze", in *Roman Mithraism: the Evidence of the Small Finds*, edd. M. Martens and G. De Boe (Brussels 2004) 303–17.

Martens M. (2004) "The mithraeum in Tienen (Belgium): small finds and what they can tell us", in *Roman Mithraism: the Evidence of the Small Finds*, edd. M. Martens and G. De Boe (Brussels 2004) 25–56.

Martin L. H. (2015) *The Mind of Mithraists: Historical and Cognitive Studies in the Roman Cult of Mithras* (London 2015).

Martin L. H. (1989) "Roman Mithraism and Christianity", *Numen* 36 (1989) 2–15.

Mattingly D. (2006) *An Imperial Possession: Britain in the Roman Empire* (London 2006).

McLynn N. (1996) "The fourth century 'taurobolium'", *Phoenix* 50 (1996) 312–30.

McCormack T. J. (1956) transl. *The Mysteries of Mithra* (orig. F. Cumont, *Les mystères de Mithra* (Brussels 1913)) (London 1956).

Meyer E. (1990) "Explaining the epigraphic habit of the Roman empire: the evidence of epitaphs", *JRS* 80 (1990) 74–96.

Meyer M. (1976) *The 'Mithras Liturgy'* (Missoula, Montana 1976).

Milburn R. (1988) *Early Christian Art and Architecture* (Berkeley 1988).

Moorhead S. (2012) "The coinage of the later Roman Empire, 364–498", in *The Oxford Handbook of Greek and Roman Coinage*, edd. W. Metcalf (Oxford 2012) 601–32.

Moretti A. M. S. (1979) "Nota preliminare su un Mitreo scoperto a Vulci", in *Mysteria Mithrae*, edd. U. Bianchi (Leiden 1979) 259–77.

Mráv Z. (2013) "Septimius Severus and the cities of the middle Danubian provinces", in *Studia Epigraphica: in Memoriam Géza Alföldy* (Bonn 2013) 205–40.

Mrozek S. (1973) "A propos de la réparition chronologique des inscriptions latines dans le haut-empire", *Epigraphica* 35 (1973) 113–18.

Müller R. (2006) "Római kori épület Héviz—Egregyen", *Ókar* 5 (2006) 89–92.

Mulryan M. (2011a) "'Paganism': regional studies and material culture", in *The Archaeology of Late Antique 'Paganism'*, edd. L. Lavan and M. Mulryan (Late Antique Archaeology 7) (Leiden 2011) 41–86.

Mulryan M. (2011b) "'The temple of Flora or Venus by the Circus Maximus and the new Christian topography: the 'pagan revival' in action?", in *The Archaeology of Late Antique 'Paganism'*, edd. L. Lavan and M. Mulryan (Late Antique Archaeology 7) (Leiden 2011) 209–77.

Nemeth-Ehrlich D. and Špalj D. N. (2003) "Municipium Andautonia", in *The Autonomous Towns of Noricum and Pannonia: Pannonia I*, edd. M. Šašel Kos and P. Scherrer (Ljubljana 2003) 107–29.

Nicholson O. (1995) "The end of Mithraism", *Antiquity* 69 (1995) 358–62.

Noll R. (1954) *Frühes Christentum in Österreich: von den Anfängen bis um 600 nach Chr.* (Vienna 1954).

Noll R. (1938) *Führer durch die Sonderausstellung 'Der grosse Dolichenusfund von Mauer A.D. Url'* (Vienna 1938).

North J. (1992) "The development of religious pluralism", in *The Jews Among Pagans and Christians in the Roman Empire*, edd. J. Lieu, J. North and T. Rajak (London 1992) 174–93.

Overbeck B. (1985) "Münzfunde aus der römischen Villa von Königsbrunn, Ldkr. Augsburg", in *Forschungen zur provinzialrömischen Archäologie in Bayerisch-Schwaben*, edd. J. Bellot, W. Czysw and G. Krahe (Augsburg 1985) 281–300.

Patrich J. (2011) *Studies in the Archaeology and History of Caesarea Maritima: Caput Judaeae, Metropolis Palaestinae* (Ancient Judaism and early Christianity 77) (Leiden 2011).

Pétry F. and Kern E. (1978) "Un mithraeum Biesheim (Haut-Rhin)", *Cahiers Alsaciens d'Archéologie d'Art et d'Histoire Strasbourg* 21 (1978) 5–32.

Piccottini G. (1994) *Mithrastempel in Virunum* (Klagenfurt 1994).

Picón C. A., Mertens J. R., Milleker E. J. and Herrmann A. (1997). "Recent acquisitions: a selection 1996–1997: ancient world", *Bulletin of the Metropolitan Museum of Art* 55 (1997) 8–17.

Planson E., Lagrange A., Minot A. and Hérard L. (1973) "Le mithraeum des Bolards à Nuits-Saint-Georges", *Archéologia* 54 (1973) 54–63.

Plouin C. (2004) "Le mithraeum de Biesheim (Haut-Rhin)", *Chantiers historiques en Alsace* 7 (2004) 9–19.

Póczy K. (2005) *Aquincum: das römische Budapest* (Mainz 2005).

Póczy K. (1997) *Aquincum—the Roman Town in Budapest* (Budapest 1997).

Póczy K. (1980) "Pannonian cities", in *The Archaeology of Roman Pannonia*, edd. A. Lengyel and G. T. B. Radan (Budapest 1980) 239–74.

Póczy K. and Zsidi P. (1995) "Roman citizens", in *Gods, Soldiers and Citizens in Aquincum*, edd. K. Kurucz, K. Póczy and P. Zsidi (Budapest 1995) 32–38.

Poulter A. (1992) "The use and abuse of urbanism in the Danube provinces during the later empire", in *The City in Late Antiquity*, edd. J. Rich (Abingdon 1992) 99–135.

Pross Gabrielli G. (1975) "Il tempietto ipogeo del dio Mitra al Timavo", *Archeografo Triestino* 35 (1975) 5–34.

Ragolič (2014) "The territory of Poetovio and the boundary between Noricum and Pannonia", *Arheološki vestnik* 65 (2014) 323–51.

Rees R. (2004) *Diocletian and the Tetrarchy* (Edinburgh 2004).

Ricci M. (2004) "Il mitreo della Crypta Balbi a Roma (note preliminari)", in *Roman Mithraism: the Evidence of the Small Finds*, edd. M. Martens and G. De Boe (Brussels 2004) 157–65.

Richardson L. (1992) *A New Topographical Dictionary of Ancient Rome* (London 1992).

Richmond I. A., Gillam J. P. and Birley E. (1951) "The temple of Mithras at Carrawburgh", *Archaeologia Aeliana* 29 (1951) 1–92.

Rodgers A. (2011) *Late Roman Towns in Britain* (Cambridge 2011).

Rorison M. (2001) *Vici in Roman Gaul* (BAR-IS 993) (Oxford 2001).

Ruprechtsberger E. M. (2005) *Neue Beiträge zum römischen Kastell von Lentia/Linz* (Linz 2005).

Ruprechtsberger E. M. (1999) *Das spätantike Gräberfeld von Lentia (Linz): Ausgrabung Tiefer Graben/Flügelhofgasse* (Mainz 1999).

Rushworth A. (2009) *Housesteads Roman Fort—the Grandest Station: Excavation and Survey at Housesteads, 1954–95* (Swindon 2009).

Saguì L. (2004) "Il mitreo della Crypta Balbi a Roma e i suoi reporti", in *Roman Mithraism: the Evidence of the Small Finds*, edd. M. Martens and G. De Boe (Brussels 2004) 167–78.

Salzman M. R. (2002) *The Making of a Christian Aristocracy: Social and Religious Change in the Western Roman Empire* (London 2002).

Salzman M. R. (1990) *On Roman Time: the Codex-Calendar of 354 and the Rhythms of Urban Life in Late Antiquity* (Oxford 1990).

Salzman M. R., Sághy M. and Testa R. L. (2016) *Pagans and Christians in Late Antique Rome: Conflict, Competition, and Coexistence in the Fourth Century* (New York 2016).

Santa Maria Scrinari V. (1979) "Il mitreo dell'Ospedale di S. Giovanni in Roma", in *Mysteria Mithrae*, edd. U. Bianchi (Leiden 1979) 219–24.

Saradi H. and Eliopoulos D. (2011) "Late paganism and Christianisation in Greece", in *The Archaeology of Late Antique Paganism*, edd. L. Lavan and M. Mulryan (Late Antique Archaeology 7) (Leiden 2011) 263–309.

Šašel-Kos M. (2010) "The early urbanization of Noricum and Pannonia", in *Roma e le province del Danubio: atti del I Convengo Internazionale Ferrara—Cento, 15–17 Ottobre 2009*, edd. L. Zerbini (Soveria Mannelli 2010) 209–30.

Sauer E. (2011) "Religious rituals at springs in the late antique and early medieval world", in *The Archaeology of Late Antique 'Paganism'*, edd. L. Lavan and M. Mulryan (Late Antique Archaeology 7) (Leiden 2011) 505–50.

Sauer E. (2004) "Not just small change—coins in Mithraea", in *Roman Mithraism: the Evidence of the Small Finds*, edd. M. Martens and G. De Boe (Brussels 2004) 327–53.

Sauer E. (2003) *The Archaeology of Religious Hatred in the Roman and Early Medieval World* (Stroud 2003).

Sauer E. (1996) *The End of Paganism in the North-Western Provinces of the Roman Empire: the Example of the Mithras Cult* (BAR-IS 634) (Oxford 1996).

Schejbal B. (2004) "Municipium Iasorum (Aquae Balissae)", in *The Autonomous Towns of Noricum and Pannonia: Pannonia II*, edd. M. Šašel Kos and P. Scherrer (Ljubljana 2004) 99–129.

Scherrer P. (2002) "Cetium", in *The Autonomous Towns of Noricum and Pannonia: Noricum*, edd. M. Šašel Kos and P. Scherrer (Ljubljana 2002) 213–44.

Schmotz K. (2000) "Der Mithrastempel von Künzing, Lkr. Deggendorf. Ein Vorbericht", in *Vorträge des 18. Niederbayerischen Archäologentages*, ed. K. Schmotz (Leidorf 2000) 111–43.

Schuddeboom F. L. (2016) "The decline and fall of the mithraea of Rome", *Babesch* 91 (2016) 225–45.

Schütte A. and Winter E. (2004) *Doliche—eine kommagenische Stadt und ihre Götter: Mithras und Iupiter Dolichenus* (Bonn 2004).

Schütte A. and Winter E. (2001) "Die Mithräen von Doliche: Überlegungen zu den ersten Kultstätten der Mithras-Mysterien in der Kommagene", *Topoi* 11 (2001) 149–73.

Schwertheim E. (1974) *Die Denkmäler Orientalischer Gottheiten im Römischen Deutschland* (Leiden 1974).

Sears G. (2011) "The fate of temples in North Africa", in *The Archaeology of Late Antique Paganism*, edd. L. Lavan and M. Mulryan (Late Antique Archaeology 7) (Leiden 2010) 229–59.

Selem P. (1980). *Les religions orientales dans la Pannonie romaine, partie en Yougoslavie* (Leiden 1980).

Sergejevskij D. (1937) *Das Mithräum von Jajce* (Sarajevo 1937).

Sfameni Gasparro G. (2011) "Mysteries and oriental cults. A problem in the history of religions", in *The Religious History of the Roman Empire: Pagans, Jews and Christians*, edd. J. North and S. Price (Oxford 2011) 276–324.

Shepherd J. (1998) *The Temple of Mithras, London: Excavations by W. F. Grimes and A. Williams at the Walbrook* (London 1998).

Sheridan J. J. (1966) "The altar of Victory—paganism's last battle", *L'Antiquite Classique* 35 (1966) 186–206.

Smith R. R. R. (2012) "Defacing the gods at Aphrodisias", in *Historical and Religious Memory in the Ancient World*, edd. B. Dignas and R. R. R. Smith (Oxford 2012) 283–326.

Smith R. (1995) *Julian's Gods: Religion and Philosophy in the Thought and Action of Julian the Apostate* (London 1995).

Sogno C. Q. (2006) *Aurelius Symmachus: a Political Biography* (Ann Arbor 2006).

Stark R. and Bainbridge W. S. (1997) *Religion, Deviance, and Social Control* (New York 1997).

Stark R. and Finke R. (2000) *Acts of Faith: Explaining the Human Side of Religion* (London 2000).

Stark R. and Iannacone L. R. (1997) "Why the Jehovah's Witnesses grow so rapidly: a theoretical application", *Journal of Contemporary Religion* 12 (1997) 133–57.

Steidl B. (2008) "Neues zu den Inschriften aus dem Mithraeum von Mühlthal am Inn", *Bayerische Vorgeschichtsblätter* 73 (2008) 53–85.

Swift E. (2000) *The End of the Western Roman Empire: an Archaeological Investigation* (Stroud 2000).

Tantillo I. (1997) *La prima orazionne di Guiliano a Constanzo. Introduzione, traduzione e commento* (Rome 1997).

Thévot E. (1948) "La station antique des Bolards à Nuits-Saint-Georges (Côte-d'Or)", *Gallia* 6 (1948) 289–347.

Thomas C. (1981) *Christianity in Roman Britain to AD 500* (London 1981).

Tolland J. (1722) *Hypatia: or the History of a Most Beautiful, Most Vertuous, Most Learned, and Every Way Accomplish'd Lady; who was Torn to Pieces by the Clergy of Alexandria, to Gratify the Pride, Emulation, and Cruelty of their Archbishop, Commonly but Undeservedly Styled St. Cyril* (London 1722).

Tóth I. (1988) "Addenda Pannonica Mithriaca", *Specimina Nova Dissertationum Ex Instituto Historico Universitatis Quinqueecclesiensis De Iano Pannonio Nominatae* 4 (1988) 17–73.

Tóth I. (1973) "Destruction of the sanctuaries of Iuppiter Dolichenus at the Rhine and in the Danube Region (235–238)", *ActaArchHung* 25 (1973) 109–16.

Trombley F. (1993–94) *Hellenic Religion and Christianization c. 370–529*, 2 vols. (Leiden 1993–94).

Trout D. (1995) "Christianizing the Nolan countryside: animal sacrifice at the tomb of St. Felix", *Journal of Early Christian Studies* 3 (1995) 281–98.

Turcan R. (1996) *The Cults of the Roman Empire* (Oxford 1996).

Turcan R. (1984) "Les motivations de l'intolérance chrétienne et la fin du mithriacisme au IVe siècle ap. J.-C.", in *Proceedings of the VIIth Congress of the International Federation of the Societies of Classical Studies*, ed. J. Harmatta (Budapest 1984) 209–26.

Turcan R. (1975) *Mithras Platonicus: recherches sur l'hellénisation philosophique de Mithra* (Leiden 1975).

Tušek I. (1990) "Das fünfte Mithräum in Ptuj", *Arheološki Vestnik* 41 (1990) 267–71.

Ulbert C. (2004) "Das Mithraeum von Bornheim-Sechtem bei Bonn: Baubefunde und Fundumstände", in *Roman Mithraism: the Evidence of the Small Finds*, edd. M. Martens and G. De Boe (Brussels 2004) 81–88.

Ulbert C., Wulfmeier J.-C. and Huld-Zetsche I. (2004) "Ritual deposits of Mithraic cult-vessels: new evidence from Sechtem and Mainz", *JRA* 17 (2004) 354–70.

Vermaseren M. J. (1974) *Mithriaca II: the Mithraeum at Ponza* (Leiden 1974).

Vermaseren M. J. (1971) *Mithriaca I: the Mithraeum at S. Maria Capua Vetere* (Leiden 1971).

Vermaseren M. J. and van Essen C. J. (1965) *The Excavations in the Church of Santa Prisca in Rome* (Leiden 1965).

Visconti C. L. (1885) "Del larario e del mitrèo scoperti nell'Esquilino presso la chiesa di S. Martino ai Monti", *BCM* (1885) 27–38.

Volken M. (2004) "The development of the cult of Mithras in the western Roman empire: a socio-archaeological perspective", *Electronic Journal of Mithraic Studies*: https://www.academia.edu/10364062/The_development_of_the_cult_of_Mithras_in_the_Western_Roman_Empire_a_socio-archaeological_perspective._EJMS_vol_IV_2004 (last accessed 23.4.16).

Voltaire (1764) *Dictionnaire philosophique portatif* (Geneva 1764).

Vomer-Gojkovič M. (2001) *Ptuj im Römischen Reich, Mithraskult und seine Zeit.* (Archaeologia Poetovionensis 2) (Ptuj 2001).

Walsh D. (2016) "The fate of temples in Noricum and Pannonia", *AJA* 120 (2016) 221–38.

Walters V. (1974) *The Cult of Mithras in the Roman Provinces of Gaul* (Leiden 1974).

Ward-Perkins B. (2011) "The end of temples: an archaeological problem", in *Spätantiker Staat und Religiöser Konflikt: Imperiale und Lokale Verwaltung und die Gewalt Gegen Heiligtümer*, ed. J. Hahn (Berlin 2011) 187–99.

Ward-Perkins B. (1984) *From Classical Antiquity to the Middle Ages: Urban Public Building in Northern and Central Italy AD 300–850* (Oxford 1984).

Watts D. (1998) *Religion in Late Roman Britain: Forces of Change* (London 1998).

Watts E. (2015) *The Final Pagan Generation* (Oakland, California 2015).

White L. M. (2012) "The changing face of Mithraism in Ostia", in *Contested Spaces: Houses and Temples in Roman Antiquity and the New Testament*, edd. D. Balch and A. Weissenrieder (Tübingen 2012) 435–92.

Wiblé F. (2008) *Martigny-la-Romaine* (Martigny 2008).

Wiblé F. (2004) "Les petits objets du mithraeum de Martigny/Forum Claudii Vallensium", in *Roman Mithraism: the*

Evidence of the Small Finds, edd. M. Martens and G. De Boe (Brussels 2004) 135–45.

Wiblé F. (1995) "Le mithraeum de Forum Claudii Vallensium/Martigny (Valais)", *ArchSchw* 18 (1995) 2–15.

Wiblé F. and Cusanelli Bressenel L. (2012) "Les graffitis sur récipients en terre cuite en relation avec le culte de Mithra de Forvm Clavdii Vallensivm (Martigny, VS)", in *Inscriptions mineures: nouveautés et réflexions*, edd. M. Fuchs, R. Sylvestre and C. Schmidt Heidenreich (Oxford 2012) 45–60.

Wigg-Wolf D. (2016) "Supplying a dying empire? The mint of Trier in the late 4th-Century AD", in *Produktion und Recyceln von Münzen in der Spätantike /Produire et recycler la monnaie au bas-empire*, edd. J. Chameroy and P.-M. Guihard (Mainz 2016).

Wightman E. M. (1970) *Roman Trier and the Treveri* (London 1970).

Wilkes J. J. (1969) *Dalmatia* (London 1969).

Will E. (1950) "La date du mithréum de Sidon", *Syria* 27 (1950) 261–69.

Winter E. (2000) "Mithraism and Christianity in Late Antiquity", in *Ethnicity and Culture in Late Antiquity*, edd. S. Mitchell and G. Greatrex (London 2000) 173–82.

Woolf G. (2014) "Isis and the evolutions of religion", in *Power, Politics and the Cult of Isis*, edd. L. Bricault and M. J. Versluys (Leiden 2014) 62–92.

Woolf G. (2009) "World religion and world empire in the ancient Mediterranean", in *Die Religion des Imperium Romanum: Koine und Konfrontationen*, edd. H. Cancik and J. Rüpke (Tübingen 2009) 19–35.

Wulfmeier, J.-C. (2004) "Ton, steine, scherben—skulpturen und reliefkeramik aus dem mithraeum von Bornheim-Sechtem", in *Roman Mithraism: the Evidence of the Small Finds*, edd. M. Martens and G. De Boe (Brussels 2004) 89–94.

Zotović L. (1973) *Mitraizam na tlu Jugoslavije* (Beograd 1973).

Zsidi P. (1995) *Gods, Soldiers and Citizens in Aquincum. An Exhibition to Celebrate the 100 Year Centennial of the Founding of the Aquincum Museum: Guide to the Exhibition* (Budapest 1995).

Index

Acumincum 51n26
Ad Enum 18, 19n7, 27, 57, 74, 92
Aedesius, Sextilius Agesilaus 27
Aguntum 18
Aion 15, 68
Alammani 85, 86, 92, 89
Alans 19
Alatheus 59
Albinus, Caeionius Caecina 28
Aleppo 84
Alexander Severus 50
Alexandria
    church 79
    mithraeum 12, 78, 79
    number of temples in 42, 43
    Serapeum 2, 42, 88, 92, 97
    violence in 78, 88, 97
Alexandros, bishop 84
Alise-Sainte-Reine
Alster, River 87
Altars
    at Martigny 49n14
    at Tawern 83
    deposited in Coventina's Well 63
    Mithraic 1, 4, 10–12, 14, 21, 25, 26, 28, 30, 32, 67, 74, 80, 81, 93, 94
        dedicated by the Tetrarchs 1, 26, 43, 67, 87, 93
    of Nantosvelta and Sucellus 18
    of Victory 50, 84
Ambrose, bishop 82, 83
Ambrosiaster 31, 41, 97
Ammianus 3, 57, 85, 87, 90
Andautonia 51n26
Angera 25
Antioch 3, 84
Antium 28
Aper, Flavius 26
Aphrodisias 3
Aphrodite 79
Apollo 82, 83, 90
    Apollo-Moritagus 18
    Helios-Apollo 29
Apollodorus, Petronius 27
Apuleius 62
Aquae Iasae 51n26
Aquincum
    civic building in 51n26
    decline of 57, 95
    mithraea 9, 18, 19, 39, 57, 58, 65
        membership of 27
        patronage of 60
        fate of 68
    Temple to Jupiter 26, 51
Arcadius 84
Ardashir II 88
Army, Roman
    and the cult of Mithras 4, 13, 19, 26, 27, 41, 44, 57–59, 65, 89, 93, 96, 99
    changing social networks of 59, 65, 95
Artemis 83
Arupium 19, 33, 74, 77n17

Augentius, Aurelius Victor 28
Auguntum 51n26
Aurelian 50
Autun 85
Axiopolis 26

Bagnall, Roger 43
Barbarian incursions 74, 85–87, 92, 93, 98
Bath (Aquae Sulis) 83
Bayliss, Richard 2, 12, 79, 89
Beck, Roger 7–9, 12, 21
Bedaium 26
Berlin 87
Biesheim 62, 68, 74, 77, 87
Birdoswald 57n1, 59
Bjørnebye, Jonas 29
Boar 11–12
Borcovicium 18n5, 57, 83, 87
Bornheim-Roisdorf 63
Bornheim-Sechtem 19, 33, 38, 39, 49, 55, 60, 63, 76, 89, 98
Bourbonne-le-Bains, Nîmes 63
Britain
    barbarian incursions into 87
    Christianity in 83, 85, 97
    cult of Mithras in 4, 95, 98
    fate of pagan statuary in 89
    mithraea in 44, 49, 77, 87, 89, 92, 95
    repair of temples in the 4th c 43
Brocolitia
    Coventina's Well 18n5, 63, 83
    fort 57n1
    mithraeum 9n38, 10, 11, 18n5, 33, 44, 49, 58, 63, 68, 87
    nymphaeum 18n5
Brontis 27
Bulls 11
Burdigala
    Christianity in 82
    mithraeum 18n3, 77, 68, 89
Burgaski Bani 63

Caelicolists 89
Caeonii Family 27
Caerwent 43
Caesarea Maritima 4, 10n42, 17, 21, 68
Caesarius of Arles 51
Cameron, Alan 3, 16, 43
Capua 9n38, 10n40, 74, 79
Carnuntum
    civic building in 51n26
    decline of 57, 90, 91, 95
    dedications to Mithras at 4, 43
        by the Tetrarchs 1, 26, 27, 43, 67, 87, 93
    mithraea
        general 9, 18, 19, 27, 93, 95, 98
        Mithraeum I 74, 80, 81, 85, 86n67, 91, 92
        Mithraeum III 1, 26, 39, 68, 80, 81
    Septimius Severus proclaimed emperor at 27
    'Temple to Diana' 51n27
Celeia 51n26
Celle Civita 62

INDEX

Cetium 51n26
Chenault, Robert 84
Chickens/Cockerels 11, 30–32, 64
Christianity
  among the aristocracy 60, 84
  and the destruction of temples 2
  approaches towards depictions of animals 80, 81
  church councils 82
  desecration of mithraea 12, 77–79, 92, 94, 97–99
  feasting 63
  in Britain 83, 85, 97
  in Dalmatia 84
  in Gaul 82, 83, 89, 92
  in Germany 97
  in Noricum and Pannonia 83, 85, 97
  in Rome 84, 85, 92, 97
  in the Eastern Provinces 84, 85, 92
  in Trier 64, 66
  persecution of 79
  targeting of nude sculptures 79
Churches 2, 42, 66, 68, 77–79, 82–85, 97
Cibalae 51n26
Cirpi 51
Cirta 28, 57, 61, 49
Civic building 49–55
Claudius 25
Clauss, Manfred 4, 12, 43
Clermont-Ferrand 85
Codex Calendar of AD 354 3
Coins
  as votives 32–33, 55, 60, 61–65, 67, 68, 74, 87, 94, 95, 97
  circulation of 55, 67, 85, 95
Constans 43
Constantine I 2, 27, 42, 87
Constantinople 3, 29
Constantius Chlorus 1, 87, 89
Constantius II 28, 57, 59, 42n4
Cos 25
Croxford, Ben 89
Cumont, Franz 12
Cyrene 90

Dalmatia
  barbarian incursions into 85
  Christianity in 84
  mithraea in 12, 19, 21, 23, 25, 31n61, 32, 33, 40, 44, 55, 74, 77, 90, 94, 95
Dardagana 23–24
Deichman, Friedrich 2
Deprivation Theory 58
Dexter, Appius Claudius Tarronius 28
Dieburg 19, 86, 87, 90
Diocletian 50
Doliche 17, 75n12, 79, 88, 92, 97
Drava, River 57
Dražinović 39
Duces 1, 26, 28, 87
Dura-Europos 4, 9n38, 17

Egypt
  cult of Mithras in 5, 30–31, 62, 78, 79
  temples 3, 43
Eleusinian Mysteries 62–62
Epidaurum 19, 21, 33, 68

Eugenius 59
Eutactus, C. Rufius 25, 30

Fauduet, Isabelle 42, 51, 99
Faustinus, Materninius 30
Faventinus, Ulpius Egnatius 27, 30
Feasting
  general 3, 11, 31–32, 63–65, 94
  in Mithraic iconography 7, 29, 76
Felix, St. 63
Fertörakos 12n53
Festivals 3, 50, 63
Flavia Solva 51n26
Flavian, bishop 84
Flavianus, Virius Nicomachus 59
Flechtorf 87
Florus, Valerius 27, 79
foederati 56, 59, 65
Fowden, Garth 2
Frankfurter, David 2
Franks 85
'free-riders' 61
Frigidus, Battle of 2
Furlenboden 62

Gallienus, Iunius 28
Gaul
  aristocracy of 60
  Christianity in 60, 82, 83, 89, 92
  civic building in 51
  coin circulation in 55
  cult of Mithras in 17, 18, 32, 40, 95
    membership of 25
  declining urban centres 57
  mithraea in 25, 32, 44, 49, 51, 54–55, 75–77, 89, 90, 92, 94, 95, 97, 98
  presence of barbarians in 59
  rural sanctuaries in 62
  temples in 3, 42, 54, 51, 82, 83, 87, 99
Gergios, bishop 78
Germany
  barbarian incursions into 59, 85, 86, 92, 93
  Christianity in 97
  cult of Mithras in 7, 19
  mithraea in 30, 25, 26, 44, 55, 68, 74, 76, 77, 80, 86, 87, 89, 90, 92, 94, 95, 97, 98
  temples in 4
Gerontios, Fl. 15
Gholaia 87
Gibbon, Edward 2
Gimmeldingen
  mithraeum 19, 21–22, 41, 44, 49, 64, 74, 77, 86, 87, 90, 92, 94, 97
    inscriptions from 26, 39
Goddard, Christophe 63
Goodman, Penelope 83
Gordon, Richard 12, 24
Gorsium 3, 51
Goths 59, 85
Governors 1, 26, 27, 49n14, 57, 79
Gracchus, prefect of Rome 78, 84, 97
Gratian 50, 64, 66, 89, 98
Gregory I, Pope 3
Gregory of Tours 85
Gregory Nazianzen 29

140 INDEX

Griffiths, Alison 43
Groß-Krotzenburg 7
Grotta Bella 62
Güglingen 9–10

Hadrian's Wall 4, 16, 18, 57, 58–60, 83, 87, 92, 93, 98
Halle 87
Hamburg 87
Harting 87
Hawarte
    church 79, 84, 85
    mithraeum
        general 17, 19, 20, 40–41, 49, 66, 68
        architecture of 21, 94
        evidence for Mithraic rituals 31–33
        fate of 77, 79, 84, 85, 88, 92, 97
        iconography 25, 30
Hayling Island 62
Hecate 15, 24, 27
Helios(-Apollo) 24, 29
Herodina 50
Hilarianus, Caelius 27, 30
Hinton St Mary 83
Hunt, David 89
Hypatia 2, 88, 92

Ilion 82
Incense 10n43
Inn, River 18, 57
Isis, cult of 15–16, 61–62
Italy
    aristocracy of 60
    Christianity in 60
    civic building in 49, 54
    mithraea 50, 54, 55, 76, 77, 95 97
    temples 49, 50, 54, 99

Jajce 19, 21, 32, 44, 68, 86n67, 90, 98
Jehovah Witnesses 44n12
Jerome, St. 11n44, 78, 84, 97
Jews 89
Jouffroy, Helene 49
Julian 2, 3, 16, 29, 41, 82, 85, 88
Julianus Valens, bishop 83
Jupiter Dolichenus, cult of 16, 83, 88, 89n78
Jupiter Hammon 87
Jupiter Optimus Maximus 26, 51, 63
Jupiter Ultor 50
Justin Martyr 78
Justinian 42

Kamenius, Alfenius Caeionius Iulianus 27, 28, 30
Koenigshoffen 10, 75n12
Königsbrunn 14, 63
Konjic 19, 21, 29, 32, 39, 76, 86n67, 90, 98
Krefeld-Gellep 59
Künzing 10

La Courtavaux 18
Lactantius 62
Lambaesis 1, 27, 32, 41, 57, 58, 68, 77, 79
Lampadius, Caeonius Rufius Volusianus 27
Lane-Fox, Robin 2
Lauriacum 51n26

Lavinium 28
Laws against 'paganism' 1, 12, 42, 43, 63, 64, 89
Lentia
    Castle Hill 57, 59
    Christianity in 83
    mithraeum 18–21, 26, 32, 40, 74, 86n67, 92, 94
    Temple of *Dea Roma* and *Genius Augusta* 19, 40, 51, 57, 94
Les Bolards 18, 32, 33, 76, 77, 80, 81, 85, 92, 97
Libanius 3, 29
Liber 27
Lioux 62
Londinium 4, 11, 18n5, 39, 44, 49, 60, 65, 68, 74, 95
Lucius (*Metamorphoses*) 62
Lucus Augusti 60n24, 68, 77, 79
Lullingstone 83
Luna 5, 23, 24, 32, 90

Mackwiller 18, 33, 60, 63, 74, 77, 92
MacMullen, Ramsey 2
Macrobius 77
Magna Mater, cult of 15, 16, 27, 61
Magnus Maximus 89, 90, 98
Main, River 86
Mandeleiu 63
Manichaens 88, 97
Marcus, bishop 83
Marin Piranomonte 62
Mark the Deacon 79, 84, 85
Martialis, Martius 25, 30
Martigny
    Christianity in 82, 85
    decline of 57
    Gallo-Roman temple 18, 57, 62
    mithraeaum 18, 32, 49, 51, 62–64, 68, 76, 77, 82, 85
    nymphaeum 18
Martin of Tours, St. 1, 82
Martin, Luther 61
Maternus, Firmicus 78, 88, 97
Mauer an der Url 89n78
Maxentius 27, 50
Maximian 26, 27
Maximinus Thrax 89
Maximinus, praefectus annonae 31
Mercury 74, 76, 80, 83, 86, 87, 97
Metamorphoses 62
Metz 51
Minerva 39
Mithraea
    architecture of 7–9, 10n42, 15, 20–22, 40, 65, 94
    as sources of *spolia* 14, 74, 89
    at Alexandria 12, 78, 79
    at Doliche 17, 75n12, 79, 88, 92
    at Königsbrunn(?) 14
    at Lucus Augusti 60n24, 68, 77, 79
    at Serdica 14
    Christian graffiti carved into 79, 82, 92, 97–99
    close proximity to water features 17–18
    comparison with modern Kingdom Halls 44n12
    converted for different uses 12n53, 14, 62, 68, 74
    cooking spaces in 7, 32
    in Britain
        general 44, 49, 77, 87, 89, 92, 98
        at Borcovicium 18n5, 57, 87
        at Brocolitia 9n38, 10–11, 18n5, 33, 44, 49, 58, 63, 68, 86n67, 87

Mithraea (cont.)
- at Londinium   4, 11, 18n5, 39, 44, 49, 60, 65, 68, 74, 95
- at Segontium   14
- at Vindobala   15
- in Dalmatia
  - general   21, 31n61, 44, 77, 94, 95
  - at Arupium   19, 33, 74, 77n17
  - at Epidaurum   19, 21, 33, 68
  - at Jajce   19, 21, 32, 44, 86n67, 90, 98
  - at Konjic   19, 21, 29, 32, 39, 76, 86n67, 90, 98
- in Gaul
  - general   25, 32, 44, 49, 51, 54–55, 64, 75–77, 89, 90, 92, 94, 95
  - at Burdigala   18n3, 77, 68, 89
  - at Les Bolards   18, 32, 33, 76, 77, 80, 81, 85, 92, 97
  - at Martigny   18, 32, 49, 51, 62–64, 68, 76, 77, 82, 85
  - at Orbe(?)   14, 63
  - at Pons Saravi   11, 18, 54, 74, 75, 92
  - at Septeuil   18, 32, 33, 49, 51, 86n67, 89, 90, 98
  - at Tienen   11, 18n5, 30, 39, 57, 68
  - at Trier   31, 33, 39, 54–56, 64, 66, 76, 85, 95, 97
  - at Venetonimagus   18, 76, 77
- in Germany
  - general   25, 26, 30, 44, 55, 77, 98
  - at Aquae Mattiacae   14
  - at Bieshiem   62, 68, 74, 77, 87
  - at Bornheim-Sechtem   33, 38, 39, 49, 55, 60, 63, 76, 89, 98
  - at Dieburg   19, 68n7, 86, 87, 90
  - at Gimmeldingen   19, 26, 21, 22, 39, 41, 44, 49, 64, 74, 80, 92, 94, 97
  - at Güglingen   9, 10
  - at Koenigshoffen   10, 75n12
  - at Mackwiller   18, 33, 60, 63, 74, 92
  - at Nida-Heddernheim   4, 9–11, 19, 39
  - at Reichweiler   19, 74, 77
  - at Rockenhausen   19, 44, 49, 55, 74
  - at Stockstadt   19, 68n7, 86, 87, 89n78
- in Italy
  - general   50, 54, 55, 76, 77
  - at Capua   9n38, 10n40, 74, 79
  - at Ostia
    - general   9, 4, 20, 33, 20, 44, 49, 60, 68n6
    - House of Diana   20, 29, 30
    - of Felicissimus   10, 20, 29
    - of Fructosus   20
    - of the Serpents   20
    - of the Seven Spheres   8
    - patronage of   60
    - Porta Romana   20
  - at Ponza   79, 92
  - at Rome
    - general   9, 20, 44, 49, 50, 54, 60, 68, 97
    - Baths of Caracalla   29
    - Castra Peregrinorum (S. Stefano Rotondo)   20, 68, 76
    - Crypta Balbi   20, 29, 49
    - Foro Boario   12, 20, 29, 49, 69
    - House of the Olympii   20, 21, 27–28, 49
    - Ospedale San Giovanni   20, 74
    - Phrygianum (Vatican Hill)   20, 49
    - San Clemente   33, 76
    - Santa Prisca   76
    - Via Giovannia Lanza   20, 21, 23, 40, 41, 49, 68, 94
  - at Spoletium   44, 76
  - at Timavo   19, 21, 33n72, 76, 86n67
  - at Vulci   81, 85, 86n67, 92, 97
- in Noricum
  - general   51, 54, 77
  - at Ad Enum   18, 19n7, 27, 57, 74, 92
  - at Lentia   18–21, 26, 32, 40, 74, 86n67, 92, 94
  - at Schachadorf   18, 32, 74, 83, 92, 93, 98
  - at St Urban   21, 32, 49
  - at Virunum   1, 18, 26, 32
- in North Africa
  - at Cirta   28, 49
  - at Lambaesis   32, 27, 58, 68, 77, 79
- in Pannonia
  - general   51, 54, 77
  - at Aquincum
    - general   9, 18, 19, 27, 95
    - Mithraeum II   60, 95
    - Mithraeum IV   57, 68
    - Mithraeum V   58
  - at Carnuntum
    - general   9, 18, 19, 27, 68, 93, 95, 98
    - Mithraeum I   74, 80, 81, 85, 86n67, 91, 92
    - Mithraeum III   1, 26, 39, 68, 80, 81
  - at Fertörakos   12n53
  - at Poetovio
    - general   1, 9, 18, 26, 27, 32, 57, 65, 85, 92, 95
    - Mithraeum I   19
    - Mithraeum II   19, 33, 54, 57, 74, 80, 81, 86n67
    - Mithraeum III   9n38, 54, 74, 80, 81, 86n67
    - Mithraeum IV   74
- in Syria
  - general   25, 30, 31, 33, 49
  - at Caesarea Maritima   4, 10n42, 17, 21, 68
  - at Dura-Europos   4, 9n38, 17
  - at Hawarte
    - general   17, 19, 20, 40–41, 49, 66, 68
    - architecture of   21, 94
    - evidence for Mithraic rituals   31–33
    - fate of   77, 79, 84, 85, 88, 92, 97
    - iconography   25, 30
  - at Šaʿara   17, 79, 80, 88, 92
  - at Sidon   15
- installed in caves   19
- installed in pre-existing structures   14, 18, 68
- modern damage to   76n14, 77n17
- on the Danube Frontier   44, 51
- patronage of   60, 65, 95
- referred to as a *fanum*   41, 94
- referred to as *spelaea*   7

Mithras Liturgy   30, 31

Mithras, cult of
- and accusations of sorcery   31
- and the army   4, 13, 19, 26, 27, 41, 44, 57–59, 65, 89, 93, 96, 99
- and the summer solstice   11
- and women   10n39
- described by Christian authors   78
- dividing of congregations   9
- feasts   11, 29, 30–32, 63–65, 95
- grades
  - general   1, 10, 11, 29, 30, 78, 97
  - and secular status   11, 28
  - *corax*   27–29, 39, 41, 94
    - *hieroceryx*   27
    - *hieroceryx sacrorum*   27
    - *hierocoracica*   28
  - depiction of   29

142   INDEX

heliodromus 29
leo 11, 29, 30, 39
maintained in 4th c 30
nymphus 39
 pater 25–30, 94
  pater patrum 25, 27, 28
  pater sacrorum 27
 roles when feasting 11
iconography
 archaeological evidence for 11
 bull-slaying scene 1, 5, 15, 19, 22–25, 42, 68, 74, 76, 79, 81, 86, 90, 94, 98
 carved into natural rock 19, 94
 depicting animals 24n27, 80
 depicting feasts 7, 29, 76
 depicting sacrifices 11
 depictions of Luna 23, 24, 90
 depictions of Mithras
  birth of 5, 98
  head removed 68, 74, 76, 80, 86, 90, 93
  performing the water-miracle 7
  wrestling with the bull 7, 76
 depictions of Sol 23, 24, 90
 fragments found in Barbaricum 87
 in Dalmatia 23, 24
 in the Capua Mithraeum 10n40
 in the Hawarte Mithraeum 24
 in the London Mithraeum 74
 nudity in 79, 80
 on ceramics 8n32, 10n40, 39
 Rhine and Danube style 7, 23
 ritual fragmentation of 33, 38, 39, 89, 90, 98
 the torch-bearers 5, 15, 23, 74, 79, 86n67, 90
 variation in the 4th c 23–24
 variation in the fourth century 24
 Zodiac 8, 80
initiations
 general 7, 10, 11, 30–31, 33, 41, 60, 66, 94, 95, 97
 compared with other cults 15, 62
 described by St. Jerome 11n44
 importance of 61, 65, 95
 of children 31
 scripts 5, 30, 62
lack of literary sources on 5
lack of popularity in certain regions 4
membership
 among the aristocracy 20, 27, 28, 60, 65, 84
 among the staff of the *portoria* 4, 57
 at Ad Enum 27
 at Aquincum 27
 at Poetovio 26
 at Trier 30
 at Ventonimagus 26, 30
 being male-only 10, 59, 60
 children 28
 depictions of members 29
 in Gaul 25
 in Rome 27, 29, 94
 Julian 29, 41
offerings
 altars 1, 4, 10–12, 14, 25, 26, 28, 30, 32, 36, 74, 79, 80, 81, 94
 ceramics 32
 coins 32–33, 55, 60, 61–65, 67, 68, 87, 94, 95, 97
 for eye diseases 18

 reliefs 26, 28, 32
  replica body parts 32
 origins and expansion of 4
 Persian aspects of 88, 92
 processions 8n32
 purification rituals 18
 sacrifices 2, 11, 31
 terminology 15
 Tetrarchic support for 26, 27, 43, 58
 the torch-bearers 5, 8, 15
Mithras
 and Persian Mithra 4
 and Sol 5, 7, 11
 appearance 4
 as a healer 25, 32, 40, 64, 65, 94
 as a military god 87, 93, 94, 95, 98
 as the 'eternal spring' 64
 combined with Helios 30, 31, 39
 dedications to 26
 depictions of 24
 pater acts as Mithras in rituals 29
 rock-birth 7, 19, 64, 95
 slaying the bull 5
 viewed as Persian 88, 97
 water-miracle 7, 18, 95
 wrestles with the Bull 7
Mormons 58
Mount Olympus, Turkey 4
Municipium Iasorum 51n26
Mursa 18

Nantosvelta 18
Narona 84
Neapolis 28
Nicasius 25
Nida-Heddernheim 4, 9–11, 19, 39
Nola 63
Noricum
 barbarian incursions into 85, 92, 93
 Christianity in 83, 85
 civic building 51n26, 54
 declining urban centres 66
 mithraea in 51, 54, 74, 77, 98
 temples in 51, 99
North Africa
 mithraea in 28, 32, 27, 49, 58, 77
 temples 3, 43, 99
Novae 4
Numidia 27
Nymphaea 18

Ober-Florstadt 12n50
Olympii, family 20, 21, 27, 28, 31, 49
Olympius, Aemilianus Corfo 28
Olympius, Aurelius Victor 28
Olympius, Nonius Victor 28
Olympius, Tamesius Augentius 28, 49
Orbe 14, 63
Ovilava 18, 83

Pannonia
 barbarian incursion into 59, 85, 92, 93
 Christianity in 83, 85
 civic building in 51n26, 54

INDEX

Pannonia (cont.)
   declining urban centres 66
   mithraea in 51, 54, 77, 95, 98
   temples in 51, 54, 99
Pannonhalma 51n26
Paulinus of Nola, St. 3, 28, 63
Pegasius, bishop 82
Pennes-Mirabeau 62
Persia 4, 13, 24, 88, 97
Pertosa 62
Phaeton 86
Philae 42
Physicians 25
Picts 87
Pliva, River 19
Plutarch 4, 62
Poetovio
   Castle Hill 59
   Christianity in 83, 85
   decline of 57, 95
   mithraea in 1, 9, 18, 26, 27, 32, 57, 65, 85, 92, 95
      Mithraeum I 19
      Mithraeum II 19, 33, 54, 57, 74, 80, 81, 86n67
      Mithraeum III 9n38, 54, 74, 80, 81, 86n67
      Mithraeum IV 74
      Mithraeum V 57
   presence of barbarians 59
   springs in 18
Pons Aeni 19, 27, 57
Pons Saravi 11, 18, 54, 57, 74, 75, 92
Ponza 79, 92
Porphyry, bishop 84, 85
Porphyry, philosopher 3, 8
Portoria 4, 57, 95
Postumianus, Iunius 27
Praetextatus, Vettius Agorius 27, 50, 77
Priesthoods 27, 28, 60
Procopius 42

Quadi 85

Reichweiler 19, 74, 77
Religious Capital 61, 65
Religious Market-Place 58n12
Riegel 10
Rockenhausen 19, 44, 49, 55, 74
Rome
   aristocracy of
      and Christianity 59
      and cult of Mithras 1, 20, 27–31, 49, 59, 65, 95, 96
      importance of status to 28
   Campus Martius 20
   Christianity in 59, 84, 85, 97
   civic building in 50
   cult of Jupiter Dolichenus in 16
   cult of Mithras in 1, 4, 20, 27, 31, 33 40, 59, 95–96
   Esquiline Hill 20
   Forum 43, 62
   mithraea in 9, 12, 21, 20, 28, 41, 40, 44, 49, 50, 54, 55, 60, 68, 78, 97
   Senate House 50
   Vatican Hill 20, 27

Šaʿāra 10, 17, 79, 80, 88, 92, 97
Sabinus, Rufius Caeionius 27

Sacrifices 1–3, 11, 12, 31
Salle, River 87
Salona 84
Salzman, Michelle 60, 97
Samaritans 85, 89
Saphrac 59
Sarapis 39, 74
Sarre, River 75
Sauer, Eberhard 12, 54
Savaria 51n26
Scarbantia 51n26
Schachadorf 18, 32, 74, 83, 92, 93, 98
Sculptures
   as focus of votive offerings 62
   barbarian desecration of 86, 87
   Christian desecration of 2, 12, 79
   decapitated 68, 76, 83, 86n67, 90, 98
   from Gholaia
   from Hochscheid 82
   from Narona 84
   from Tawern 83, 87
   in bronze 15, 76
   in silver 84
   laws concerning 43
   Mithraic 68
      from Ad Enum 74
      from Aquincum IV 68
      from Biesheim 62, 68
      from Brocolitia 68, 86n67
      from Burdigala 68
      from Carnuntum I 80, 86n67
      from Carnuntum III 68, 81
      from Dieburg 86, 87, 90
      from Gimmeldingen 74
      from Jajce 86n67, 90
      from Les Bolards 33, 81
      from London 39, 74
      from Martigny 76
      from Poetovio II 74, 80, 86n67
      from Poetovio III 74, 80, 86n67
      from Pons Saravi 74
      from Rome 23
      from Schachadorf 74
      from Septeuil 86n67, 90
      from Sidon 15
      from Stockstadt 86, 87
      from Timavo 19, 86n67
      from Vulci 81, 86n67
      of Aion 15, 68
      of animals 33, 80, 81, 98
      of Mithras 39, 74
         carrying the bull 15
         of the rock-birth 74, 80, 86n67, 90, 92
         slaying the bulk 15, 19, 76, 81, 86n67
      of the torch-bearers 15, 23, 74, 81, 86n67, 90
      ritual fragmentation of 33, 38, 39, 89, 90, 98
   of Aphrodite 79
   of Apollo 82, 83
   of Artemis 83
   of Bacchus 74n9
   of emperors 84
   of Fortuna 87
   of Hecate 15
   of Mercury 74, 76, 83, 86, 87, 97

144 INDEX

of Minerva   39, 74
of Sarapis   39, 74
of Sirona   82, 83
of Venus   15, 82n29, 84, 86
of Victory   87
Sears, Garth   42
Segontium   14
Septeuil   18, 31n61, 32, 33, 49, 51, 86n67, 89, 90, 98
Septimius Severus   27
Serdica   14
Servius   67
Severianus, C. Magius Donatus   27
Shapur I   88
Shapur II   88
Shenoute of Atripe, St.   1
Shrines
    at Borcovicium   57
    at Celle Civita   62
    at Grotta Bella   62
    at Lioux   62
    at Marin Piranomonte   62
    at Pennes-Mirabeau   62
    at Pertosa   62
    of Coventina   18n5, 83
    of Mars Thincus   57
Sidon   15
Silchester   84
Silvanus, Ulpius   60
Sirmium   18, 51, 54
Sirona   82, 83
Siscia   51n26
Smith, Rowland   29
Social Capital   58, 60, 65, 95
Sol   5, 7, 11, 23, 24, 29, 80, 90
sorcery   31
Sozomen   62
Spain
    cult of Mithras in   4, 60n24
    Temples   3
Spoletium   44, 76
Springhead   62
Springs   18, 19, 25, 64, 65, 67
St Margarethen   83
St Urban   21, 32, 49
Stark, Rodney   58
Statius   4, 28
Stifis   26
Stockstadt   19, 68n7, 86, 87, 89n78
Stridon   84
Sucellus   18
Suetonius   62
Symmachus, Quintus Aurelius   59, 82

Taq Bostan   88
Tarsus   3
Taunum   12n50
Taurobolium   27, 61n31
Tawern   87
Temples
    Christian desecration of   79
    converted to churches   2, 68
    destruction of   2–4, 67
    in Britain
        at Hayling Island   62

    at London   74
    at Springhead   62
    at Vindolanda   16
    at Worth   84
in Cyprus   90
in Dalmatia   84
in Egypt
    general   3, 43
    at Alexandria   2, 42, 88, 92, 97
    at Philae   42
in Gaul
    general   3, 42, 51, 54, 82, 83, 99
    at Champallement   51
    at Clermont-Ferrand
    at Furlenboden   63
    at Hochscheid   82, 83
    at Martigny   18, 57, 62
    at Matagne-la-Grande   51
    at Matagne-la-Petite   51
    at Tawern   82, 83, 82
in Germany
    at Trier   18, 64, 66
in Italy
    general   49, 50, 54, 99
    at Cosa   74n9
    at Herodina   50
    at Ostia   50
    at Rome   20, 27, 43
    at Verona   50
in Pannonia
    general   1, 51, 54, 99
    at Aquincum   51
    at Carnuntum   91
    at Cirpi   51
    at Gorisum   3, 51
    at Sirmium   51
in Noricum
    general   1, 51, 54, 99
    at Bedaium   51
    at Lendorf   83
    at Lentia   19, 40, 51, 57, 86n67, 94
    at Mauer an der Url   89n78
    at St Margarethen   83
in North Africa
    general   3, 43
    at Cyrene   90
    at Gholaia   87
    at Lambaesis   57
in Spain   3
laws concerning   1, 42, 89
non-religious uses of   43
of Apollo   82, 90
of Asclepius   57
of Bacchus(?)   74
of Bona Eventus   51
of Diana   50
of *Dea Roma* and the *Genius Augusta*   19, 40, 51, 57, 94
of Herculius   50
of Isis   42
of Jupiter   51, 63
of Jupiter Dolichenus   16, 83, 88, 89n78
of Jupiter Hammon   87
of Jupiter Ultor   50
of Liber Pater   74

INDEX 145

Temples (cont.)
    of Magna Mater 20, 27, 49
    of Mars 83
    of Mars Latobius 83
    of Sarapis 50, 64, 88, 92, 97
    of Saturn 50
    of Silvanus 51
    of the Divine Romulus 50
    of the Imperial Cult 84
    of Venus and Roma 50
    of Venus(?) 50
    of Victory 51
    of Zeus 90
Tertullian 78
Tetrarchs 1, 3, 26, 27, 43, 51, 58, 67, 87, 88, 93
Teurnia 51n26, 83
Theodore, Publius Ancilius 49
Theodoret, bishop 79
Theodorus, bishop 82
Theodosius I 12, 43, 59, 87
Theodosius, *comes* 87
Theopilus of Alexandria, bishop 1, 2, 78n22
Tienen 11, 18n5, 30, 39, 57, 68
Timavo 19, 21, 33, 76, 86n67
Tolland, John 2
Transitus 24
Trier
    Christianity in 64, 66, 82, 97, 98
    Frankish period 76
    mithraeum 25, 30, 31, 33, 39, 54–56, 64, 66, 76, 85, 95, 97
    the imperial court at 60, 98
    temples in 18, 64, 66
Trombley, Frank 79
Trout, Dennis 63
Turcan, Robert 29

Ulcisia Castra 26
Unification church 58

Valens 50, 59
Valentinian I 28, 31, 57n3, 82, 90
Valentinian II 50, 82
Venetonimagus 18, 25, 30, 76, 77
Venus 15, 82n29, 84
Veramand 59
Verona 50
Verulamium 43
Vicarello 63
Victory 26, 50, 84, 87
Villas 14
Vindobala 15, 16, 57n1
Vindolanda 16, 83
Virilis, C. Rufius 25
Virunum
    civic building in 51n26
    cult of Mithras in 1, 7n30, 9, 18, 26, 32
    dolichenum 83
Visigoths 85
Voltaire 2
Volusiana, Rufia 27
Volusianus, Ceonius Rufius 27
Vulci 81, 85, 86n67, 92, 97

Wallsend 57n1
Will, Ernest 15
Woolf, Greg 16
Worth 84

Xenephon 25

Zenofilus, Domitius 57
Zeus 24
Zichron Ja-akov 63
Zoroastrianism 24, 88, 97
Zosimus, author 85
Zosimus, Fl. Septimius 20, 27

LATE ANTIQUE ARCHAEOLOGY

Series Editor
LUKE LAVAN

Late Antique Archaeology is published annually by Brill, based on papers given at the conference series of the same title, which meets annually in London. Its *Supplementary Series* aims to publish thematic monographs which address life within the Roman Empire or its successor states in the period A.D. 283–650, as informed by material evidence, supported by other sources. All publication proposals are subject to satisfying the comments of two anonymous referees, managed at the discretion of the editor. We take the unusual route of accepting PhD theses plus examiner's reports for review. We then produce a potential publication plan for candidates to satisfy, with an idea of the support we can provide. The editorial committee includes Albrecht Berger, Will Bowden, Kimberly Bowes, Averil Cameron, Beatrice Caseau, James Crow, Jitse Dijkstra, Sauro Gelichi, Jean-Pierre Sodini, Bryan Ward-Perkins, Emanuele Vaccaro and Enrico Zanini. Journal abbreviations follow those used by the *American Journal of Archaeology*, whilst literary sources are abbreviated according to the *Oxford Classical Dictionary* (3rd ed. Oxford 1999) xxix–liv and when not given here, following A. H. M. Jones *The Later Roman Empire* (Oxford 1964) vol.2, 1462–76, then G. W. H. Lampe *A Patristic Greek Lexicon* (Oxford 1961).

For notes for contributors, with contact details, visit:
www.lateantiquearchaeology.wordpress.com
For submissions and ordering information visit:
www.brill.com/publications/late-antique-archaeology
www.brill.com/products/series/late-antique-archaeology-supplementary-series

Printed in the United States
By Bookmasters